# The Eisenhower Years: A Social History of the 1950's

*Also by Richard T. Stanley, Ed.D.*

*Lessons of American History*

*A Humorous Account of America's Past: 986 to 1898*

*A Humorous Account of America's Past: 1898 to 1945*

*A Humorous Account of America's Past: 1945 to 2001*

# The Eisenhower Years:
# A Social History of the
# 1950's

RICHARD T. STANLEY

iUniverse, Inc.
Bloomington

# The Eisenhower Years: A Social History of the 1950's

*Copyright © 2012 by Richard T. Stanley.*

*All rights reserved. No part of this book may be used or reproduced by any means, graphic, electronic, or mechanical, including photocopying, recording, taping or by any information storage retrieval system without the written permission of the publisher except in the case of brief quotations embodied in critical articles and reviews.*

*iUniverse books may be ordered through booksellers or by contacting:*

iUniverse
1663 Liberty Drive
Bloomington, IN 47403
www.iuniverse.com
1-800-Authors (1-800-288-4677)

*Because of the dynamic nature of the Internet, any web addresses or links contained in this book may have changed since publication and may no longer be valid. The views expressed in this work are solely those of the author and do not necessarily reflect the views of the publisher, and the publisher hereby disclaims any responsibility for them.*

*Any people depicted in stock imagery provided by Thinkstock are models, and such images are being used for illustrative purposes only.*
*Certain stock imagery © Thinkstock.*

ISBN: 978-1-4759-2647-7 (sc)
ISBN: 978-1-4759-2648-4 (ebk)

*Printed in the United States of America*

*iUniverse rev. date: 06/05/2012*

# DEDICATION

This book was written for future generations so they may better understand and appreciate American society during the Eisenhower years.

# Contents

PREFACE ................................................................................. ix

Chapter 1 INTRODUCTION ...................................................... 1
Chapter 2 MOVIES ..................................................................23
Chapter 3 TELEVISION ...........................................................51
Chapter 4 SPORTS ...................................................................71
Chapter 5 MUSIC ..................................................................100
Chapter 6 BUSINESS .............................................................111
Chapter 7 EDUCATION ........................................................127
Chapter 8 LITERATURE ........................................................142
Chapter 9 CONCLUSION .....................................................153

EPILOGUE ...........................................................................169
BIBLIOGRAPHY ...................................................................175
INDEX ..................................................................................181

# PREFACE

Two of the most intriguing and romanticized decades of 20th Century American history are the "Roaring Twenties" and the "Fabulous Fifties" (or the "Eisenhower Years"). During both decades, the White House was occupied by relatively conservative Republican Presidents—Calvin Coolidge (1923 to 1929) and Dwight Eisenhower (1953 to 1961). Both men favored less government and more private enterprise. Both clearly preferred equality of opportunity over equality of condition. And both "Silent Cal" and Ike were masters at maintaining positive public images as trustworthy father figures presiding over a dynamic society often viewed by some of their contemporaries as out-of-control (e.g., bathtub gin and rock 'n' roll).

"Keep Cool with Coolidge" provided some centripetal force—some stabilizing influence—to an otherwise "Lost Generation" of Americans who were sick and tired of the Progressive reforms begun by Theodore Roosevelt (a Republican) and disillusioned by the results of Democrat Woodrow Wilson's war-time domestic policies and internationalism. As President Harding, who succeeded Wilson in a landslide victory in November 1920, so accurately predicted prior to Election Day, Americans simply wanted to return to "normalcy." Translated, "normalcy" meant it was time for the national government to take a nap so average Americans, freed from most recent governmental restrictions (except Prohibition), could get on with their lives as *they* saw fit.

To the generation of the Roaring Twenties, their newly-found freedom soon created a "normalcy" that included wild parties in "Speak-Easies" where bootleg booze and bathtub gin flowed like water.

Normalcy included men with slicked-back hair dressed in tuxedoes dancing "The Charleston" with scantly-clap female "Flappers" with "bobbed" hair and easy smiles. Jazz music was "it." Even the normally stoic President Coolidge would occasionally ham-it-up for the White House press corps, as when he famously posed for photographs wearing a genuine Indian feather headdress and a sly grin.

In the spring of 1927, Charles A. Lindbergh dared to attempt to fly "solo" over the stormy Atlantic Ocean from New York City to Paris, France. Lindbergh departed New York City as that young daredevil, "fool hardy" aviator in his "Spirit of St. Louis." His primitive airplane was filled with little more than aviation fuel, a compass, some food and water, and its optimistic pilot. Landing safely in Paris on May 21$^{st}$, however, "Lucky Lindy" instantly became the international hero of the decade, beloved by millions on both sides of the Atlantic for his daring accomplishment. Millions of Americans also came to idolize baseball's Babe Ruth, especially after he hit a record 60 home runs in 1927 for the New York Yankees. While most Americans had difficulty remembering the name of their own Congressman, any red-blooded American male that year could name the starting lineup for the 1927 Yankees, or knew that "Gentleman" Gene Tunney was the Heavyweight Boxing Champion of the World, or that Knute Rockne was the head football coach of the "Fighting Irish" of Notre Dame. Certainly, by the mid-1920's, American men and women could name more Hollywood movie stars or radio personalities than they could identify world leaders. As long as they and their friends and families were kept safe (Coolidge's job; and later, Ike's), *normalcy* was what really mattered to them.

Knowledge of *social history* can be fleeting. Today's social happenings can become tomorrow's forgotten past in the blink of an eye. Why? Because it is usually *political and military history* that most often survives for future generations to study and evaluate. And, for a majority of historians, it seems, those 20$^{th}$ Century American Presidents most worthy of study are those whose philosophical inclinations and actions led to the *expansion* of government in our daily lives—Theodore Roosevelt, Woodrow Wilson, Franklin Roosevelt, Harry Truman, John Kennedy, Lyndon Johnson. Turn the pages of any recently-published U.S. History textbook, for example, and flip those pages concerning the beginning of Theodore Roosevelt's Administration in 1901 to the last page regarding Franklin Roosevelt's first eight-and-one-half years in office prior to December 7, 1941, and you will surely find a disproportionate number of pages devoted to the years *activist* Presidents were in office, as if the rich social history of the 1920's and early '30's during the administrations of Warren Harding, Calvin Coolidge, and Herbert Hoover is not worthy of remembering. Similar oversights are obvious regarding the Eisenhower Years. Unfortunately, the Eisenhower Years are also fading from America's memory as more and more of those of us who lived them are expiring.

The Eisenhower Years, generally speaking, were happier, more stable, more prosperous, more optimistic, and simpler times then the preceding decades of the 1930's and '40's (Hoover, FDR, and Truman) and the increasingly turbulent 1960's and '70's (Kennedy, Johnson, Nixon, Ford, and Carter) that followed. Those of us who were fortunate enough to grow up during the Fabulous Fifties still have fond memories of President Eisenhower's reassuring smile. Memories of cute "sweater girls" with hoop skirts, petticoats, and bobby socks. Young guys with "crew cuts" or Elvis-style pompadours wearing white tee-shirts, blue Levis with the little tags showing, and brown leather jackets. Drinking milk shakes through a straw and spooning thick malts made with real ice cream at genuine soda fountains. Eating burgers and fries served by roller skating waitresses at local drive-in cafes. Listening to Elvis Presley, Doris Day, Nat "King" Cole, or Frank Sinatra's voice coming from jukeboxes and car radios. Old Western movies on TV. Hearing Bing Crosby's recording of "White Christmas" each winter, played again and again. Fathers and sons watching the "Friday Nite Fights" on TV. Families dressing up for church on Sunday mornings and watching "The Ed Sullivan Show" on TV together Sunday evenings. And so much more.

The Fabulous Fifties were times worth remembering. The Eisenhower Years produced amazing contributions to our American culture—and to other cultures around the world. In so many ways, *Americans innovated, and the world imitated*—from Elvis Presley and rock 'n' roll to the Salk anti-polio vaccine. America's contributions to the world included motion pictures and the Broadway stage; radio and television; amateur and professional sports; jazz, the "blues," country-and-Western music, traditional ballads and popular songs, and rock 'n' roll; domestic and international business and trade; public and private educational opportunities; and a rich and varied literature.

Richard T. Stanley

While Americans did not invent all these categories, they nevertheless took each to new heights during the Eisenhower Years, and shared their bounty with the world. It would truly be a shame to forget about America's many cultural contributions during the 1950's simply because they may not have much political or military merit in the eyes of some traditional historians.

# Chapter 1

# INTRODUCTION

On Tuesday, January 20, 1953, Dwight D. Eisenhower became the thirty-fourth President of the United States. Less than nine years earlier, on June 6, 1944, General Eisenhower commanded the largest amphibious invasion force in the history of the world—a force which even his childhood hero Hannibal, the great Carthaginian warrior, would have truly been envious. Within weeks, Ike was leading an army of nearly three million men on the continent of Europe with one firm goal: The unconditional surrender of Nazi Germany. Now, on this Inauguration Day, Dwight D. Eisenhower became the sworn servant and protector of the American people—all two hundred and fifty-five million of them.

"Little Ike," as President Eisenhower was once called by his older brother Edgar (Edgar was known as "Big Ike"), had come a long way from his family's humble home in Abilene, Kansas, just before the turn of the century. At age sixty-two, Eisenhower was the oldest man ever elected to the Presidency.[1] Born David Dwight Eisenhower on October 14, 1890 in Denison, Texas, "Little Ike" entered a world without many of the modern marvels his Inauguration Day audience of thousands in attendance and millions more watching on television generally took

---

[1] Ronald Reagan would later break Ike's record by seven years.

for granted, including automobiles, airplanes, radios, motion pictures, and, most recently, TV sets, TV trays, and frozen TV dinners.[2]

Since the beginning of our Republic, military men were not uncommon candidates for President, beginning, of course, with George Washington. Yet, while 19th Century Presidential campaigns were often dominated by former military officers, Ulysses S. Grant was the *only* West Point graduate to occupy the White House until Dwight D. Eisenhower. Nevertheless, Presidents Benjamin Harrison and James A. Garfield once held the rank of *general*. Theodore Roosevelt became famous as a *colonel* leading his "Rough-Riders" during the Spanish-American War. William McKinley served as a *major* during the Civil War. And Harry Truman fought as a *captain* of artillery in World War I. With the exception of Teddy Roosevelt and Harry Truman, however, the rest of America's Presidents during the first half of the 20th Century—William Howard Taft, Woodrow Wilson, Warren Harding, Calvin Coolidge, Herbert Hoover, and Franklin Roosevelt, had no record of military service. (Although F.D.R. did serve as Assistant Secretary of the Navy during World War I, he was a *civilian*.) With the election of Dwight D. Eisenhower, there was a West Pointer in the White House for the first time since 1877.

Eisenhower, as a proven master tactician in the art of war, was considered by most (if not all) of his Inauguration Day audience capable of defending the nation against the threat of communist aggression and possible atomic annihilation. But would he also be up to the task of redirecting the nation's wobbly economy? His opponent for the Presidency during 1952, Adlai Stevenson, was the intellectual darling of America's liberals and a polished public speaker. By comparison, Dwight Eisenhower was neither. But Eisenhower was a beloved and admired national hero; Stevenson was not. And on October 24th, when Ike dropped the campaign bombshell—*Elect me President, and I'll end the Korean War!*, the election's outcome suddenly became obvious.

---

[2] Upon Ike's enrollment at West Point in 1911, his name was mistakenly transposed by a clerk on the Academy's official records as *Dwight David* Eisenhower, and the Academy's error stuck. From then on, David Dwight was *Dwight David*. Ike didn't seem to mind, as long as he got a free education. See Carlo D'Este's *Eisenhower: A Soldier's Life* (New York: Henry Holt and Company, 2002), p. 47.

Not only did Ike win the electoral vote by a margin of 442 to 89; he won the popular vote by more than 6,500,000 *and both houses of Congress.* Eisenhower won every single state outside the Democrat's "Solid South," including Stevenson's home state of Illinois, and he also carried Florida, Tennessee, Texas, and Virginia. "I Like IKE!" *indeed!* But now began the true test. Now was the time to begin fulfilling his campaign promises—both foreign and domestic. Sincerely humbled by his latest triumph, Eisenhower began his First Inaugural Address with a *prayer.*

> Almighty God, as we stand here at this moment my future associates in the executive branch of government join me in beseeching that Thou will make full and complete our dedication to the service of the people in this throng, and their fellow citizens everywhere.
>
> Give us, we pray, the power to discern clearly right from wrong, and allow all our words and actions to be governed thereby, and by the laws of this land. Especially we pray that our concern shall be for all the people regardless of station, race, or calling.
>
> May cooperation be permitted and be the mutual aim of those who, under the concepts of our Constitution, hold to differing political faiths; so that all may work for the good of our beloved country and Thy glory. Amen.

After seeking Divine guidance from his Higher Power, as witnessed by that vast audience, President Dwight D. Eisenhower began to deliver his Inaugural Address.

> *My fellow citizens:*
> The world and we have passed the midway point of a century of continuing challenge. We sense with all our faculties that forces of good and evil are massed and armed and opposed as rarely before in history.

Richard T. Stanley

* * * * * *

In the swift rush of great events, we find ourselves groping to know the full sense and meaning of these times in which we live. In our quest of understanding, we beseech God's guidance. We summon all our knowledge of the past and we scan all signs of the future. We bring all our wit and all our will to meet the question:

How far have we come in man's long pilgrimage from darkness toward light? Are we nearing the light—a day of freedom and of peace for all mankind? Or are the shadows of another night closing in upon us?

* * * * * *

Freedom is pitted against slavery; lightness against the dark.

The faith we hold belongs not to us alone but to the free of all the world.

This common bond binds the grower of rice in Burma and the planter of wheat in Iowa, the shepherd in southern Italy and the mountaineer in the Andes. It confers a common dignity upon the French soldier who dies in Indo-China, the British soldier killed in Malaya, the American life given in Korea.

We know, beyond this, that we are linked to all free peoples not merely by a noble idea but by a simple need. No free people can for long cling to any privilege or enjoy any safety in economic solitude. For all our own material might, even we need markets in the world for the surpluses of our farms and our factories. Equally, we need for these same farms and factories vital materials and products of distant lands. This basic law of interdependence, so manifest in the commerce of peace, applies with thousand-fold intensity in the event of war.

So we are persuaded by necessity and by belief that the strength of all free peoples lies in unity; their danger, in discord.

> To produce this unity, to meet the challenge of our time, destiny has laid upon our country the responsibility of the free world's leadership.

President Eisenhower went on to pledge that, during his administration, the United States, as leader of the Free World, would be guided by nine "fixed principles": (1) To always exercise "statesmanship" from a position of "strength"; (2) to never settle for "appeasement" by "trading honor for security"; (3) for its citizens to place "country" before *self*; (4) to never force America's "cherished political and economic institutions" upon others; (5) to expect other nations, "within the limits of their resources," to assist the United States in the "common defense of freedom"; (6) to encourage "productivity and profitable trade" throughout the Free World; (7) to promote regional groupings of free peoples through "the framework of the United Nations" in accord with their differing needs; (8) to "hold all continents and peoples in equal regard and honor"; and (9) to respect "the United Nations as the living sign of all people's hope for peace."

President Eisenhower stated earlier in his Inaugural Address, "Great as are the preoccupations absorbing us at home" . . ."each of these problems is dwarfed by [the Cold War] . . . ." Following his "fixed principles" for the benefit of the United States and the Free World would be the primary focus of his Presidency. Ike proved true to his word.

While the primary focus of Dwight Eisenhower's Presidency was foreign policy due to his own philosophy of limited government and the extraordinary demands of the Cold War, Ike moved quickly to get his administration's domestic house in order. First, he began by creating the position of "Assistant to the President" to help make the White House—and his Presidency—run smoothly. The position of Assistant to the President (or Chief of Staff) was patterned after the model of military organization Ike was most familiar with and confident about. Ike had served as Chief of Staff for General Douglas MacArthur during the 1930's, and General Bedell Smith had done a splendid job as Ike's Chief of Staff during much of World War II. Ike reasoned, *If it could work for me then, it can work for me now.* So Sherman Adams, a Dartmouth graduate, the former Republican Governor of New Hampshire, and

Ike's tough, no-nonsense campaign manager was quickly selected as his Assistant to the President.

Next, Eisenhower established the Office of Congressional Relations to promote improved communication between the White House and Congress. He appointed General Wilton B. Persons, who was one of the Army's chief liaison officers with the Congress during World War II, to facilitate patronage requests and promote the administration's legislative programs. And, on February 6, 1953, President Eisenhower issued an executive order that abolished all Federal controls on wages in an effort to stimulate the economy.

From the beginning, President Eisenhower involved the members of his Cabinet more than most Presidents—certainly more than FDR had—in the nation's governance.[3] Eisenhower's Cabinet included John Foster Dulles as Secretary of State. Dulles had served Presidents from Wilson to Truman and was a powerful member of the Washington "establishment." Ike chose the former CEO of Hanna Steel, George M. Humphrey, as his Secretary of the Treasury. Humphrey was thrifty by nature, well-organized, affable, and soon became one of Ike's rare confidants as well as a highly influential voice during Cabinet meetings. Charles E. ("Charlie") Wilson was Ike's pick for Secretary of Defense. Charlie Wilson had been the outgoing and sometimes garrulous and overconfident President of General Motors. Winston Churchill had once called John Foster Dulles, now Ike's Secretary of State, "Dull." Charlie Wilson could be called anything but "dull." And he had a particular penchant for irritating liberals with such well-known statements attributed to him as, "What's good for General Motors is good for the country."[4] But Ike valued his administrative expertise as Secretary of Defense. And he served in the Cabinet until mid-1957.

The Cabinet member Dwight Eisenhower knew best prior to becoming President was his Attorney General, Herbert Brownell, Jr. Brownell acted as a key advisor to Ike during the Presidential campaign. Ike was especially intrigued by how the highly intelligent Brownell could maintain his social idealism and personal integrity while

---

[3]  See Lewis L. Gould's *The Modern American Presidency* (Lawrence: The University of Kansas Press, 2003), p. 118.

[4]  See Jim Newton's *Eisenhower: The White House Years* (New York: Doubleday, 2011), p. 86.

demonstrating time and again his practical acumen for the rough and tumble world of domestic politics. Another key Cabinet member in Eisenhower's administration was his Secretary of Commerce, Sinclair Weeks. Known to Ike and other close associates as "Sinny," Sinclair Weeks soon became a major contributor to Ike's successful push for funding from the Congress for his highly ambitious National Highway Program, the largest venture of its kind in American history. Meanwhile, Ike's choice for Secretary of Labor—not the most prestigious post in a Republican administration—was Martin Durkin. Within one year, Durkin was replaced as Labor Secretary by James P. Mitchell, who loyally served in that same position for the remaining seven years of Eisenhower's Presidency.

For Postmaster General, President Eisenhower selected Arthur Ellsworth Summerfield. Summerfield remained in office for Ike's full tenure. So too with Ezra Taft Benson, Ike's Secretary of Agriculture. Summerfield proved non-controversial; Benson was anything but. Ezra Taft Benson, an apostle of the Mormon Church, was the first clergyman of the 20$^{th}$ Century to hold a Cabinet post. It was not Secretary Benson's faith that made him Ike's most controversial Cabinet officer; it was his opposition to Federal farm subsidies that made him so. Since the early days of the New Deal, many farmers had received Federal payments to *not* grow certain crops or raise animals on their lands in order that commodity prices would remain relatively high due to limited supply. Many farmers came to view such subsidies as "entitlements"—a sort of rural welfare. Farmers argued that without subsidies, they risked losing their lands during economic hard times. As head of the Department of Agriculture, Benson opposed most subsidies, and often battled with members representing agricultural districts from both parties in Congress. Ike loyally stood by Benson throughout his eight years as Secretary of Agriculture.

The traditional number of nine Cabinet positions was completed with the appointment of Douglas McKay as Ike's Secretary of the Interior. McKay was replaced by Frederick A. Seaton in June of 1956, but each successfully managed millions of acres of Federal lands, including their oil, mineral, timber, grazing, and water resources without the slightest hint of scandal.

While President Eisenhower continued to pursue his plans to shrink the size of the Federal bureaucracy, he increased the number of his

Cabinet departments to ten. On April 1, 1953, with Senate approval, Eisenhower added the newly created Cabinet position of Secretary of Health, Education, and Welfare, with Oveta Culp Hobby as its first Secretary. Mrs. Hobby actively managed the influential *Houston Post* with her husband (a former Texas governor) and had been a force behind the Women's Army Corps in Washington, D.C., during World War II. In spite of being a life-long Southern Democrat, in 1952, Oveta Culp Hobby spearheaded the political action group "Democrats for Eisenhower." Her group's support helped Ike carry many traditionally Democratic states, including Florida, Tennessee, Texas, and Virginia. But Eisenhower chose Hobby not simply because she had helped him politically; he chose her because she was an ethical and highly capable workaholic. And she got results.

As President, Dwight Eisenhower scheduled weekly meetings of his full Cabinet. He made it clear to each Secretary that the information they shared and the recommendations they made regarding their respective departments was *important* to him. Ike made it a point to *listen*. He was not a micromanager. He *delegated*, held his managers *accountable*, and offered a "guiding hand" when he deemed it necessary.

In addition to organizing his White House, Dwight Eisenhower was quite aware of the importance of maintaining a cordial and ongoing relationship with his constituency—namely, the American people. And he had long ago appreciated the political wisdom of a keen observation made in 1831 by a celebrated Frenchman named Alexis de Tocqueville while visiting the United States: "the periodical press is still, after the people, the first of powers."[5] Ike fully recognized the power of the press in the United States, and, following his election in November 1952, he made appointing a highly-qualified individual as his Press Secretary one of his first priorities. Whom did he choose? James Haggerty. For the next eight long and eventful years, James Haggerty managed to shield his boss from the slings and arrows of a free White House press corps while maintaining a cordial relationship with many in the news media.

President Eisenhower surrounded himself with highly qualified, successful, and ultimately powerful Cabinet members and other

---

[5] Alexis de Tocqueville, *Democracy in America* (Chicago: The University of Chicago Press, 2000), p. 178.

subordinates. That was his *modus operandi* as a successful military commander of vast armies during World War II, and it served him—and his nation—well. As President, why change? When one operates in a political galaxy of several stars, however, one risks having one of those other stars shine more brightly from time to time than one's self. As one or more of his subordinates took center stage on major issues from time to time, Ike came to be viewed by a growing number of his fellow Americans as a beloved but part-time President, perhaps guilty of spending too much time on his golf game, or schmoozing with his inner-circle of bridge buddies and barbecue pals (or even reading his favorite Western novels) than he spent on substantive matters. In other words, to some, Ike was still basking under the continuing public adulation for past military victories while his Cabinet and other advisors were actually steering the Ship of State. After all, the American public's memory of what Presidents *do* was mainly formed by one man during their own lifetimes—Franklin D. Roosevelt—from 1933 to 1945. Compared to any past President except for his "Bully!" cousin Theodore, FDR was a noisy, one-man-band. Even the feisty President Truman (with his "Give 'em Hell, Harry!" attitude) was dwarfed by FDR's gigantic shadow. Had Ike never earned his reputation as a great war hero, it is highly likely that his lack of *public* activism as President would have diminished his popularity, especially with political pundits, even further.

Since the Fabulous Fifties, abundant evidence of Eisenhower's behind-the-scenes command of events, both domestic and foreign, has slowly come to light. Also, more Americans of the 21$^{st}$ Century have come to appreciate that Ike's antipathy towards big government had little to do with alleged laziness and much to do with proven wisdom. Privately, Eisenhower was often even more calculating and Machiavellian than the old master, Franklin Roosevelt. As a case in point, take his relationship with the Dulles Brothers.

The Dulles Brothers—John Foster Dulles and Allen Dulles—were the most powerful and influential team of brothers in American history during the 20$^{th}$ Century, until John F. Kennedy and his brother Bobby came to power in 1961. During the Eisenhower Administration, John Foster Dulles served as Ike's loyal Secretary of State from 1953 until just before his death in 1959. And his younger brother, Allen, was Ike's dedicated Director of the Central Intelligence Agency (CIA) from

1953 to 1961. Except for President Eisenhower himself, no two men held more power and influence in Washington, D.C., than did the Brothers Dulles. Not even J. Edgar Hoover, the notorious Director of the FBI, who was "rumored" to have secret dossiers on nearly every politician and political activist in town (he *did*), was more powerful.[6] Both brothers had lengthy family ties to the Washington Establishment. Their grandfather, John Watson Foster, had served as Secretary of State under the Republican President, Benjamin Harrison. And their uncle, Robert Lansing, was Secretary of State under Democrat Woodrow Wilson. Both brothers graduated from Princeton and George Washington University (brother John also attended the University of Paris). During World War II, Allen Dulles directed America's spy service from Bern, Switzerland (officially called the U.S. Office of Strategic Services), while brother John practiced law in New York City and served as a consultant on international law. In 1951, President Truman appointed John Foster Dulles to negotiate America's peace treaty with Japan. To say that these two brothers had connections with people in high positions is an understatement.

As President, Dwight Eisenhower followed the same basic management style that had made him so successful as a military commander of millions: Appoint the best and brightest advisors and *delegate* authority, while reserving the right of ultimate decision making. No micromanager, *Ike* made the important decisions after carefully considering "expert" advice. And none of his advisors were more expert than the Dulles Brothers.

While Eisenhower's grin could be disarming, he was far less jovial than FDR. He was also even more *Machiavellian* than his former Commander-in-Chief when it came to getting done what he believed had to be accomplished in the interest of the nation, including *deadly covert operations against foreign enemies*. That's where the Dulles Brothers served him best. While Secretary of State John Foster Dulles publicly conducted America's official business with the world's diplomatic community, his brother Allen at the CIA coordinated America's rapidly-growing spy networks around the world quietly and secretly. To put it in blunt terms, foreign leaders who "messed

---

[6]  See Anthony Summers', *Official and Confidential: The Secret Life of J. Edgar Hoover* (New York: G.P. Putnam's Sons, 1993).

with Eisenhower's man," Secretary John Foster Dulles in public, could expect a visit from his brother Allen's CIA boys in private. Just like in the movie, *The Godfather*. Frankly, America's foreign policy *Godfather* was *Eisenhower*.

During his eight years in office, President Eisenhower, in his behind-the-scenes manner, utilized the enormous talents of the Dulles Brothers to their fullest in keeping the Free World *free*. It was no accident that Mao Tse-tung and his Red Army did not invade Formosa during the Eisenhower years, or that Mao *willingly* pulled his forces from combat in Korea. Mao was made an offer he could not refuse—*leave, or face a nuclear attack*! Formosa remained free, and the Korean War (as promised during Ike's campaign) came to a screeching halt on July 27, 1953.

As an added precaution, and to make certain that the powerful Dulles Brothers did his bidding on foreign affairs, President Eisenhower had, from the very beginning of his administration, his own personal "mole" within the State Department and the CIA. Who was he? General Bedell Smith, Ike's former Chief-of-Staff during World War II and President Truman's CIA Director. Demonstrating his loyalty to Ike by accepting his demotion from CIA Director to Undersecretary of State, Bedell Smith became Eisenhower's loyal eyes and ears at both the State Department and through his old contacts at the CIA. How Machiavellian on Ike's part was that?

In 1953, other world trouble spots included the Middle East nation of Iran, where the CIA was very much involved in a coup to topple Iran's anti-American (and anti-British) regime. Muhammed Mossadegh, leader of the so-called Persian "National Front," assumed dictatorial powers as the Shah's Prime Minister against the monarch's wishes. The Shah of Iran, Muhammed Riza Pahlavi, fled to exile in Rome on August 16th, as his nation erupted in violence. Within one week, however, Prime Minister Mossadegh was in prison, charged with treason, and the Shah was back on his throne in Tehran. Persian loyalists celebrated the Shah's return to power by demonstrating in the streets of Tehran, while in London and New York City, oil company executives and their stockholders gave sighs of relief. And in the White House, at the State Department, and at CIA Headquarters, smiles were legion, and credit for jobs-well-done was quietly and modestly accepted.

By January 1954, America's Cold War military strategy was dramatically changing. Truman's *defensive* strategy of *containing* Communist aggression by committing American ground troops to whatever trouble spots arose in the world did not lend itself to *reducing* the size of the military and *cutting* defense costs—both major objectives of President Eisenhower and Secretary of State Dulles (and *resisted* by many in the military establishment). With more than enough atomic bombs to destroy *any* enemy, Eisenhower and Dulles decided to go on the *offensive*. On January 12, 1954, John Foster Dulles announced through the State Department that the United States planned to *cut back* on the size of its military forces while relying on its *nuclear stockpile and the threat of "massive retaliation."* Simply put, "massive retaliation" meant *Beware: While America is a peace-loving nation that is cutting back on its defense spending, the air and sea forces of the United States have the necessary mobility and nuclear weapons to reach and destroy any nation on earth when provoked.*

Back on December 8, 1953, President Eisenhower gave his "Atoms for Peace" speech before the United Nations General Assembly. To prevent the Soviets from mistaking his speech calling for *peaceful* applications of atomic energy as a sign of weakness, Eisenhower soon ordered the U.S. Air Force Strategic Air Command (SAC) to maintain long-range B-52 bombers, armed with *atomic bombs,* on constant 24-hour alert. In addition, Admiral Hyman Rickover's new-fangled nuclear-powered submarine fleet (beginning with the *Nautilus* in January 1954), would be lurking, armed with atomic weapons, in the oceans of the world. Teddy Roosevelt, one of Ike's favorite Presidents, would no doubt have approved of his "speak softly, and carry a big stick" approach to protecting the Free World.

By the spring of 1954, it was Guatemala's turn to experience the "hidden-hand" of President Eisenhower. A growing dispute with the American-owned United Fruit Company, plus Guatemala's own sordid history of one dictatorship after another, resulted in a communist-controlled government led by Jacobo Arbenz. When Allen Dulles' CIA agents operating behind the Iron Curtain and in Central America discovered that President Arbenz was receiving arms and money from the Soviet Union via Communist Czechoslovakia, he immediately informed President Eisenhower and his brother at the State Department. They decided that John Foster Dulles, as Secretary of State, would publicly peruse the matter as a threat to *all* the North, Central, and South American states, while his brother and the CIA would take whatever covert actions were deemed necessary to remove Arbenz. At the Inter-American Conference held in March 1954, Secretary Dulles received the unanimous support of the Latin American republics (except Guatemala) in condemning the Arbenz regime. In April, following a well-publicized appeal by the Roman Catholic Archbishop of Guatemala to overthrow the God-less communists, Arbenz responded by declaring marshall law and by arresting many of the anti-communist leaders and their followers. On April 18th, a "liberating army" from neighboring Honduras, led by Colonel Carlos Armas and aided by CIA-trained soldiers, invaded Guatemala. By July 8, 1954, Colonel Armas was *President* Armas of Guatemala. Again, in the White House, at the State Department, and at CIA Headquarters, smiles were legion, and credit for jobs-well-done was quietly and modestly accepted. By 1954, it was generally understood in Washington that it was the CIA's job—in the interest of "national security"—to utilize covert operations to destabilize Third World nations with anti-American regimes: Use Latins against Latins, Asians against Asians, Arabs against Arabs, Africans against Africans, Persians against Persians, with a little help from their friends at the CIA.

During Eisenhower's watch, the recovering occupation zones of American, British, and French-controlled Germany peacefully united into one sovereign, free, and independent nation, the Federal Republic of Germany (West Germany) on April 1, 1955. In May, West Germany became a member of NATO, under the military umbrella of the West. President Eisenhower gladly gave much of the credit for West Germany's amazing recovery to his pal, George C. Marshall, and to his "Marshall Plan" (to the consternation of some conservatives, who had once branded General Marshall as being "soft on communism"). Meanwhile, the Russian zone—East Germany—languished under the oppression of their Soviet masters, making the contrast between Western democracy and Eastern totalitarianism all the more apparent as thousands of disconsolate East Germans risked their lives by escaping to West Germany. Many more died trying.

While West Germans (and quietly, Ike and the Dulles Brothers) were celebrating the birth of their new nation under the able leadership of Chancellor Konrad Adenauer, trouble was brewing in Egypt. The world's most important man-made waterway—the Suez Canal—has connected the Mediterranean Sea and Europe with Africa and the Middle East *through Egypt* since it first opened in 1869. By international agreement in 1888, the Suez Canal was to remain open to the ships of *all* nations during peace *and* war. Since 1936, the British had provided military protection for the Suez Canal Zone. Following World War II and Franklin Roosevelt's call to the world for "self-determination," increasing pressure from Egyptian nationalists caused the British, in early 1954, to agree to remove the last of their troops from the Canal Zone. Within one month of the departure of the last British "Tommy," President Gamal Abdel Nasser of Egypt ordered the seizure of the Suez Canal and promptly denied access to the canal for ships from the Jewish state of Israel. According to President Nasser, after the United States and Great Britain withdrew their offers to finance the construction of the Aswan High Dam on the Nile River, Egypt desperately needed the revenues generated by the Suez Canal to finance the billion-dollar project. Nasser went on to declare that Israel was the enemy of all Arab nations—*and had no right to exist.* Hence, Israel's banning was *justified*.

In response to President Nasser's unprecedented move on the Suez Canal, Israel invaded Egyptian territory in Gaza and on the Sinai Peninsula, while the British Royal Air Force began a series of air strikes on Egypt along the Canal Zone. Meanwhile, French forces were mobilized to prepare to join Israel and the United Kingdom against Egypt. On October 31, 1956, President Eisenhower surprised the world when he publicly condemned the Israeli-British attack on Egypt, while Secretary of State John Foster Dulles appealed to the United Nations to mobilize a police force to restore peace in Egypt. According to President Eisenhower and Secretary Dulles, the "Suez Canal" was a matter for the *United Nations* to settle, not a hastily-formed coalition of *colonial powers* plus Israel.[7]

The Israelis and their European allies, however, continued to fight. While the Israeli Army captured the entire Gaza Strip and the Sinai Peninsula, British and French forces invaded Port Said, Egypt, on November 5, 1956. But President Eisenhower and the Dulles Brothers

---

[7] See David A. Nichols' *Eisenhower 1956: Suez and the Brink of War* (New York: Simon & Schuster, 2011) for an excellent in-dept analysis.

had been feverishly working behind the scenes. On November 6th, the invasion was halted when a "UN cease-fire" was announced. By December 22nd, all the Anglo-French forces had withdrawn from Egypt due to immense pressure from the United States and the UN. President Eisenhower had made it clear to both Britain and France that *their* military days of dominance and dominion were over, and that the United States, in "partnership" with the United Nations, now ruled the roost in the Free World.

During President Eisenhower's first few years in office, his State Department and the CIA were often credited with numerous foreign policy accomplishments, including (1) Communist China's abandonment of its plans for the invasion of the island of Formosa (Taiwan) held by the Nationalist Chinese; (2) establishing a lasting "cease-fire" at the 38th parallel on the Peninsula of Korea; (3) ordering the Strategic Air Command on a continuous, 24-hour alert, and announcing the arming of its aircraft with atomic bombs as a deterrent to Soviet aggression; (4) sending America's new fleet of long-range nuclear submarines armed with atomic weapons to surreptitiously roam the ocean depths around the world; (5) replacing President Arbenz's communist regime in Guatemala with one more favorable to America; and (6) ending the crisis over the Suez Canal by forcing an end to the hostilities between Egypt and Israel and her European allies, Great Britain and France. While much credit was due to the Dulles Brothers and their many associates, make no mistake about the extent of Ike's involvement. President Eisenhower's "guiding hand" directed each operation from its beginning. The consummate skill demonstrated during the completion of each of the foreign operations listed in no way indicates a lack of Presidential leadership.

On the domestic scene, Secretary of Agriculture Ezra Taft Benson was often in the news about his controversial statements regarding such hot topics as price supports and farm subsidies. And Charles Wilson, Ike's Secretary of Defense, sometimes elaborated on his answers to reporters' questions to the extent that he would unintentionally make a statement he would later regret. President Eisenhower, on the other hand, was most often seen by the public in newspaper and magazine photos and on television playing golf, greeting school children or foreign heads of state at the White House, smiling at his wife Mamie, or otherwise acting *Presidential*. In some ways, Ike had become the picture of the ideal grandfather. "I Like IKE!" was not just a campaign slogan. Republicans *and* Democrats truly liked Ike.

While the relatively minor controversies swirling around Secretaries Benson and Wilson in the national spotlight were numerous, they were often overshadowed by sensational stories emanating from the notorious anti-communist Junior Senator from Wisconsin, Joseph R. McCarthy. Few political figures in our nation's history have added words to our American lexicon. From our 8th President, Martin Van Buren and his nickname "Old Kindernook," we have *okay*, or "O.K." And from our 29th President, Warren G. Harding, we have "normalcy," his mispronunciation in a speech of the word, normality. Both words have positive meanings. During Ike's first term in office, thanks to CBS commentator Edward R. Murrow, United States Senator Joseph "Joe" McCarthy gave us a negative word, a word of derision: "McCarthyism."

Initially a Democrat, Joseph R. McCarthy was first elected to the United States Senate as a Republican in 1946. The Junior Senator from Wisconsin soon joined many of his fellow Republicans (and some Democrats, including Congressman John F. Kennedy) in blaming the Truman Administration for "losing China to the communists." According to Senator McCarthy and many others in Congress, President Truman and his special envoy to China, General George C. Marshall, were "Communist dupes." Many Americans agreed with this point of view regarding the fall of Nationalist China. Their fears were reinforced by the conviction in 1950 of a top New Deal official, Alger Hiss, as a Russian spy, and the equally notorious case of Julius and Ethel Rosenberg, convicted of passing on atomic secrets to the Soviets. Meanwhile, Senator Joseph McCarthy suddenly grabbed the national spotlight in a speech he gave on February 9, 1950, in Wheeling, West Virginia. In that speech, McCarthy declared that he held in his hand *a list of two-hundred-and-five communists currently working at the U.S. State Department.* Suddenly, Senator McCarthy was the Truman Administration's most vocal and notorious critic in Congress. *McCarthyism*—sensational political remarks and, at times, unsubstantiated accusations of wrongdoing, including wrongful claims of guilt by association—was born.

For the first half of the 1950's, Joe McCarthy was the most well-known member of the United States Senate due to the popularity—and *notoriety*—of his increasingly wilder accusations of communists in the government and the private sector, especially the motion picture industry. As a result of pressure from Senator McCarthy in particular, and the American public in general, the Communist Party in America was *outlawed* in 1954. On August 24, 1954, the Communist Control Act passed both houses of Congress and was signed by President Eisenhower. The Communist Control Act of 1954 was an act "To outlaw the Communist Party, to prohibit members of Communist organizations from serving in certain representative capacities, and for other purposes." Passage of the act could have been the highlight of Senator McCarthy's career. As Chairman of the Senate's Subcommittee on Investigations of Governmental Operations, Senator McCarthy had launched a highly publicized investigation into alleged communist infiltration of the Voice of America and the Army Signal Corps in early 1953. Truman, however, was no longer President; *Eisenhower* was. Ike, already privately angered by McCarthy's accusations that his long-time friend, superior officer and mentor, General Marshall, was a "communist dupe," decided to keep a close watch on the Senator *behind-the-scenes*. It was soon determined that many of McCarthy's accusations were simply self-serving hot air. McCarthy was rapidly becoming a *liability* to the Eisenhower Administration and *to the nation*.

In the spring of 1954, Senator McCarthy accused the United States Army of being "soft on communism" by promoting a *dentist* who was a "communist." Behind-the-scenes, Eisenhower sprang into action. Ike encouraged the creation of a special Congressional committee to investigate an earlier attempt by Senator McCarthy and his Chief Counsel, Roy Cohn, to gain special treatment for one of McCarthy's former aides who have been drafted. On April 22, 1954, the "McCarthy Hearings" began. McCarthy retaliated by claiming that the Secretary of the Army had concealed foreign espionage activities. The "hearings" were broadcast nationwide on radio and television. Noted CBS commentator Edward R. Murrow proceeded to excoriate Senator McCarthy in a series of televised reports.

On July 30, 1954, Senator Ralph Flanders of Vermont called for McCarthy's formal censure by the Senate. The drama played out in the Senate and on TV for months. Accusations of alcoholism and abuse of power by Senator McCarthy abounded. Senator McCarthy fell from grace with a thud. While the Senate finally cleared McCarthy of any "criminal" wrongdoing, he was *censured* by a resolution passed by the full Senate (67 to 22) on December 2, 1954. McCarthy remained in the Senate until his death in 1957, but his political power was shattered. Only his pejorative *McCarthyism* lived on. Meanwhile, from the sidelines, a smiling Ike quietly continued to play golf and act *Presidential*.

\* \* \* \* \* \*

On Inauguration Day, January 20, 1953, while Dwight D. Eisenhower solemnly took the oath of office as the thirty-fourth President of the United States, his devoted wife, Marie "Mamie" Geneva Doud Eisenhower stood proudly by his side, beaming upward. Mamie could not have been more delighted for her Ike. Besides, after thirty-seven years of marriage, Mamie, now America's "First Lady," would finally experience the luxury of living in the same home for more than one or two years in a row since she had been a young girl. And to think that her first regular home since she married Ike would be the *White House*!

Born in Boone, Iowa, and raised in Denver, Colorado, Mamie lived a rather pampered childhood as the "prettiest" of the four daughters of John and Elvira Doud. John Doud was highly successful as the owner of a large meatpacking business—so successful that as early as 1904, he was rumored to be a millionaire.[8] While Doud was a rugged man, his wife and daughters were small, quite feminine, and somewhat frail. Sparing no expense, Mr. Doud annually sent his family south for the winter to the warmer climate of San Antonio, Texas. That is where Mamie met Ike. Ike, after graduating from West Point, was stationed in San Antonio. As a First Lieutenant in the United States Army, Ike earned the grand sum of $147 a month. Mamie's allowance from her father may have been larger. No matter. Both soon fell in love, and on Valentine's Day 1916, they became engaged. And, on July 1st, the couple were married in the Doud family home in Denver. After a brief honeymoon in nearby Eldorado Springs, the newlyweds left by train to the modest Eisenhower home in Abilene, Kansas, so Mamie could

---

[8] See Newton, *Eisenhower*, p. 16.

meet Ike's parents, David and Ida, and his brother Milton for the first time. All went well.

Now, thirty-seven years later, Ike was President, and Mamie was First Lady. Nearby, their son, Major John Sheldon Doud Eisenhower, also a West Point graduate just like his pop, was in the audience. Only one member of the immediate family was missing on that auspicious and memorable day—Doud Dwight "Icky" Eisenhower. Born in 1917 to Captain and Mrs. Dwight Eisenhower, their first-born pride and joy suddenly died of scarlet fever in 1921. Neither parent ever fully recovered emotionally from their devastating loss of Icky. To his dying day, Ike maintained that the loss of his son Icky was the worst thing that had ever happened to him. But few outside their immediate family and some close friends ever sensed the depth of Ike and Mamie's loss. After all, they were seasoned *troopers*.

As a seasoned trooper, Mamie Eisenhower was actively involved in a series of moves during Ike's long military career. She averaged moving the Eisenhower household nearly once every year.[9] Years before the Eisenhowers moved into the White House, Mamie had her color schemes and special interior decorating touches down pat. Pink was her favorite color, accompanied by various shades of green. Pink and green became the Eisenhowers' trademark interior colors. Mamie's taste in home decorating may best be described as cheerful, middle-class, and comfortable. Soon, the White House reflected her taste. No one ever accused Mamie Eisenhower of having pretentious tastes when it came to home decorations or her own personal manner of dressing. Mamie took pride in admitting that, even as First Lady, she often bought her clothes off department store racks. And she preferred wearing costume jewelry to the real thing.

As First Lady, Mamie Eisenhower's "bangs" became all the rage in women's hair styles. Her bangs and her affinity for wearing pink strapless evening dresses for White House parties, often snapped by photographers whose photos later appeared in prominent magazines, became known in the fashion world as the "Mamie Look." Unlike her two most recent predecessors as First Lady, Eleanor Roosevelt and Bess Truman, she abhorred dressing like "an old lady," and she loved playing

---

[9] See Betty Boyd Caroli's *The First Ladies* (New York: Madison Park Press, 2008), pp. 210-16.

hostess at White House functions. With so many recent improvements in international air travel, the Eisenhowers entertained an increasing number of foreign heads of state, as well as the usual variety of foreign diplomats and American dignitaries, at the White House.

While Mamie grew up in a home with servants to do most culinary chores, Ike learned to cook in his mother's kitchen. Who would have guessed back in Abilene during Ike's youth that the young boy who sometimes made tamales in his mother's kitchen, faithfully following her recipe, and then sold them door-to-door in his neighborhood for spending money, or later, the young Army Lieutenant who loved to grill steaks over an open fire for other officers and their wives at small dinner parties would one day become President of the United States? Ike often cooked simply to relax. But he was not limited to tamales or steaks. Ike even had his own special recipe for vegetable soup—*from scratch*.

Dwight Eisenhower also smoked cigarettes, a habit he first picked up while a cadet at West Point. He often smoked as many as sixty cigarettes per day. During the D-Day invasion, he functioned in a perpetual cloud of smoke. Not until he was President of Columbia University and was hospitalized for ileitis did Ike quit smoking. And in his typical stubborn fashion, he managed to quit *cold turkey*.

Both Eisenhowers were avid card players. Ike and Mamie were especially expert at poker and bridge. Ike was so competitive at bridge that only a few of his friends who were equally expert at the game would dare to be his partner. Ike had an explosive temper, and he hated to lose, particularly due to a less-competent partner. Ike despised incompetency.

One of Dwight Eisenhower's most famous acquaintances from the many months he was stationed in England as Allied Commander during the war was Winston Churchill, Britain's Prime Minister. Churchill, like Eisenhower, was often under great pressure to succeed. Failure to win the war against Hitler and the forces of Nazi Germany's giant fighting machine would likely result in death for both men and the destruction and enslavement of their respective nations for generations to come. The proverbial weight of the world was upon their shoulders. The stress they felt from their responsibilities was nearly overwhelming at times. To relieve tension, Eisenhower smoked cigarettes by the pack; Churchill smoked cigars by the box and drank Scotch by the case.

Churchill's less well-known tension-releasers were two of his favorite get-away hobbies: laying bricks, and painting pictures by brushing oils on canvas at his country estate outside London. Churchill found great pleasure from his painting. Perhaps it was at one of Ike's meetings with the great man that he decided to take up painting himself one day. Who knows? What we do know is that Ike began painting with oils on canvas while he was President of Columbia University. As Ike often told his friends, he started painting after a highly talented New York artist, Thomas E. Stephens, began to paint Mamie's portrait at their newly adopted home, Columbia's formidable marble and dark oak president's mansion at Sixty Morningside Drive in Morningside Heights.[10] After Ike's first experimentation with oils, Stephens encouraged him to paint. Soon, Ike was painting during breaks from his busy schedule in the relaxing seclusion of a converted water tower room atop the old formal mansion—Ike's "penthouse" retreat and art studio at Columbia.

When Eisenhower became President of the United States, a small room on the second floor of the White House was set aside as an art studio, complete with oil paints, easel, and canvases. Ike used his White House studio often, especially for brief periods of time before lunch. Ike was never one to compliment his own art work, whether his painting was a landscape, a still life, or a portrait. But his former Vice President Richard Nixon proudly displayed one of Ike's landscapes on a prominent wall in his bedroom for many years. And a large painting by Eisenhower of Winston Churchill hangs above the mantel in the formal living room of the Presidential Suite in Ward Eight of Walter Reed Hospital in Washington, D. C.[11]

As President and First Lady, Ike and Mamie had the world at their fingertips. Yet, at heart, they were still simple folks. Mamie still addressed her female friends as "girls," or "kiddo." Her favorite flowers were common gladiolus, not exotic orchids. Mamie, at least according to Ike, made the White House "livable and comfortable." And, when she and Ike weren't entertaining presidents, prime ministers, kings, and queens at formal state dinners, they preferred to dine together upstairs

---

[10] See Dwight D. Eisenhower's *At Ease: Stories I Tell to Friends* (New York: Doubleday & Company, Inc., 1967), pp. 336-41.

[11] See David Eisenhower's *Going Home to Glory* (New York: Simon & Schuster, 2010), pp. 249-50.

in their private quarters while seated in front of TV trays watching television and eating good old American food such as roast turkey, baked ham, meat loaf, beef stew, fried chicken, pork chops, or steaks. And, if Mamie should decide to retire to a nearby room after dinner to play a game of solitaire, Ike would happily flip the channels on their television set until he just happened to come across a re-run of one of his favorite forms of entertainment—an old cowboy movie.

# CHAPTER 2

# MOVIES

During the mid-1920's, Major Dwight D. Eisenhower served with the Twentieth Infantry Brigade at the United States Army base in Panama. Major Eisenhower was personally selected by the base commander in Panama, Brigadier General Fox Conner, to leave the states as soon as possible and report for duty as his military aide. Fox Conner had been the Army's Chief of Operations during World War I, and he had a well-known reputation within the Army of having a brilliant mind and a penchant for spotting up-and-coming officers. To be summoned by General Conner to serve at his side—even if it meant service in the jungles of Panama—was to a young and ambitious Major Eisenhower, the chance of a lifetime. And so, it was not long before Ike, his wife Mamie, and their son John (born John Sheldon Doud Eisenhower on August 3, 1922 back in Mamie's home town of Denver, Colorado) were busy dodging mosquitoes, avoiding snakes, lizards, and bed bugs, and seeking shelter from the hot tropical sun and the drenching rains of Panama. Duty and ambition called. And Fox Conner soon proved to be one of the best mentors Dwight Eisenhower ever had.

Meanwhile, back in the United States, a section of the City of Los Angeles known as "Hollywood" was rapidly becoming the "Motion Picture Capital of the World." While Ike and his wife and son seldom saw more than the Panama Canal, their military base, and the surrounding jungles, Hollywood was turning out movies at an astounding rate. Many movies were distributed worldwide. Hollywood's motion pictures were already having a profound impact upon the cultures of the world.

The sprawling Southern California ranch originally purchased in 1886 by a retired Kansas City real estate developer named Wilcox and renamed "Hollywood" by his wife Deida far exceeded even its founder's wildest dreams. Created in an "illegal" attempt to break the stranglehold of Thomas Edison's Motion Picture Patents Company of New York City (even America's first "Westerns," including Edwin S. Porter's *The Great Train Robbery*, were shot in the "wilds" of New Jersey, thanks to Mr. Edison's strict control), Hollywood soon thrived, thanks to a handful of risk-takers. It all began when Colonel William N. Selig fled Edison's span of control to establish the first large motion picture studio in the Los Angeles area in 1909, the same year Ike graduated from high school. Not only was the warm and dry climate of Southern California ideally suited for filming outdoors—the Mexican border was close by if a quick escape from pursuing lawmen proved necessary. Other daring entrepreneurs soon followed, including Cecil B. DeMille, Jesse L. Lasky, and Samuel Goldfish. Mr. Goldfish soon changed his name to Goldwyn. In 1913, they picked the quiet village of Hollywood and, with DeMille as director, produced the early Western classic, *The Squaw Man*. The popularity of *The Squaw Man*, together with a flood of films soon to follow, made Hollywood synonymous with motion pictures. Then, in 1915, came D.W. Griffith's *The Birth of a Nation*, Hollywood's first worldwide "blockbuster."[12] *Hurray for Hollywood!*

By 1950, Hollywood had long been established as the movie capital of the world (although most of the major studios were located in Burbank or Culver City). But, following 1946, the industry's most profitable year in its history to date, two unforeseen events rocked the motion picture industry. First, in 1947, the House Un-American Activities Committee began holding hearings into the alleged infiltration of the movie industry by communists; Second, the United States Supreme Court ruled in May 1948 in favor of the Federal government's antitrust suit against Paramount Studios and the other four "majors." As a result of the Congressional probes, the "Hollywood Ten" were branded as

---

[12] See Melvyn Stokes' *D.W. Griffith's The Birth of a Nation* (New York: Oxford University Press, 2007) for an excellent account.

"communist traders," and were eventually found guilty in Federal court and were sent to prison. Many others who were shown to have had communist sympathies were "black listed" by the industry and had to seek other employment. As a result of *The United States v. Paramount Pictures, Inc., et al* (first filed in 1938), the "Big Five" studios named in the suit were forced by the Supreme Court to sell their theatres across the country—their main source of power and income. To make matters even worse for movie moguls and their millions of fans, foreign nations, including Great Britain, began to levy limits on the profits American film companies could make abroad in order to shore-up their own war-weary economies. And finally, there was the rapidly growing competition within the entertainment industry itself from *television*. By 1950, even some movie industry insiders began to ask, *Can Hollywood survive?*

In light of Hollywood's many post-war challenges, it seems altogether fitting that one of 1950's most memorable movies was about a washed-up, delusional silent film star from the good old days, *Sunset Boulevard*. Gloria Swanson, one of director Cecil B. DeMille's favorite silent screen actresses, and one of Paramount's brightest movie stars of the mid-1920's, played the role of a neurotic, faded silent screen star opposite a much younger William Holden as her writer-gigolo. The famous silent film director Erich von Stroheim played the flamboyant, ramrod-spined Prussian director who promised to facilitate Miss Swanson's "comeback." In the film, any possibility of Miss Swanson's comeback as a screen star again (similar to Hollywood's plight?) was simply a figment of her imagination.

Thankfully, quality movies, including *Sunset Boulevard*, helped Hollywood to survive its many misfortunes of the late 1940's and early 50's. While the annual number of movies produced by the studios continued to decrease, the overall quality of their films seemed to increase. For example, Humphrey Bogart's *The African Queen* (1951), Vivian Leigh's *A Streetcar Named Desire* (1951), and Gary Cooper's *High Noon* (1952) were excellent motion pictures. Some claim *High Noon* was the first modern adult Western. All three films are still well-known motion picture classics today. Furthermore, the array of A-list movie stars available on screen to America's movie going public, and to fans around the world during the Eisenhower Years, was truly amazing. From 1952 through the end of the decade, film aficionados had their pick of movies starring, in alphabetical order, June Allyson, Fred Astaire, Lauren Bacall, Ingrid Bergman, Humphrey Bogart, Ernest Borgnine, Marlon Brando, Yul Brynner, Richard Burton, Leslie Caron, Cyd Charisse, Maurice Chevalier, Montgomery Clift, Lee J. Cobb, Gary Cooper, Tony Curtis, Doris Day, James Dean, Kirk Douglas, José Ferrer, Henry Fonda, Glen Ford, Clark Gable, Ava Gardner, Greer Garson, Cary Grant, Susan Hayward, Audrey Hepburn, Katherine Hepburn, Charlton Heston, William Holden, Judie Holliday, Rock Hudson, Van Johnson, Jennifer Jones, Shirley Jones, Gene Kelly, Grace Kelly, Deborah Kerr, Alan Ladd, Burt Lancaster, Janet Leigh, Vivien Leigh, Jack Lemon, Shirley MacLaine, Gordon MacRae, Victor Mature, Robert Mitchum, Marilyn Monroe, Ricardo Montalban, Yves Montand, Paul Newman, David Niven, Kim Novak, Maureen O'Hara, Jack Palance, Gregory Peck, Anthony Perkins, Sidney Poitier, Tyrone Power, Elvis Presley, Vincent Price, Anthony Quinn, Lee Remick, Debbie Reynolds, Cesar Romero, Jane Russell, Eva Marie Saint, Randolph Scott, Frank Sinatra, Jimmy Stewart, Elizabeth Taylor, Gene Tierney, Spencer Tracy, Lana Turner, Robert Wagner, Richard Widmark, Cornel Wilde, Joanne Woodward, John Wayne, Natalie Wood, and Jane Wyman. And that was just the *A-list*. Arguably, there were many others who could be added to that list of *movie* stars, including Brigitte Bardot, Bing Crosby, Judy Garland, Betty Grable, Sir Alec Guinness, Rita Hayward, Bob Hope, Tab Hunter, Danny Kaye, Howard Keel, Fernando Lamas, Dorothy Lamour, Hope Lange, Piper Laurie, Peter Lawford, Gina Lollobrigida, Sophia Loren, Dean Martin and Jerry Lewis, Marcello Mastroianni, Virginia Mayo, Auddie Murphy, Debra Pagent, Aldo Ray, Barbara Rush, Robert Ryan, Red Skelton, Robert Taylor, Claire Trevor, and Shelly Winters. Get the picture?

During the Eisenhower Years, Americans certainly had many excellent movies they could choose to watch. 1953, Ike's first year as President, was an especially good year for motion picture fans. One of the finest military films ever made won the coveted Oscar for "Best Picture" in 1953—*From Here to Eternity*, starring Burt Lancaster and Deborah Kerr. For his role in *Eternity*, Frank Sinatra won the Oscar for "Best Supporting Actor" (Sinatra's role as Angelo Maggio resurrected his show business career), and Donna Reed—famous for director Frank Capra's classic 1945 film *It's a Wonderful Life*, co-starring Jimmy

Stewart, and later, TV's "The Donna Reed Show" (1958-66), won for "Best Supporting Actress."

For his outstanding performance in another war-related drama, *Stalag 17*, William Holden won the 1953 Oscar for "Best Actor." Like many other Hollywood actors of the day, Holden's movie career had been interrupted by World War II. After playing the boxing hero in *Golden Boy* (1939) and George Gibbs in *Our Town* (1940), Holden served as a lieutenant in the U.S. Army during the war. His career resumed following the war when he played a psychotic killer in *The Dark Past* (1949), as Gloria Swanson's boy-toy in *Sunset Boulevard* (1950), and as Judy Holliday's tutor in the comedy *Born Yesterday* (also 1950). But the film that established him as one of Hollywood's leading stars and a top box-office attraction of the 1950's was Billy Wilder's *Stalig 17*. William Holden would go on to star in such romantic classics as *Love Is a Many-Splendored Thing* (1955) and *Picnic* (1956).

Unlike William Holden, Audrey Hepburn skyrocketed to movie stardom within a matter of months. Audrey Hepburn was retained in Belgium by the Nazis during World War II. The young daughter of an English banker and a Dutch baroness, she and her mother had just left London and were vacationing in Brussels when Hitler's armies suddenly attacked and overran Belgium in 1939, thus trapping them. Following the war, Miss Hepburn, a petite, graceful, and radiant young lady, began acting in British and French films. In 1951, the young European film star was enticed to come to America to play the lead role in the Broadway production of "Gigi" in New York City. "Gigi" made her an instant star of the Broadway stage. Her next stop? Hollywood. In 1953, Audrey Hepburn won the Oscar for "Best Actress" in her first American film, *Roman Holiday*, co-starring box-office idol Gregory Peck. By the beginning of Ike's second year in office, Audrey Hepburn was both a Broadway star *and* a leading Hollywood actress.

In 1953, Elizabeth Taylor, at age twenty-one, had already been under contract with MGM Studios for ten years. The London-born beauty of American parents living in England before the war, Elizabeth became a child star as the result of her movie role in *Lassie Come Home* (1943), as Velvet Brown in *National Velvet* (1944), as the loving daughter in *Life with Father* (1947), as Meg in *Little Women* (1949), and as Spencer Tracy's beloved daughter in *Father of the Bride* (1950). Finally, in 1953, she played the beautiful grown-up in the lead role of *The Girl Who Had*

*Everything.* Constantly under the public's microscope, her private life soon became as infamous as her screen persona was famous. Already divorced at age seventeen from Nicky Hilton, the heir to the Hilton Hotel empire and a notorious playboy, she married the much older and more mature Michael Wilding in 1952. After divorcing Wilding in 1957, she married the flamboyant producer of the smash movie hits *Oklahoma!* (1955) and *Around the World in 80 Days* (1956), Mike Todd. Married to Todd less than a year, she suddenly became a widow when Mike Todd's private plane named "The Lucky Liz" crashed on a business trip en route to New York City. The Best Man at Mike and Elizabeth's wedding had been singer Eddie Fisher. Fisher did more than console the Widow Todd; he dumped his wife, the perky and popular Debbie Reynolds, and married the former Mrs. Todd in 1959. The press went ballistic, and the public ostracized Elizabeth as a home-wrecker.

But Elizabeth Taylor's film career continued to sizzle. Liz was nominated for an Oscar for her splendid performances in *Raintree County* (1957), *Cat on a Hot Tin Roof* (1958), and *Suddenly Last Summer* (1959). By then, she was one of the world's highest-paid performers. During President Eisenhower's last year in office, Elizabeth Taylor won her first Oscar as "Best Actress" for *Butterfield 8*. Some claimed she was still the most beautiful woman in the world.

Every generation has its naysayers. Even during the "Happy Days" atmosphere of the Eisenhower Years, there were a few prominent rebels in the public spotlight, including Marlon Brando and James Dean. Marlon Brando and James Dean were the big screen's chief iconoclasts of the 1950's. James Dean, a former UCLA student, was still playing bit parts on Broadway and in TV dramas in 1953. But he soon became the personification of restless American youth when he vaulted to stardom in the film version of John Steinbeck's *East of Eden* in 1955, and co-starred with Rock Hudson in the 1956 blockbuster *Giant*. But, following his tragic death in a horrible car crash while speeding in his new Porsche to compete in an auto race near Salinas, California, James Dean is still best remembered for his role as the "Rebel" in the 1955 film, *Rebel Without a Cause*. James Dean enjoyed his super-stardom for less than one year. Dean died in 1955 some months before the movie *Giant* was released. Not so, Marlon Brando. Brando's career would span generations.

In 1953, Marlon Brando's star was rapidly rising when he was nominated for an Academy Award for his performance as Marc Anthony in *Julius Caesar*. A Nebraska native who had the dubious distinction of being expelled from a Minnesota military academy before escaping to New York City and enrolling in drama classes, Marlon Brando focused his rebellious personality on Broadway. Under the guidance of director Elia Kazan and aided by his Actors Studio "method" training, Brando became a Broadway star in 1947 as a result of his forceful portrayed of the S.O.B. Stanley Kowarski in playwright Tennessee William's "A Streetcar Named Desire."

By 1950, Marlon Brando was starring in his first Hollywood film, *The Men*, directed by Stanley Karmer. In *The Men*, Marlon Brando brilliantly portrayed an embittered paraplegic. He then starred in the film version of *A Streetcar Named Desire* in 1951, and as the flamboyant Mexican General Emiliano Zapata in *¡Viva Zapata!* in 1952. And, in 1953, Ike's first year as President, Marlon Brando *was* Marc Anthony in the film *Julius Caesar*. But his most outstanding performance to date came in his role as Terry Malloy, the ex-pugilist, in *On the Waterfront* in 1954. *On the Waterfront* won the Oscar for "Best Picture," "Best Director" (Elia Kazan), "Best Actor" (Marlon Brando), and "Best Supporting Actress" (Eva Marie Saint).

In 1954, Marlon Brando starred as Napoleon in *Désirée* and also in *The Wild One*. In 1955, it was *Guys and Dolls*; in 1956, *The Teahouse of the August Moon*; in 1957, *Sayonara*; and in 1958, *The Young Lions*—all highly successful movies. Most Americans during the mid and late 1950's considered Marlon Brando as one of the greatest actors who ever lived. Certainly, there were those who disapproved of his rebellious nature off-camera. But even his harshest personal critics agreed that his on-camera performances made Brando the "method actor" a super-star. Such acting tributes were never extended to another 1950's super-star, Marilyn Monroe.

In 1953, Marilyn Monroe was one of the biggest stars under contract to 20$^{th}$ Century Fox Studios and Hollywood's number one "sex goddess." In an age known for its family values and modest rules of decorum, movie fans flocked to Marilyn Monroe's teasing, light-hearted, sexy, 1953 comedies *Gentlemen Prefer Blondes* and *How to Marry A Millionaire*. Born the illegitimate daughter of a mom who was a mentally ill movie studio worker in Hollywood, Norma

Jean Baker grew up in a succession of foster homes in Los Angeles after her mother was placed in a mental institution. A high school drop-out who married at sixteen, Norma Jean eventually became a paint sprayer in an aircraft factory after her husband was sent overseas as a merchant marine during World War II. She was first discovered by an army photographer visiting the factory where she worked. Soon, she was posing for "pin-ups" intended to boost the morale of our G.I.'s overseas. They did.

After the war, and following her divorce from husband number one, a struggling young magazine editor named Hugh Hefner convinced Marilyn to pose for his first issue of *Playboy*. By this time, Norma Jean Baker had gone from brunette to blond, and had changed her name to Marilyn Monroe. And the rest, as they say, is history. *Playboy* soon became America's favorite sex-oriented magazine for men, and Marilyn Monroe soon became America's favorite female sex symbol.

In 1954, Marilyn Monroe, America's erotic, yet wholesome and funny sex symbol, married baseball hero Joe DiMaggio, the retired super-star centerfielder for the New York Yankees. The highly popular "Yankee Clipper" and she held the world's spotlight for much of the entire nine months of their marriage, from January through October 1954. Meanwhile, Marilyn Monroe completed two more big hits, *There's No Business Like Show Business* (1954), and *The Seven Year Itch* (released in 1955). While still working on the *Itch*, Marilyn divorced DiMaggio. Next, she gave a surprisingly subtle performance in the 1956 film, *Bus Stop*. Then, desperately seeking more serious acting parts, she left Hollywood for New York City to study acting at the same Actors Studio Marlon Brando once graced. Marilyn dreamed of becoming a serious actress. The renowned Lee and Paula Strasberg became her teachers. Meanwhile, Miss Monroe also hobnobbed with Manhattan's intellectual crowd, including award-winning playwright Arthur Miller (he of "Death of a Salesman" fame).

In June 1956, Marilyn Monroe and Arthur Miller were married. Again, as had been the case with her marriage to Joe DiMaggio, the press went wild. Pictures and articles about the famous couple were in all the newspapers and magazines, and they were constant topics on radio and television. Speculation as to the future success or failure of their marriage abounded. The newlyweds fled to England. While in England with her husband, Marilyn starred in the film *The Prince and the Showgirl*, opposite the world-acclaimed English actor, Sir Lawrence Olivier. The film became one of her few commercial flops. And the couple returned to America.

Marilyn Monroe returned to Hollywood to make yet another light-hearted, sexy comedy, *Some Like it Hot*, in 1959. *Some Like it Hot*, the 1920's comedy co-starring Tony Curtis and Jack Lemmon, was a tremendous success. Elizabeth Taylor may have been a far better actress and "the most beautiful women in the world" during the decade of the 1950's, but Marilyn Monroe was undeniably America's favorite "sex goddess." With both Miss Taylor and Miss Monroe to inspire the vast majority of America's men (and many women), how could the generally prosperous 1950's not be viewed as "Happy Days"?

Another female box office mega-star of the Eisenhower Years had her brief but spectacular film career end with a true-life, fairy-tale wedding. Her name? Grace Kelly. Her fairy-tale wedding? When she became Princess Grace of Monaco in 1956.

Grace Kelly was figuratively born with a silver spoon in her mouth. With a former "cover girl" as her loving mother and a wealthy businessman as her doting father, young Grace grew up amidst Philadelphia's high society. As a young aspiring actress, she literally projected serene beauty and sophistication. In an age when smoking tobacco was "in," the young, beautiful, and "classy" model/actress first gained public notice in cigarette commercials on local television in the nation's number one advertising market, New York City. In 1949 at age twenty-one, she finally won a part in a Broadway play. Acting with Ramond Massey, her fine performance in *The Father* caught Hollywood's eye. In only her second movie, she was cast opposite long-time film star Gary Cooper as his loyal wife in the Western classic *High Noon* (for which Cooper won the 1953 Academy Award for "Best Actor"). An instant success as a serious actress, young Grace was nominated for an Oscar as "Best Supporting Actress" for her portrayal of an adulteress in her next motion picture, *Mogambo*, opposite another long-established super-star, Clark Gable (also known as "The King"). In 1954, in the same year that *On the Waterfront* nearly swept the Academy Awards, Grace Kelly won the Oscar for "Best Actress" for her role as the embittered wife of an alcoholic actor-singer in *The Country Girl*. Again, she played opposite another aging super-star, Bing Crosby.

Grace Kelly's first three major motion pictures featured her opposite three established actors, each more than twice her age—Gary Cooper, Clark Gable, and Bing Crosby. Her next film role? Director Alfred Hitchcock selected her to play the love interest of yet another aging film star, the ever-handsome and dapper, Cary Grant, in *To Catch a Thief* (1955). Filmed on sound stages at Paramount Studios in Hollywood and on the French Riviera, young Grace met still another older man while filming in Europe, the royal playboy of the tiny principality of Monaco, Prince Rainier III. Smitten, and in need of an eventual heir to the throne, Prince Rainier proposed marriage to the young American beauty . . . and she accepted. Meanwhile, just before their marriage, Grace Kelly the actress completed two more movies for release in 1956, *The Swan*, and a more memorable film as her last swan song, *High Society*. *High Society* was a splendid success, and Grace Kelly was more popular with motion picture fans around the world than ever before. At her spectacular 1956 wedding in Monaco with all its royal pomp and circumstance, the little rich girl from Philadelphia and Hollywood completed her fairy-tale life to date by becoming the smiling Princess Grace of Monaco. From then on, instead of studio publicity photos, her beautiful face would grace the official postage stamps of the country of Monaco. Postage stamp sales in her adopted country skyrocketed. In the opinion of many Americans, Grace Kelly was one of the luckiest women in the world. Had she not fulfilled every young all-American girl's dream that, as Walt Disney's Snow White once sang, "Some day my Prince will come . . ."?

On the masculine side, besides Bill Holden, Gregory Peck, Rock Hudson, Clark Gable, Jimmy Stewart, Spencer Tracy, Richard Widmark, Marlon Brando, and James Dean, any list of Hollywood's box office super-stars of the 1950's would be woefully incomplete without the inclusion of John Wayne, Randolph Scott, Cary Grant, Kirk Douglas, and Charlton Heston.

Charlton Heston, after completing speech and drama classes at Northwestern University, served three years in the Army Air Force during World War II. Returning from the war, he began his acting career on Broadway. But his first national exposure began during the early years of television in the late 1940's, playing such well-known leading characters as Anthony in "Julius Caesar," Heathcliff in "Wuthering Heights," and Petruchio in "The Taming of the Shrew."

By 1953, Charlton Heston was appearing on the big screen in motion picture theatres across the county as Andrew Jackson in *The President's Lady* and as Buffalo Bill Cody in *Pony Express*. He went on to portray still another famous American, William Clark of Lewis and Clark Expedition fame in *The Far Horizons* (1955).

In 1956, Charlton Heston played perhaps his most memorable role as Moses in *The Ten Commandments*. While *The Ten Commandments* was a Hollywood spectacular of epic proportions, it faced stiff competition at the 1956 Academy Awards ceremony from *Around the World in 80 Days* ("Best Picture"), *Giant* (George Stevens, "Best Director"), *The King and I* (Yul Brynner, "Best Actor"), and *Anastasia* (Ingrid Bergman, "Best Actress"). Heston resumed his portrayal of Andrew Jackson in 1958's *The Buccaneer*. And, in 1959, he finally won an Academy Award for "Best Actor" for his lead role in the remake of the old silent film classic, *Ben-Hur*. As President Eisenhower's second term in office was nearing its end, Charlton Heston's *Ben-Hur* also won the Oscar for "Best Picture," "Best Director" (William Wyler), and "Best Supporting Actor" (Hugh Griffith). Of all the movie stars during the Eisenhower Years, Charlton Heston was without a doubt Hollywood's resident epic hero.

Kirk Douglas, another Hollywood action hero of the 1950's, was also known for his excellent portrayals of off-beat characters. Seven years older than Charlton Heston, Kirk Douglas, following a stint in the Navy during the war, got a slight head start on Heston when he was nominated for an Academy Award in 1949 for his leading role as an unscrupulous boxer in *Champion*. Following his success in *Champion*, Douglas starred in a succession of highly successful films, including *The Glass Menagerie* and *Young Man With a Horn* in 1950, *Along the Great Divide* in 1951, *The Big Sky* in 1952, *The Bad and Beautiful* in 1953, and the Jules Verne classic *20,000 Leagues Under the Sea* in 1954. In 1955, he was *The Indian Fighter*. But perhaps his most memorable movies during the Eisenhower Years were *Lust for Life* (1956), in which he played the tormented artist, Vincent Van Gogh, and as the lead in the action thriller *Spartacus* (1960). During the 1950's, Kirk Douglas earned worldwide recognition for his versatile acting talent.

In spite of his many critics, one of the greatest Hollywood stars of all time was John Wayne. Also known as "Duke," the former USC football player vaulted to stardom in 1939 when his long-time friend, director John Ford, cast him in the role of the Ringo Kid in his Western classic, *Stagecoach*. Prior to his role in *Stagecoach*, John Wayne had been typecast as the six-foot-four-inch tall, strong, silent-type star of nearly eighty low-budget films of the 1930's and 40's. "Yup," "Nope," and "Howdy" comprised the majority of his movie lines during his low-budget "B" movies career. But thanks to *Stagecoach*, and then to such memorable films as *Fort Apache*, *Red River*, and *Wake of the Red Witch* in 1948, as the aging cavalry officer in *She Wore a Yellow Ribbon* in 1949, and for his leading roles as a Marine hero in the *Sands of Iwo Jima* in 1950, and in *Flying Leathernecks* in 1951, John Wayne forged his image as the all-American hero. By 1953, President Eisenhower's first year in office, John Wayne had become one of the brightest box-office stars in Hollywood history.

In 1953, John Wayne starred in and co-produced one of his greatest hits ever, *Hondo*, followed by a succession of other successful films, including *The High and the Mighty* (1954), *Blood Alley* (1955), *The Searchers* (1956), the *Wings of Eagles* and *Legend of the Lost* (1957), *The Barbarian and the Geisha* (1958), *Rio Bravo* and *The Horse Soldiers* (1959), and, as Davy Crockett in *The Alamo* (1960). During the Eisenhower Years, aside from the President himself, John Wayne personified the American hero and patriot.

Last but not least of the Technicolor Western heroes of the 1950's was Randolph Scott. Born way back in January 1898, just before the Spanish-American War broke out (and before Ike turned eight years old), Randolph Scott was still riding high in the saddle during the Eisenhower Years to the delight of millions of his fans. At the age of only fourteen, the tall and husky Virginia lad lied about his age and went off the fight in World War I.[13] Returning to the United States after the war to study engineering at Georgia Tech and the University of North Carolina, Scott then went west to California. Deciding he'd rather act than work as an engineer, Randolph Scott joined the Pasadena Community Playhouse. Following a chance meeting on a local golf course with the legendary millionaire industrialist, playboy,

---

[13] Contrary to his public image, John Wayne never served in the military due to an injury he suffered while performing a movie stunt at a Hollywood studio during his student days at USC. The injury also ended his football career with the Trojans.

aviator, and movie producer Howard Hughes, Randolph Scott landed his first bit part in a Hollywood movie. The year? 1927.

Eventually, Randolph Scott was featured in a host of low-budget films, including *Wild Wagon Wheels* (1934), *Home on the Range* and *Rocky Mountain Mystery* (1935), *The Last of the Mohicans* and *Go West Young Man* (1936), *High, Wide and Handsome* (1937), *Rebecca of Sunnybrook Farm, The Texans,* and *The Road to Reno* (1938), *Jesse James,* the *Frontier Marshall* (as Wyatt Earp), and *Coast Guard* (1939), *Virginia City* (1940), and *Belle Star* (1941). Throughout World War II, Randolph Scott, a veteran of the Great War, continued to make movies to entertain the troops and the folks back home.

By the early 1940's, Randolph Scott had become one of Hollywood's *richest* men. By 1953, his personal wealth in oil, real estate, his production company (Ranown), and stocks and bonds was estimated to be approximately one hundred million dollars (a giant sum for a time when the average total price of a new "tract" home in the suburbs of Southern California was *nine thousand dollars).* While Randolph Scott's personal fortune may not have matched that of Bob Hope (or possibly Gene Autry's or Bing Crosby's), both Hope, the world's wealthiest comedian, and Scott, the Hollywood prototype of the rugged and aging cowboy hero, continued working well past the time they needed to do so for economic reasons *because they loved to entertain the folks.*

During the Eisenhower Years, Randolph Scott starred in eighteen films, from *Man Behind the Gun* in 1953 to *Comanche Station* in 1960. Randolph Scott never won an Academy Award for his acting, but he was one of Hollywood's best known and most beloved movie stars during America's "Happy Days."

Another of America's most beloved movie stars for more than three decades was Cary Grant. Cary Grant was once Randolph Scott's roommate during their early days in Hollywood. Mr. Grant was as handsome and stylishly dapper as Mr. Scott was authentically Western and rugged. Fans flocked to the movies to see Cary Grant play *Cary Grant.* Sophisticated, charming and debonair yet manly, Cary Grant's distinctive English accent was recognizable worldwide long before Dwight Eisenhower earned the rank of general.

Born into poverty in Bristol, England in 1904 as Archibald Leach, Cary Grant ran away from home at the age of thirteen. He traveled about England as part of an acrobatic troupe. He performed as a song-and-dance man, as a juggler, and, after coming to America in 1920, as a lifeguard on New York's Coney Island. He later appeared in several Broadway musicals in between such unusual side jobs as carrying advertising signs down New York City sidewalks while walking on stilts. He even appeared in numerous operettas in St. Louis, Missouri, as he slowly headed west towards Hollywood.

Cary Grant finally arrived in Hollywood in the fall of 1931, during the midst of the Great Depression. He was soon "discovered," and began appearing in movies. After appearing in seven feature films in 1932, including *Blond Venus*, starring Marlene Dietrich, Mae West gave his movie career a major boost when she picked him to co-star in her hit film *She Done Him Wrong*. Cary Grant had become one of Hollywood's romantic leading men.

By the late 1930's, Cary Grant had developed his unique screen personality. He had a rare knack for sophisticated comedy unmatched by any other Hollywood personality. And, like the popular and seemingly ageless female star Loretta Young, he seemed to remain forever young—dashing and dapper on screen to the end. During the 1950's, he played the romantic attraction of many young female stars who were half his age, including Grace Kelly in *To Catch a Thief* (1955) and Sophia Loren in *Houseboat* (1958). And he did so with a convincing style and panache. To his millions of fans, Cary Grant seemed ageless, and certainly one-of-a-kind.

As great as many of Hollywood's motion picture stars were as box office attractions during the Eisenhower Years, they certainly did not have a monopoly on the sale of movie tickets in America. Suddenly in 1956, from the music world of rock-'n-roll sprang Elvis Presley. Elvis Presley's sudden influence on American pop music in particular and on society in general was truly amazing. The former movie theatre usher and truck driver from Memphis, Tennessee by way of his birthplace of Tupelo, Mississippi, Elvis ("The Pelvis") Presley's pelvic gyrations while singing caused him to be idolized by teenagers of both genders, while many parents, especially across the "Bible Belt," declared his singing style and theatrics a serious threat to the morals of American youth. A young Frank Sinatra may have wowed teenage girls with his soulful voice during the 1940's, but even most of their parents loved his singing. Sinatra perfected contemporary songs; Presley popularized a whole new kind of music.

At first, Elvis Presley, as a newcomer to show business, toured parts of the South as "The Hillbilly Cat." But not for long. In 1955, Elvis Presley signed with RCA Records and became an instant hit on radio, television, and in concert halls coast-to-coast. "Love Me Tender," sung by Elvis, suddenly seemed to be heard everywhere. Teenage girls everywhere swooned at the sound of his voice, while teenage boys began wearing their "Levis" and slicking their hair with pomade *just like Elvis* in hopes of duplicating "The King's" luck with the girls.

Hollywood was quick to cash in on Elvis Presley's new-found-fame. First came the film *Love Me Tender* in 1956. Next, *Loving You* and *Jailhouse Rock*—also the titles of Presley's song hits—were big money-makers in 1957. All three movies were declared "duds" (or worse) by film critics. But each produced a box-office bonanza in cold hard cash. His next three films, *King Creole* (1958), *G.I. Blues* and *Flaming Star* (1960), shared similar receptions from critics and his fans. Elvis Presley was, in spite of his many critics, *the* young super-star of the late 1950's.

If Elvis Presley was the devil-in-disguise to many parents during the Eisenhower Years, Doris Day was their freckle-faced, girl-next-door sweetheart. Beginning in the 1940's as a young vocalist with the Bob Crosby and Les Brown bands, by the end of the decade she had become a highly successful recording artist. Her renditions of popular songs could be heard everywhere. As was the case with Elvis Presley, Hollywood acted quickly. Doris Day's first film appearance came in 1948 in *Romance on the High Seas*. In 1950, she starred in three films, *Young Man with a Horn, Tea for Two,* and *The West Point Story*. Film critics generally liked her light fare, and movie fans flocked to their local theatres to see her sweet and likeable image on the big screen. During the mid and late 1950's, Doris Day perfected her comical, virginal-like heroine style in romantic bedroom farces opposite such would-be seducers as Cary Grant and Rock Hudson. While Doris Day never came close to winning an Oscar for "Best Actress," she was one of Hollywood's most popular movie stars of the 1950's and one of its highest paid actresses. Among her biggest movie hits were *I'll See You in My Dreams* (1951), *April in Paris* (1952), *By the Light of the Silvery Moon* (1953), *Lucky Me* (1954), *Young at Heart* (1955), *Julie* (1956),

*The Pajama Game* (1957), *Teacher's Pet* (1958), *Pillow Talk* (1959),and *Midnight Lace* (1960). During the Eisenhower Years, Doris Day was unquestionably America's favorite romantic tease.

Near the end of President Eisenhower's first term in office, a new, young, Hollywood star was born when he burst upon the scene in 1956 in his convincing portrayal of the highly popular former Middleweight Boxing Champion of the World, Rocky Graziano, in the film *Somebody Up There Likes Me*. His name? Paul Newman. Paul Newman was bright, athletic, handsome, with a natural sense of humor and, according to his newly-found female fans, he had "Blue eyes to die for!"

Following service in the Pacific as a radioman with the Navy Air Corps, Paul Newman graduated from Kenyon College in Ohio and then attended Yale University's Drama School and the famed Actors Studio in New York City. Highly successful in 1953 in his first Broadway play, "Picnic," Warner Brothers Studios brought him to Hollywood. Following his successful performance in *Somebody Up There Likes Me*, Newman soon starred in a host of other popular films, including *The Helen Morgan Story* and *Until They Sail* in 1957, opposite Elizabeth Taylor in the smash hit *Cat on a Hot Tin Roof* in 1958, and opposite Joanne Woodward (the 1953 Academy Award winner for "Best Actress" for *The Three Faces of Eve*) in *The Long Hot Summer* and *Rally 'Round the Flag Boys!*, also in 1958. That same year, Paul Newman and Joanne Woodward were married. Somehow, Newman managed to give one more fine performance in 1958 as Billy the Kid in *The Left-Handed Gun*.

Paul Newman's next three motion pictures proved to be Hollywood classics: *The Young Philadelphians* in 1959, and *Exodus* and *From the Terrace* (co-starring Joanne Woodward) in 1960. Both Paul Newman and his wife Joanne Woodward would remain major stars and shining examples of Hollywood's more cerebral side for years to come.

Paul Newman and Joanne Woodward were certainly polished actors with cerebral reputations. So too was Gregory Peck. Tall, dark, and handsome, with a deep, resonant voice, Gregory Peck was the prototype Hollywood leading man during the Eisenhower Years. Born in La Jolla, California, Peck graduated from San Diego State College and was a pre-med student at the University of California at Berkeley when he was first bitten by the acting bug. Exempt from military service due to a sports injury, Peck left for New York City, where he had his first taste of success as an actor on Broadway in 1942.

In 1942, many of Hollywood's established leading men were overseas, fighting in the war, including Army Air Force Major Clark Gable, Navy Lieutenant and Bronze Star recipient Henry Fonda, Marine Lance Corporal Glenn Ford, British Commando Lieutenant David Niven, Army Air Force Colonel Jimmy Stewart, and Navy flight instructor Robert Taylor. As a replacement leading man, Gregory Peck quickly became a movie star during the 1940's.[14] His first Oscar nomination came as a result of his excellent acting in *The Keys of the Kingdom* in 1945.

In 1950, Gregory Peck played the lead role in the popular Western drama, *The Gunfighter*, and he gained a third Oscar nomination for "Best Actor" for his performance in the military thriller *Twelve O'Clock High*. During the Eisenhower Years, Gregory Peck starred in many hit films, including *Roman Holiday* (opposite Audrey Hepburn) in 1953; *Night People* in 1954; *The Man in the Gray Flannel Suit* and as Captain Ahab in *Moby Dick* in 1956; *Designing Woman* in 1957; *The Big Country* in 1958; as F. Scott Fitzgerald in *Beloved Infidel*, in the nuclear-age thriller *On the Beach*, and the bloody Korean War drama *Pork Chop Hill* in 1959. Gregory Peck would finally win the coveted Academy Award for "Best Actor" for his memorable performance as the highly principled and ethical attorney Atticus Finch in the civil rights classic *To Kill a Mockingbird* (1962).

Of those Hollywood leading men of the late 1930's who served with distinction during World War II, no one was more successful in films following the war than Jimmy Stewart. A Princeton University graduate with a degree in architecture, Jimmy Stewart was persuaded by classmate Joshua Logan (who would later co-author such Broadway classics as "Mister Roberts," "South Pacific," and "Fanny") to try acting. Stewart agreed. Soon, he was sharing a New York City apartment with another aspiring Broadway actor, Henry Fonda (who would later gain international fame as Tom Joad in the 1940 film version of John

---

[14] It should be noted that many of Hollywood's top directors and producers served in the Army Signal Corps during World War II, including Colonel Frank Capra, Lieutenant Colonel Daryl F. Zanuck, and Major John Houston, producing and directing "Why We Fight" documentaries.

Steinbeck's classic, *The Grapes of Wrath*). Both Stewart and Fonda were briefly roommates again when they first arrived in Hollywood in 1935. Fonda's first movie role was in *The Farmer Takes a Wife*; Stewart's was in *The Murder Man*. Both men became stars in 1939 when Henry Fonda played Lincoln in *Young Mr. Lincoln* and Jimmy Stewart in *It's a Wonderful World* and *Mr. Smith Goes to Washington*. In 1940, Jimmy Stewart won the Academy Award for "Best Actor" for *The Philadelphia Story*.

During World War II, Henry Fonda fought bravely in the Pacific while Jimmy Stewart flew twenty dangerous missions over Nazi Germany as a bomber pilot. Following the war, Fonda returned full-time to civilian life; Stewart remained in the Air Force Reserve, ultimately rising to the rank of Brigadier General. Like Fonda, Stewart also resumed his movie career. Throughout the Eisenhower Years, Jimmy Stewart was one of America's leading movie stars *and the highest-ranking entertainer in the United States military.*

It has been written that Jimmy Stewart's favorite film was the first one he made after the war, Frank Capra's sentimental 1947 classic *It's a Wonderful Life* (still commonly aired on TV during the Christmas season in its original black and white), in which Stewart played a banker with a big heart. In real life, Jimmy Stewart was also good with a buck. To his good fortune, he was one of the first movie stars during the early 1950's to accept less money up front for his work on a movie in exchange for a percentage of the film's net profits. Stewart's films made enormous profits, especially *Winchester 73, Broken Arrow*, and *Harvey* (1950); *The Greatest Show on Earth* (1952); *Thunder Bay* (1953); as band leader Glenn Miller in *The Glenn Miller Story*, co-starring the "sweet" and very popular June Allyson, and the thriller, *Rear Window* (1954); *The Far Country, Strategic Air Command*, and *The Man From Laramie* (1955); *The Man Who Knew Too Much* (1956); as the aviator Charles A. Lindberg in *The Spirit of St. Louis* (1957); *Vertigo* and *Bell, Book and Candle* (1958); and *Anatomy of a Murder* and *The FBI Story* (1959). Jimmy Stewart was truly Hollywood's most wholesome, shy, guy-next-door-type leading man during the 1950's. America loved him and respected him.

During the Eisenhower Years, America also loved and respected Walt Disney. Of all of the Hollywood motion picture producers and executives since the invention of "talkies," no one has had a greater impact upon the entertainment of children *worldwide* than Walt Disney. His invention of the beloved cartoon character Mickey Mouse in 1928 has since delighted children and adults around the globe. Over the years, beginning with his first talking cartoon featuring Mickey Mouse in *Steamboat Willie* (1928), and with his "Silly Symphony" cartoons, including *The Three Little Pigs* (1933), Walt, with his older brother Roy lending a steady hand, grew his tiny production team of talented and dedicated artists into a mighty entertainment empire. By the 1950's, The Walt Disney Company dominated the family entertainment industry.

Volunteering as a Red Cross ambulance driver in France during World War I at the age of sixteen, the Chicago-born Walt Disney returned to the United States in 1919 to work as a commercial artist in Kansas City, Missouri. Kansas City's loss was Hollywood's gain when the young Mr. Disney left for Southern California and established his own cartoon production company in 1923. It took five long and lean years before The Walt Disney Company produced its first real cartoon hit, *Steamboat Willie*. Soon, however, the successful animated cartoons featuring Mickey Mouse spawned a splendid stable of loveable, human-like characters including Mickey's girlfriend Minnie Mouse, his pal Donald Duck and Donald's girlfriend Daisy, Donald's rich Uncle Scrooge McDuck, his mischievous nephews Huey, Dewey, and Louie, Mickey's trusty dog Pluto, and his wacky friend Goofy. Each character became enormously famous.

In 1955, during President Eisenhower's third year in office, Walt Disney realized his dream of a "Magic Kingdom" for everyone who was *young at heart* when, amidst all the media hoopla and TV coverage he could muster, he personally opened the doors to Snow White's magic castle. *Disneyland*, built on what was once 160 acres of orange trees on the outskirts of the old farm town, Anaheim, California, made his "Magic Kingdom" a reality for all to behold. Walt Disney's *Disneyland* suddenly became *the* entertainment destination for the young at heart from around the world. And Mickey Mouse, Donald Duck, Pluto, Goofy, Snow White and the Seven Dwarfs, and the rest of the Disney gang were there *in person* to greet each guest.

One might make the argument that *Disneyland* was made possible primarily because of a giant gamble taken by Walt Disney many years before when he decided to risk everything in 1934—in the midst of the Great Depression—in order to make the world's first full-length, animated feature film, *Snow White and the Seven Dwarfs*. Three years in the making (each story panel had to be carefully hand painted by Disney artists), *Snow White and the Seven Dwarfs* was an instant hit following its release in February 1938. No wonder Snow White's Castle was featured in the center of Disney's giant amusement park in Anaheim.

During the Eisenhower Years, Walt Disney was as well-known and respected as any of Hollywood's biggest movie stars. One of the reasons for his fame was the fact that he never rested his reputation on past laurels alone. While steadfastly loyal to his early creations, including Mickey Mouse, he nevertheless expanded his entertainment empire beyond animated films during the 1950's to include live action motion pictures, such as his 1950 version of the classic tale, *Treasure Island*, and full-length nature documentaries, beginning with *The Living Desert* in 1953. In 1954, Disney's action adventure *20,000 Leagues Under the Sea*, starring Kirk Douglas, was a major box-office triumph. In 1955, his success grew even greater. Not only was Disneyland's opening a colossal success from the start—The Walt Disney Company released four of its most successful films that same year: *Davy Crockett—King of the Wild Frontier*, starring Fess Parker; the animated film classic *Lady and the Tramp*, featuring the incomparable and "hip" singing of jazz vocalist Miss Peggy Lee; the beautiful nature film *The African Lion*; and the humorous *The Littlest Outlaw*. Many major Disney hits of a widely varied nature soon followed, including *The Giant Locomotive Chase* and *Secrets of Life* (1956); *Sleeping Beauty* and *The Shaggy Dog* (1959); and *Kidnapped, Pollyana, The Swiss Family Robinson,* and *The Sign of Zorro* (1960). Family life in America (and perhaps in much of the world) would not have been the same during the Eisenhower Years without Walt Disney and his many dreams.

Beginning in the mid-1950's, many American women of all ages had dreams of being the love interest of a tall, young, masculine-looking and very handsome new film star called Rock Hudson. Rock Hudson, born Roy Scherer, Jr., in Winnetka, Illinois, had a certain visual wholesomeness of character, an easy smile, and a deep, sexy-sounding voice that drew audiences—especially members of the opposite sex—to his image on the big screen. Unable to win any acting roles in high school plays as a youth, Rock Hudson won *Look* magazine's award as Hollywood's "Star of the Year" in 1958.

The motion picture that made Rock Hudson an instant Hollywood movie star in 1954 was *Magnificent Obsession*. Starring opposite Jayne Wyman, who was already an established star in her own right (and Ronald Reagan's former wife), Rock Hudson was highly believable as the wholesome hero in that tearful melodrama. Jayne Wyman's penchant for playing the heroine in such classic tearjerkers as *The Lost Weekend* (1945), *Johnny Belinda* (1948), and *The Blue Veil* (1951), was again evident in her performance in *Obsession*. Together, they simply clicked, even though Jayne was nearly twelve years older than Rock.

From *Magnificent Obsession*, Rock Hudson soon starred in a series of hit films during the 1950's, including *Captain Lightfoot* and *One Desire* in 1955; *All That Heaven Allows* and the mega-hit *Giant* in 1956; *Written on the Wind* and *A Farewell to Arms* in 1957; *Twilight for the Gods* in 1958; and with Doris Day in the enormously popular romantic comedy *Pillow Talk* in 1959.

Rock Hudson was tall, handsome, and somewhat talkative, showcasing his sexy voice. He was still young and also relatively new at being a movie star. Gary Cooper, on the other hand, was tall but slimmer than Rock, still handsome but obviously weathered, and always the shy, silent-type, one of the reasons he was sometimes simply called "Coop." Gary Cooper had been a Hollywood leading man for over thirty years, since starring in the 1926 *silent* film classic, *The Winning of Barbara Worth* opposite such ancients as Ronald Coleman and Vilma Banky. "Coop" had survived the transition in the late 1920's/early '30's from silent films to sound motion pictures, and he was still going strong.

Born in Helena, Montana just after the turn of the century, Gary Cooper worked briefly as a guide at Yellowstone National Park after graduation from college. His career ambition? To be a political cartoonist for a major Western newspaper. With that purpose in mind, young Cooper set out for Los Angeles in 1924. But instead of a career as a cartoonist for the Los Angeles *Examiner* or *Times*, he found himself making ends meet by working as a door-to-door salesman and as an extra in Western movies. Gary Cooper was tall and handsome, with a shy smile and a hesitant way of speaking that soon endeared him to movie audiences—male *and* female—when Hollywood was making its sometimes painful transition from silent films to talkies. Gary Cooper was comfortable in both.

During the 1930's, Gary Cooper steadily built his reputation as Hollywood's prototype man of the west—strong, silent, an all-American man of action and few words. His many successful films included the motion picture version of Ernest Hemingway's classic novel, *A Farewell to Arms* (1932); *Mr. Deeds Goes to Town* (1936); his portrayal of Wild Bill Hickok in *The Plainsman* (1937); as Marco Polo in *The Adventures of Marco Polo* and as the cowboy in *The Cowboy and the Lady* (1938); and in the title role in *Beau Geste* (1939). By 1940, Gary Cooper had established himself as one of Hollywood's leading stars. But many of his finest films were yet to be made. In 1941, Gary Cooper won his first Academy Award for "Best Actor" for his portrayal of World War I's most decorated hero, *Sergeant York*. Next, he gained high praise as the "Iron Man" Lou Gehrig in *The Pride of the Yankees* (1942), followed by his leading role in Ernest Hemingway's monumental tale of the Spanish Revolution, *For Whom the Bell Tolls* (1942).

Ten years later, in 1952, Gary Cooper—with Grace Kelly playing his beautiful young wife—won the Oscar for "Best Actor" for his role as the rather isolated town marshall in the thrilling Western psychodrama, *High Noon*. Some critics called *High Noon* the first "modern" Western for its raw and frank portrayal of life as it really was in the Old West. During the Eisenhower Years, Gary Cooper remained one of Hollywood's leading stars, demonstrating his acting versatility not only in *High Noon*, but in his films that followed, including *Springfield Rifle* (1952); *Return to Paradise* and *Blowing Wild* (1953); *Garden of Evil* and *Vera Cruz* (1954); as General Billy Mitchell in *The Court-Martial of Billy Mitchell* (1955); in *Friendly Persuasion* (1956); *Love in the Afternoon* (1957); *Ten North Frederick* (1958); and *The Hanging Tree* (1959).

The most famous American artist and illustrator of the 1930's, '40's, and '50's—Norman Rockwell—was widely known and loved throughout the United States for his illustrations on the covers of *The Saturday Evening Post* celebrating the lives of average Americans at work, while worshiping, and at play. Perhaps of all of Hollywood's leading male stars, Gary Cooper, together with Jimmy Stewart and John Wayne, best fit Norman Rockwell's concept of what a composite of the all-American hero might look like. In the minds of many Americans during the 1950's, Cooper, Stewart, and Wayne were not only movie stars; they were *heroes* and *role models*.

The Hollywood of the Eisenhower Years also had many heroes behind the cameras whose talents and dedication helped make Gary Cooper, Jimmy Stewart, John Wayne, and a host of other actors and actresses part of the average American's psyche. Hollywood's producers, directors, and screenwriters were the men primarily responsible for the films that brought audiences into the theatres and helped the stars shine on the big screen.[15] Included among Hollywood's greatest producers, directors, and screenwriters of the 1950's were Buddy Adler, producer (*From Here to Eternity, Love is a Many-Splendored Thing, The Revolt of Mamie Stover, Bus Stop,* and *South Pacific*); Richard Brooks, director (*The Blackboard Jungle, Cat on a Hot Tin Roof,* and *Elmer Gantry*); John Ford, producer/director (*Wagonmaster, Rio Grande, The Quiet Man, Mogambo, The Wings of Eagles,* and *The Last Hurrah*); Arthur Freed, producer (*Annie Get Your Gun, Show Boat, An American in Paris, Singin' in the Rain, Brigadoon, Kismet, Silk Stockings,* and *Gigi*); Howard Hawks, producer/director (*The Big Sky, Gentlemen Prefer Blonds,* and *Rio Bravo*); Alfred Hitchcock, producer/director (*Dial M for Murder, Rear Window, To Catch a Thief, Vertigo, North by Northwest,* and *Psycho*); Elia Kazan, director (*A Streetcar Named Desire, ¡Viva Zapata!, On the Waterfront,* and *East of Eden*); Stanley Kramer, producer/director (*Death of a Salesman, High Noon, The Caine Mutiny, Not as a Stranger, The Defiant Ones, On the Beach,* and *Inherit the Wind*); Walter Lang, director (*Cheaper by the Dozen, Call Me Madam, There's No Business Like Show Business, The King and I,* and *Can-Can*); Joseph L. Mankiewiez, producer/director/screenwriter (*All About Eve, The Barefoot Contessa, Guys and Dolls,* and *Suddenly Last Summer*); Otto Preminger, producer/director (*The Man with the Golden Arm, Porgy and Bess, Anatomy of a Murder,* and *Exodus*); John Sturges, director (*Bad Day at Black Rock, Gunfight at the O.K. Corral, The Old Man and the Sea,* and *The Magnificent Seven*); Hal B. Wallis, producer (*Come Back Little Sheba, The Rose Tattoo,* and *The Rainmaker*); Raul Walsh, director (*Battle Cry, Band of Angels,* and *The Naked and the Dead*); William Wellman, director (*Across the Wide*

---

[15] It should be noted that Hollywood during the 1950's was still very much a *man's* town. Ida Lupino, the movie actress, was the only female director of Hollywood motion pictures during the 1950's.

*Missouri, Island in the Sky*, and *The High and the Mighty*); Billy Wilder, producer/director/screenwriter (*Stalig 17, Sabrina, The Seven Year Itch, Some Like it Hot*, and *The Apartment*); Robert Wise, director (*The Day the Earth Stood Still, Executive Suite, Somebody Up There Likes Me*, and *Run Silent Run Deep*); William Wyler, producer/director (*Carrie, Roman Holiday, Friendly Persuasion, The Big Country*, and *Ben-Hur*); and Fred Zinnemann, director (*High Noon, From Here to Eternity, Oklahoma!*, and *The Sundowners*). The one obvious name missing? Cecil B. DeMille.

Cecil B. DeMille, producer/director/screenwriter extraordinaire, was already a true Hollywood pioneer and a living legend when "I Like IKE!" swept the nation in 1952. Born way back in 1881 (some nine years older than Ike), DeMille was still going strong when he produced and directed the last of his mammoth spectaculars, *The Ten Commandments*, starring Charlton Heston as Moses. From 1914, when he produced Hollywood's first full-length Western, *The Squaw Man*, to *The Ten Commandments*, released in 1956, Cecil Blount DeMille produced and directed seventy motion pictures of generally high quality and assisted in the writing and production of many others. By the dawn of the 1950's, the name Cecil B. DeMille was synonymous with Hollywood movies. The son of an Episcopalian preacher, DeMille's films often contained a compelling Christian message that resonated with American audiences during the first five decades of Hollywood's existence. Especially powerful were his giant spectacles, *The King of Kings* (1927), *The Sign of the Cross* (1932), *Cleopatra* (1934), *The Crusades* (1935), *Samson and Delilah* (1949), and *The Ten Commandments* (1956).

During the Eisenhower's Years, other well-known behind-the-scene Hollywood personalities included the world-famous costume designer, Edith Head. Edith Head, with a B.A. from UCLA, an M.A. from Stanford, and a California teaching credential in art, was *the* designer for the stars (and Cecil B. DeMille) at Paramount Studios during the 1940's and '50's. During the 1950's, she won Oscars for "Best Costume Design" for *All About Eve* and *Samson and Delilah* (1950), *A Place in the Sun* (1951), *Roman Holiday* (1953), and *Sabrina* (1954). To movie fans during the 1950's, Edith Head was *the* costume designer to the stars.

How would motion pictures be made without cameramen? They wouldn't. Yet, during the 1950's, only one Hollywood cameraman was widely known by the movie-going public—James Wong Howe. Born in Canton, China, the former professional boxer first broke into the film business during the 1920's under the guiding hand of his mentor, Cecil B. DeMille. Among Howe's most memorable films of the 1950's were *Come Back Little Sheba* (1953), *The Rose Tattoo* (1955), *Picnic* (1956), *The Sweet Smell of Success* (1957), *The Old Man and the Sea* (1958), and *The Last Angry Man* (1959). When the name James Wong Howe flashed on the big screen's credits in bold letters, audiences knew they were about to see excellence in cinematography.

Silent films were all cinematography; sound motion pictures also had recorded human voices, sound effects, *and music* as integral parts of the finished product. The right music at the right time helped create the appropriate mood for the movie audience. During the Eisenhower Years, Hollywood producers and directors—and the actors whose performances they helped showcase—depended on excellent sound tracks containing the musical scores of their films. Sound tracks for dialogue and sound effects were recorded separately and then blended, or "mixed," with the film's music score to produce the final product. During the 1950's, Hollywood was blessed with a host of outstanding music composers and arrangers who wrote the scores for the sound tracks of the industry's greatest films. They included such titans of the music world as Irving Berlin, Elmer Bernstein, Leonard Bernstein, Sammy Cahn, Hoagy Carmichael, George and Ira Gershwin, Johnny Green, Oscar Hammerstein II, Jerome Kern, Frederick Loewe, Henry Mancini, Johnny Mercer, Alfred Newman, Cole Porter, André Previn, Richard Rodgers, and Dimitri Tiomkin—A "Who's Who" of the music world. Many won Oscars for their contributions to successful films.

Advertising was essential to the success of each of Hollywood's plethora of films. Competition was keen. Film critics were courted. Millions could be made or lost when a film was judged a "hit" or a "miss" based on its bottom line: gross ticket sales. After all, movie fans voted when they *bought tickets*; the movie industry was a *business*. To advertise its films in order to pack the nation's theatres with their products, each major studio—Columbia, MGM, Fox, Paramount, RKO, Warner Bros., and Walt Disney—had its own huge publicity department. But most movie fans demanded more than glowing, self-serving accounts of a film's attributes, or of its stars' on-screen performances. They read reviews of films by independent critics. And they demanded "inside information"—*gossip*—about the private lives of the stars. That was the role of the gossip columnists and their "inside" stories about the behind-the-scenes lives of Hollywood's celebrities. During the 1950's, two Hollywood gossip columnists ruled the roost—Hedda Hopper, and her rival, Louella Parsons. A former silent film actress, and a Hollywood celebrity and "insider" in her own right, Hedda Hopper began her career as a gossiper on the radio in 1936, adding her syndicated newspaper column in 1938. Famous for her flamboyant hats, her flighty chitchat style, and her public feuds with some of Hollywood's leading actresses, including Constance Bennett (*Moulin Rouge*, *Topper*, and *As Young as Your Feel*), Hedda Hopper was extremely powerful in Hollywood during the 1940's and '50's. She could make or break lives and careers. So well known was she that she played herself in *Breakfast in Hollywood* (1946) and in *Sunset Boulevard* (1950). Hedda Hopper often referred to her own mansion in Beverly Hills as "The house that fear built."

Louella Parsons was Hedda Hopper's chief rival in the gossip column business. She became famous for her frequent inside "scoops" on the private lives of Hollywood's rich and famous. Writing a syndicated column published in the nation's major cities by newspaper titan William Randolph Hearst (who, as a married man, convorted with his movie-star girlfriend Marion Davis at their 110 room mansion on the beach at Santa Monica and at his even grander *castle* just up the California coast at San Simeon), Louella Parsons also wielded enormous power over who in Hollywood became a star, and who would flop and soon disappear.

By the late 1950's, not all "hit" movies shown in America were made in Hollywood. A former school dropout and shoeshine boy from Boston, Joseph E. Levine made a fortune following World War II by buying up the rights to Japanese-made science-fiction action films, including his biggest hit, *Godzilla*, at cheap prices and then garnering huge box-office profits through clever and extravagant advertising campaigns. Levine also turned to war-torn Italy for the rights to such muscle epics as *Hercules*, and he profited handsomely. Profits earned from those foreign movies were later used by him to produce some of Hollywood's finer films. During the 1960's, Joseph E. Levine produced such American-made classics as *The Carpetbaggers* and *Where Love Has Gone* (1964), *Nevada Smith* (1966), and *The Graduate* (1967).

Certainly, not all American films made during the 1950's were ever intended to be considered for any awards. Many, especially most comedies, were simply produced with two objectives in mind: (1) Make a profit, and (2) entertain the audience. Hollywood producer Hal Wallis had a list of serious films to his credit. He also produced many movies with the simple intent to entertain at a tidy profit. With those two objectives in mind, Hal Wallis signed the young night club comedy act of Martin and Lewis to a movie contract with Paramount in 1949. The result? Seventeen Martin and Lewis comedy hits at the box-office between 1949 and 1956, before the dynamic duo of Dean Martin and Jerry Lewis suddenly split up.[16] During President Eisenhower's first term in office, the team of Martin and Lewis was the hottest comedy act in America. Together, they became two of the biggest box-office attractions in Hollywood. Never worried about winning an Oscar for their efforts on screen, Dean Martin—the handsome, singing straight-man—and Jerry Lewis—the crew-cut, nutty comic—laughed all the way to the bank, with Hal Wallis right beside them.

Not all of Hollywood's movie moguls and exhibitors were laughing all the way to the bank during the Eisenhower Years. Back during the last years of the Truman administration, the U.S. Supreme Court's decision in *The United States v. Paramount Pictures, Inc., et al* of May 1948 essentially declared Hollywood's major studios *illegal monopolies*. As a result, the famed "studio system" which had encouraged each major studio to painstakingly recruit, groom, and publicize its own stable of stars under contract since the early 1920's for the exclusive production of its films to maximize profits began to slowly crumble. In 1950, nearly all of Hollywood's actors and actresses were still under contract to one of the five major studios; by 1960, most worked in independent productions in America and abroad, or primarily in television. Of the roughly 150 Hollywood stars under contract to Paramount, MGM, or one of the other majors in 1950, perhaps a mere twenty top stars remained bound by contract to major studios by 1960.

By the mid-1950's, an increasing number of Hollywood's big name movie makers, including Stanley Kramer and Otto Preminger,

---

[16] For a revealing and in-depth review of the hit comedy team of Martin and Lewis, see Jerry Lewis and James Kaplan's *Dean & Me* (New York: Doubleday, 2005).

became highly successful independent producers who could hire the stars of their choosing for the making of a particular film. While many other Hollywood movie moguls worried about competition from independent producers within the industry, they also had to contend with the ever-growing popularity of stay-at-home TV. As a result of all this new competition, the total volume of motion pictures produced dropped, but the general quality of those films produced appeared to improve.

More than 20,000 motion picture theatres existed in 1946. By 1957, just eleven years later, fewer than 14,000 were still open for business. And, while nearly 5,000 drive-in theatres across the country continued to prosper—especially in areas where land prices and property taxes were relatively cheap—projections for future growth were dim. For theatres and drive-ins alike, competition also forced filmmakers to improve the ways their films were projected onto the big screen. Hence, the 1950's witnessed numerous technological advancements in projection systems, including Paramount's "Vista-Vision," MGM's "Panavision," and 20th Century Fox's "CinemaScope." Some major cities were also introduced to the far more expensive, three-screen "Cinerama," productions. Even "3-D" made its appearance, complete with special "3-D glasses" to be worn while viewing the big screen for "life-like" results.

Since many movie theatres were closing due to declining revenues, theatre owners attempted to attract more customers by offering two movies for the price of one, or "double features," as they came to be called. During the 1950's, an increasing number of theatres offered a "featured" movie plus another less-publicized film *and* a cartoon *and* a newsreel, with an "intermission" in the middle, all for the price of one admission. Some theatres also held nightly drawings for prizes as special promotions. But the motion picture industry could simply not hold back the rising tide of television. Would television eventually put Hollywood's motion picture studios out of business?

# CHAPTER 3

# TELEVISION

In 1950, television was in its infancy; by 1960, it was America's chief means of entertainment. Because of television, the entire entertainment industry in America—and society itself—was revolutionized during the Eisenhower Years. Dwight Eisenhower lost no time in actively cultivating his "TV image." In 1953, Robert Montgomery, the long-established movie star and former President of the Screen Actors Guild, was persuaded by Ike to serve as his Special Consultant to the President on TV and Public Communications. Together, they were masterful at maintaining a positive public image of Eisenhower on television and in the print media as someone the average American could *trust*. "I Like IKE!" was not simply a political slogan during the 1952 and 1956 Presidential campaigns; it was a carefully managed public relations strategy—and television played a major role in maintaining Ike's image as one of America's most beloved presidents.

In 1946, only a few thousand television "sets" could be found in American homes, primarily in New York City and its surrounding area. By 1956, only ten years later, more than forty-two million TV sets could be found in homes from coast-to-coast across the United States. Television had rapidly become a big industry. American-made television sets manufactured by more than a dozen competing U.S. firms, including Admiral, General Electric, Hoffman, Magnavox, Motorola, Muntz, Packard-Bell, Philco, RCA, Westinghouse, and

Zenith were locked in a fierce battle to fill the growing demand for bigger and better TVs. Some television sets were built into fancy wood consoles made to look like pieces of living room furniture and costing up to a thousand dollars. Smaller, more "portable" TVs without the wood console generally cost far less. Regardless of size or cost, Americans bought TVs at an ever-growing rate. They also bought frozen "TV dinners" to heat in the oven and then eat on "TV trays" in front of their sofas or easy chairs while watching television in their living rooms. Many also purchased "TV lights" to better illuminate their otherwise darkened viewing and eating area. And the weekly *TV Guide*, listing all of the programs available with commentaries appropriate to various viewing areas, became one of America's leading publications. *TV Guide* soon became available at most drug stores, grocery stores, liquor stores, and through home delivery by U.S. mail for a reasonable subscription rate.

During the early 1950's, it was not at all uncommon in cities large and small across America, especially during Friday and Saturday evenings, to see groups of people standing on sidewalks outside stores where TVs were sold watching television shows through plate glass windows. TVs were frequently turned on so passersby would be enticed to come inside and purchase a set of their own. In many areas, demand sometimes exceeded supply. And to many people, prices still seemed prohibitive. As a result, many viewers were compelled to watch TV at their local stores, *or visit friends and neighbors lucky enough to already own one.* "TV antennas" on the roofs of houses across America soon became *status symbols* (and magnets for visiting neighbors not yet fortunate enough to have their own TV).

To many Americans during the early 1950's, television was truly *magical.* Believe it or not, to some individuals, even the "test patterns" were worth watching. Most TV "channels" only offered regular programs from approximately 7 am to midnight. A "test pattern" with the particular station's logo was often broadcast during down time. Even New York City, Chicago, and Los Angeles offered fewer than twelve channels—2 through 13—for viewing pleasure. In 1952, as Dwight Eisenhower and Adlai Stevenson battled each other for the Presidency, the Federal Communications Commission (FCC) authorized a maximum of 2053 television stations in 1291 communities in the United States and its territories and possessions to operate locally on a total of twelve Very

High Frequency (VHF) bands. Each station operating on the same VHF band was required to be at least 170 miles apart. The nation's three largest radio networks—CBS, NBC, and the upstart ABC—were quick to establish as many stations as possible in each regional market, while many independents and smaller networks vied for the rest. In Los Angeles, for example, CBS was Channel 2, NBC Channel 4, and ABC Channel 7, while various smaller networks and independents claimed Channel 5 (Gene Autry's Golden West Broadcasters), Channel 9, Channel 11 (the Los Angeles *Times*), and Channel 13. The growing interest in television was greatly bolstered in 1951 with the introduction of coaxial cable and microwave relays coast-to-coast. Sporting events, major political conventions and Presidential speeches, breaking news of national importance, popular variety shows, and other TV offerings became eyewitness events to most Americans with television sets. By late 1956, as President Eisenhower was running for reelection, nearly five hundred separate television stations (many part of the CBS, NBC, or ABC networks) were broadcasting in the United States. And many of their broadcasts, including the evening news from New York City, were coast-to-coast.

Television was ideal for advertising. Radio was sound. Newspapers and magazines had pictures. TV had both! TV advertising fast became another billion-dollar industry created by this new technological marvel. Those viewers who even watched "test patterns" for entertainment were joined by millions more who were often mesmerized by the wide variety and appeal of TV ads. Only ads for hard liquor and certain "unmentionables" were prohibited; most other product promotions, including beer and tobacco products, were encouraged. And, as the number of TV sets in homes increased, the price of advertising on television—especially ads shown during the most popular time slots—skyrocketed. By the early 1950's, industry revenues for the major networks, the more successful independent stations, and the top advertising agencies increased dramatically. By the time Ike and Mamie settled into the White House in 1953, TV was *big business*.

As the popularity of television grew, its list of well-known personalities increased. During the 1950's, television's list of personalities was amazing in its scope and diversity. During the Eisenhower Years, television's top personalities included Fred Allen, George Burns and Gracie Allen, Steve Allen, Eddie "Rochester" Anderson, Eve Arden,

James Arness, Lucille Ball and Desi Arnaz, Gene Autry and his horse "Champion," Jim Backus, William Bendix, Jack Benny, Edgar Bergen and his wooden sidekick Charley McCarthy, Milton Berle, Leonard Bernstein, Joey Bishop, Mel Blanc, Ward Bond, Richard Boone, Ernest Borgnine, William Boyd, Charles Boyer, Walter Brennan, Lloyd Bridges, Raymond Burr, Red Buttons, Sid Caesar, Art Carney, Leo Carrillo, Dick Clark, Iron Eyes Cody, Wally Cox, Broderick Crawford, Robert Cummings, Andy Devine, Jimmy Durante, Dale Evans, Nanette Fabray, Annette Funicello, Eva and Zsa Zsa Gabor, James Garner, Jackie Gleason, Arthur Godfrey, Lorne Greene, Andy Griffith, Barbara Hale, Bob Hope, David Janssen, Michael Landon, "Lassie," Stan Laurel and Oliver Hardy, Robert Q. Lewis, Liberace, Art Linkletter, June Lockhart, Tina Louise, Darren McGavin, Steve McQueen, Guy Madison, Groucho Marx, Ray Milland, Robert Montgomery, Clayton Moore, Ozzie and Harriet Nelson and their sons David and Ricky, David Niven, Lloyd Nolan, Hugh O'Brien, Donald O'Connor, Fess Parker, Jack Parr, Tony Randall, Ronald Reagan, Donna Reed, Carl Reiner, Duncan Renaldo, Roy Rogers and his horse "Trigger," Mickey Rooney, Rod Serling, Jay Silverheels, Phil Silvers, Red Skelton, Ann Southern, Barbara Stanwyck, Ed Sullivan, Danny Thomas, "The Three Stooges" (Curly, Moe, and Larry), Jack Webb, Jane Wyatt, Loretta Young, and Robert Young. And the leading television newsmen of the day were such outstanding journalists as Edward R. Murrow, Walter Cronkite, David Brinkley, Chet Huntley, and Lowell Thomas. During the Eisenhower Years, the list of well-known television personalities was nearly endless. Such an endless pool of talent (often displayed in variety shows and dramas broadcast *live*) has led many critics to proclaim the 1950's as the "Golden Age" of television. With such a variety of talent available in one's living room each night at no additional cost except for the original purchase price of a TV set and a slight increase in one's monthly electric bill, is there any wonder why Hollywood movie studios during the 1950's cut back on the number of motion pictures they produced? Or why many movie theatres closed for lack of customers?

 The television industry in America that began its first regularly scheduled service in New York City on April 30, 1939 with the broadcast of the opening of the New York World's Fair—*live in black and white*—was rudely interrupted by World War II. Television service was resumed by a few broadcasting stations in 1946. By 1953, most major cities across America had their own local television stations, some of which were affiliated with the big radio networks—CBS, NBC, and ABC. Initially, during the late 1940's and early '50's, the motion picture industry and television *clashed*. Not nearly so with radio. Television soon became "radio with pictures," and many existing radio networks simply expanded to include TV. Old radio shows designed for living room *listening* became "new" TV shows for living room *watching and listening*. Using many of the same program formats, scripts, and most of the same stars, new TV shows were often old radio programs *alive and in person*. For example, one of American radio's all-time hit shows during the late 1940's and early '50's was "The Adventures of Ozzie and Harriett," starring Ozzie Nelson (the clean-cut former Rutgers graduate and lawyer-turned-band leader), his ex-vocalist wife Harriett, and their real-life sons David and Ricky. Their family comedy began on radio when David was eight and Ricky was four. The Nelson family's "Adventures" ran weekly on radio for eight years, beginning in 1944, and then successfully transitioned to television one night per week for another fourteen years (1952-66) as one of America's favorite *families*. They also bridged the gap between movies and television by being some of the first TV stars to make several movies together, including *Here Come the Nelsons* in 1952.

Another popular hit show that easily made the transition from radio to television on the same network was one of NBC's top programs, "The Jack Benny Show." Jack Benny's show—a full hour of song and comedy—included singer Dennis Day, Black comedian Eddie Anderson as "Mr. Benny's" wise and loyal valet "Rochester," Mary Livingston (Jack Benny's real wife), band leader and singer Phil Harris, the show's announcer Don Wilson, and the master voice impersonator (also *the* voice of Warner Bros.' Bugs Bunny, Daffy Duck, and Porky Pig) Mel Blanc, and also Jack Benny's ancient Maxwell automobile (he was too cheap to buy a new Cadillac) and his private, residential walk-in money vault with the squeaky door. Jack Benny became world-famous as the vain, selfish, wisecracking, violin-playing Hollywood miser—the exact opposite of his real-life persona.

Eve Arden, one of film land's wittiest comediennes during the 1940's, became a radio star as the caustic and single but loveable high school English teacher, "Our Miss Brooks," beginning in 1948. "Our Miss Brooks" was one of the top situational comedies on radio until

1956, when Eve Arden and her cast transitioned to television without a hitch.

Other highly popular radio shows that later became big hits on television included two well-known Westerns—"The Lone Ranger" and "Gunsmoke." "The Lone Ranger" (also highly popular as comic books) starred Clayton Moore as the "Masked Man" who shot *silver* bullets at the bad guys, and his loyal Indian sidekick "Tonto," played by Jay Silverheels (who was the son of a *real* Indian chief). "The Lone Ranger" was a mythical-like superhero who led the forces of good against evil in the Old West. His far more realistic partner in the fight matching good against evil in the Old West was "Gunsmoke," which eventually became the most popular TV Western of all time.

"Gunsmoke" began on radio as a thoughtful, adult drama who's mission was to depict the Old West as it really was—warts and all. Unlike "The Lone Ranger," which was often more thrilling fantasy than fact, or like such child-friendly cowboys as Roy Rogers and Gene Autry (whose cowboy "outfits" and "cap-guns" could be purchased at many of the nation's department stores, and whose comic books could be purchased for a dime at most newsstands) "Gunsmoke's" U.S. Marshall Matt Dillon was the hard-nosed, man-of-few-words, shoot-first-and-ask-questions-later-type who kept the peace in *the* Dodge City, Kansas, of the 1870's. Unfortunately, the *radio* Matt Dillon, played by the excellent actor William Conrad—he of the deep, commanding voice—was nearly as wide as he was tall. Conrad was ideal for the part on radio. But, like many of the silent movie stars who had fine physiques but voices like Mickey Mouse, poor Mr. Conrad's husky voice could not hide the fact that, in front of the camera, he looked more like Porky Pig than Marshall Dillon. Enter six-foot-seven James Arness.

James Arness, a former war hero, wanted to star in movies (so did his younger brother Peter Graves). But, for many movie roles, James' commanding height was a disadvantage. Fortunately for him, he had a true friend in another tall actor named John Wayne. John Wayne secured parts for James Arness in several of the motion pictures he starred in and co-produced, including *Big Jim McLain* in 1952 and *Hondo* in 1953. When the producers of "Gunsmoke" finally decided to transition from radio to television, John Wayne recommended James Arness for the lead role as Marshall Dillon. Arness had both the commanding voice *and* the towering physique. Was John Wayne correct? "Gunsmoke," which aired its first episode in 1955, starring James Arness as U.S. Marshall Matt Dillon of Dodge City, Kansas, and co-starring Amanda Blake as "Miss Kitty," the town's pretty and practical saloon keeper, lasted a record-breaking *twenty years*, from 1955 to 1975. Another good judge of talent was Arthur Godfrey.

Arthur Godfrey had been popular as a combination entertainer and talk show host on CBS radio, coast-to-coast, for years. Affectionately nicknamed "The Old Redhead" (with his trademark ukulele always nearby), Arthur Godfrey endeared his radio listeners with his easy-going manner, his wide-ranging, unscripted monologues, musical performances, and celebrity guests on his late-morning radio show, "Arthur Godfrey Time," which aired Monday through Friday each week. As Godfrey's national popularity grew during the late 1940's, CBS supplemented his morning show with a prime-time variety hour, "Arthur Godfrey's Talent Scouts," in 1947. In 1948, CBS began broadcasting "Talent Scouts" *simultaneously* on radio and television. Soon, "Talent Scouts" became the most popular show on television. And sponsors—especially Lipton Tea, Frigidaire appliances, Pillsbury cake mixes, and Chesterfield cigarettes—loved him for his folksy and convincing promotions of their products. In 1949, CBS added the weekly part-time show "Arthur Godfrey and his Friends." It too became a big hit, while Arthur Godfrey became one of the busiest (and richest) men in television.

During the Eisenhower Years (Ike and Arthur were friends), "Arthur Godfrey's Talent Scouts" was ranked number one nationwide in terms of total viewing audience. His "Arthur Godfrey and Friends" was ranked number six, behind only "I Love Lucy" (CBS, #2); Groucho Marx's "You Bet Your Life" (NBC, #3); Jack Webb's "Dragnet" (NBC, #4); and "The Jack Benny Show (CBS, #5). In addition, Arthur Godfrey's shows helped jumpstart the careers of many up-and-coming young performers, including Don Adams, Steve Allen, Tony Bennett, Pat Boone, Lennie Bruce, Roy Clark, Patsy Cline, Eddie Fisher, Marilyn Horne, Julius LuRosa, and "The Cordettes." For old radio hands like Godfrey, Jack Benny, and the Nelson Family, television was little more than "radio with pictures."

The "Golden Age" of television did not, however, just depend on adapting existing programs, including "Amos 'n Andy," "Burns and

Allen," "The Red Skeleton Show," or the long-running soap opera, "The Guiding Light," to TV. "I Love Lucy," the highly popular half-hour comedy show first aired on CBS in 1951 (and "Lucy" is still popular as TV re-runs) was *original* to television.[17] Starring Lucille Ball as "Lucy," and her husband Desi Arnaz as Cuban bandleader "Ricky Ricardo," "I Love Lucy" topped the rating charts from 1951 through 1957.

Lucille Ball began in show business as a Chesterfield Cigarette Girl back in the 1930's, and eventually found her niche as one of Hollywood's foremost female clowns, co-starring with Bob Hope in *Fancy Pants* and Red Skeleton in *The Fuller Brush Girls*, both in 1950. By then, Lucille Ball had already been married to Desi Arnaz for nine years. Desi Arnaz, the son of a wealthy Cuban landowner, fled Cuba during the Batista dictatorship at age sixteen. Desi found fame and fortune in America as the singing, bongo-playing leader of a popular Latin American band. Desi met Lucy while making his first motion picture, RKO's *Too Many Girls*, in 1940. They were the film's co-stars. They soon married. But it was not until they decided to create their own comedy show for television that their wildest career dreams came true. By Ike's first year in office, Lucille Ball and Desi Arnaz had solidified their position as the most famous and successful husband-and-wife-team in television history.

Comedy shows on television—situation comedies like "I Love Lucy," "The Danny Thomas Show," "Burns and Allen," "Ozzie and Harriett," and comedy-oriented variety shows—were highly popular during the "Happy Days" of the Eisenhower Years. But the bar for comedic variety shows on television had already been set by Milton Berle back in 1948 with his highly successful "Texaco Star Theater." Comedian Milton Berle, nicknamed "Uncle Miltie," was "Mr. Television" to the average American by 1950. But, although Berle's TV variety show remained on the air through 1956, he was replaced as the king of TV slapstick comedy by the zany, yet loveable antics of television's most famous male clown, Red Skeleton.

---

[17] In truth, the "I Love Lucy" show was loosely based upon the earlier CBS radio hit "My Favorite Husband," starring Lucille Ball and Richard Denning. However, Denning was certainly no Cuban bandleader, making the TV show co-starring Desi Arnaz appear "original."

Red Skeleton had starred in many MGM movies featuring his comedic talents in the past, and had also been highly successful on radio. But Red Skeleton reached the zenith of his shown business career during the 1950's and '60's on television with "The Red Skeleton Show." Star of motion pictures, radio, and now television playing himself, and a variety of his famous characters, including "Clem Kadiddlehopper," the clumsy oaf, and "Freddie the Freeloader," the loveable hobo, Red Skeleton was one of TV's brightest stars.

Lucille Ball and Desi Arnaz, Jack Benny, George Burns and Gracie Allen, "Uncle Miltie," and, of course, Red Skeleton, when grouped together, were enough to make any decade "golden" when it came to comedy. But the 1950's offered many more great comedy stars, including Sid Caesar, Jackie Gleason, and the incomparable Bob Hope. Sid Caesar, assisted by the ingenious Imogene Coca, became a national sensation with his realistic, yet off-the-wall impersonations of foreign dialects in comedy skits during his "Your Show of Shows," in the early 1950's. And Jackie Gleason, the once-youthful pool hall prodigy turned vaudevillian, became one of television's all-time stars as the result of a series of comedy hits, including "Cavalcade of Stars" (1950-52), "The Jackie Gleason Show" (1952-55/1956-59/1961-70), and "The Honeymooners" (1955-56), all on CBS. Jackie Gleason created and brought to the TV screen such memorable characters as "Ralph Kramden" (the frustrated bus driver in "The Honeymooners"), the down-to-earth "Joe the Bartender," "Reggie Van Gleason III" (the spoiled rich guy), and the totally obnoxious "Charlie the Loudmouth." Jackie Gleason remained one of television's most popular comedians for at least twenty years.

Bob Hope was one of Hollywood's top ten money-making movie stars from 1941 to 1947, and again from 1949 through 1953. During the 1950's, Bob Hope continued to make tons of money for himself and for Paramount Studios with such hit comedy movies as *Fancy Pants* (1950), *The Lemon Drop Kid* (1951), *Son of Paleface* (1952), the *Road to Bali* with his buddy Bing Crosby (1953), *Casanova's Big Night* (1954), *The Seven Little Foys* (1955), *That Certain Feeling* (1956), *Beau James* (1957), *Paris Holiday* (1958), and *Alias Jesse James* (1959). Always a busy movie star, Bob Hope nevertheless made numerous trips to entertain American's troops overseas, especially during the Korean War and later in Vietnam. He also made annual visits to military posts located in various parts of the globe every Christmas season in order to bring a bit of holiday joy to young men and women in uniform far from home. Hope filmed the many variety shows he brought to our servicemen overseas and then shared them with American audiences nationwide in a series of Bob Hope "Specials" on the NBC television network. Bob Hope's "Specials" always drew huge television audiences during the Eisenhower Years. Over the years, Bob Hope reached far more Americans through his television specials than he did via his many hit movies, causing many of his fellow countrymen to view him primarily as a TV star. Regardless, to President and Commander-in-Chief of the Armed Forces Dwight Eisenhower, Bob Hope, for his service to America's lonely G.I.'s far from home, was *a patriot and a hero.*

Nearly as famous as Bob Hope, yet totally untalented by comparison, was Ed Sullivan. Ed Sullivan entered the living rooms of millions of Americans every Sunday night via television as the host of his New York City-based variety show, "Toast of the Town" (from 1948 to 1955), and "The Ed Sullivan Show" (1955 to 1971). An ex-boxer and former sports writer, during the 1930's and early '40's Ed Sullivan became a major rival of New York's long-establishing gossip columnist and show business star maker, Walter Winchell. Sullivan finally surpassed Winchell in fame and fortune as his CBS Sunday night variety show, "Toast of the Town," became a rapidly growing source of entertainment for families across the country. By September 1955, when CBS renamed his show "The Ed Sullivan Show," the entertainment icon with the lousy posture, bugging eyes, odd accent, mechanical movements, and no discernable talent, had become one of America's leading showmen. How? By booking and introducing to his TV audiences each week a head-spinning variety of acts, including animal acts, opera singers, comedians, comediennes, ballet dancers, country-and-Western singers, pop singers, ventriloquists, jugglers, acrobats, trapeze artists, circus performers, Broadway casts performing portions of their shows, knife throwers, plate-spinners, famous athletes, rock 'n roll groups, movie stars, TV stars, and an occasional world leader (including Fidel Castro). Ed Sullivan kept his audiences focused and tuned in. Ike and Mamie often watched his show from their private quarters in the White House.

Children were not forgotten by TV executives during the 1950's. Cowboy stars Gene Autry and Roy Rogers made fortunes off TV re-runs of their old movies and new programs produced exclusively for television. Before World War II, Gene Autry—"The Singing Cowboy"—was the only Western film star to be listed among the top ten money-makers in Hollywood motion pictures. Autry was Republic Studios' top star. In addition, his network radio show was highly successful, and he wrote and recorded hundreds of popular songs, including "Here Comes Santa Claus" and "Back in the Saddle Again." During World War II, Gene Autry served as an officer in the Army Air Force. During Autry's absence overseas, another of Republic's singing cowboys under contract took over as the new 'King of the Singing Cowboys." His name? Roy Rogers. Along with his whiskered sidekick Gabby Hayes and his heroine (and wife) Dale Evans, Roy Rogers starred in many popular Western movies, including *Sons of the Pioneers* and *Romance on the Range* (1942), *King of the Cowboys* and *Song of Texas* (1943), *The Cowboy and the Senorita* (1944), *Don't Fence Me In* (1945), *My Pal Trigger* (1946), *Springtime in the Sierras* (1947), and numerous other films during the late 1940's and early '50's. But, as the heyday of the low-budget Western motion pictures faded with the advent of TV, Roy Rogers switched to television, starring in "The Roy Rogers Show" from 1951 through 1957.

Both Roy Rogers and Gene Autry were highly astute businessmen who made a smooth and profitable transition from movies to television. Both established their own TV production companies during the 1950's. During the 1950's, nearly every child in America with access to a television set knew that Gene Autry's horse was named "Champion," and that Roy Rogers' horse was "Trigger." Gene Autry primarily focused on his Flying-A Picture Production Company, his own Golden West Broadcasting Network of radio (including KMPC Los Angeles) and television stations (including KTLA Los Angeles), his ranches, and his quest to own his own major league baseball team (eventually, the American League's Los Angeles Angels in 1961). Roy Rogers focused on the manufacture and distribution of Roy Rogers and Dale Evans Western costumes for kids, cap guns, and other theme-oriented Western gear, school lunch boxes, and various toys and dolls. He even ventured into selling desert lots in "Apple Valley" near Victorville, California, and established a chain of Roy Rogers Restaurants in Southern California. But Roy Rogers and Gene Autry, however famous, did not surpass the popularity of *Hopalong Cassidy* with America's youth during the Eisenhower Years.

Dwight Eisenhower was a Major in the United States Army stationed at Camp Meade, Maryland, when William Boyd appeared in his first Hollywood motion picture, *Why Change Your Wife?*, as an extra in 1920. At age twenty-five, William Boyd was only five years younger than our future President. William Boyd soon became a popular star in several of director Cecil B. DeMille's silent motion picture spectaculars, including *The Volga Boatman* (1926), and *The King of Kings* (1927). Unfortunately for the rising star, another stage actor with the same name became involved in a major gambling scandal, causing *both* William Boyds to suffer career-wise. Ironically, however, William Boyd's unfair loss of lead acting roles due simply to guilt by name association eventually turned into a pot of gold at the end of the rainbow for him in a new genre—leading-man in low-budget ("B") Western movies.

William Boyd starred in his first "B" Western, *Hopalong Cassidy*, in 1935. Little did he know that when he made the last of his sixty-six Hopalong Cassidy movies in 1948, he would soon become rich and famous beyond his wildest dreams. Bill Boyd hit the jackpot soon after he bought the rights to all of his old Hopalong Cassidy films for a relative song. By the time former Major Dwight Eisenhower was sworn in as our thirty-fourth President in 1953, William Boyd, a.k.a. "Hoppy," and his trusty horse "Topper" could be found everywhere—on shirts, hats, pants, "cap guns" sets, school lunch boxes, comic books, story books, drinking glasses and cups, toys, on the covers of breakfast cereal boxes . . . .

Gene Autry, Roy Rogers, and Hopalong Cassidy (kids knew him as "Hoppy," or Hopalong Cassidy, not as William Boyd) all shared some of their stardom with their horses—Champion, Trigger, and Topper. But their horses always got second billing. Not so with two very special dogs during the Eisenhower Years—"Lassie" and "Rin Tin Tin." "The Adventures of Rin Tin Tin" was a popular television show, especially for children, from 1954 through 1959. Parents and *grandparents* approved of the program because the canine hero had been one of *their* childhood favorites since the original animal star appeared in its first Warner Bros. movie back in 1922. The original Rin Tin Tin was a German shepherd found abandoned in an enemy trench by American

Army Captain Lee Duncan during World War I. Captain Duncan brought the bright and loveable pooch to Hollywood and trained him to act in the movies. Soon, with assistance from Darryl F. Zanuck, he became Warner Bros. most popular—and profitable—star during the silent era of the 1920's.

Lassie had a different origin. Lassie the collie was the fictional heroine of Eric Knight's novel *Lassie Come Home*. Lassie starred in six motion pictures, including *Lassie Come Home* (1943), *Son of Lassie* (1945), *Courage of Lassie* (1946), and *Challenge to Lassie* (1950). Lassie also had "her" own radio show on ABC, beginning in 1947 (all the movie and TV Lassies were *male* dogs). Lassie was so popular with rug rats and their parents that she/he/*they* starred in "Lassie" on TV—first in black and white and then in color—from 1954 through 1973. Lassie and Rin Tin Tin's shows outlasted many popular, human-led programs on television during the 1950's, including the hilarious "Phil Silvers Show."

Phil Silvers acted in numerous motion picture comedies, beginning in 1940. But he first became a star on Broadway in 1951 in the musical comedy "Top Banana." His greatest claim to fame, however, came from television in his hit role as U.S. Army Master Sergeant Ernest G. Bilko, the rascally NCO who was always getting the better of Army brass and fellow "grunts" by hook or crook. No doubt President Eisenhower was amused by Sgt. Bilko's hilarious scenes on more than one occasion between the show's premier (originally titled "You'll Never Get Rich") in 1955 and its last season in 1959. To most Americans—and especially to those who had served in the U.S. Army—Phil Silvers' Sgt. Bilko was both hilarious and all too real at times.

The Fabulous Fifties offered an amazing variety of television shows that appealed to both children and adults alike. An early Mexican-American Western, "The Cisco Kid", with Leo Carrillo as his loyal and humorous sidekick "Pancho," was widely popular. While acting in movies for MGM in 1932, Duncan Renaldo was briefly jailed as an illegal alien (he was born in Spain, lived in Europe, and came to America aboard a Brazilian ship). By the late 1930's, Duncan Renaldo was back acting in motion pictures at Republic Studios, starring as the early-California hero Zorro in the movie serial *Zorro Strikes Again* (1937), and as the Cisco Kid in *The Cisco Kid Returns* (1945). But his popularity as the Cisco Kid peaked on episodes made especially for television. Leo Carrillo, by contrast, was born in Los Angeles to a long-established California family. Leo Carrillo was well-known as a Latin character actor in a wide variety of moves during the 1930's and '40's. Together, The Cisco Kid and his sidekick Pancho brought both laughter and a respect for "justice" to many children and their parents who joyfully followed their many adventures in "Old California" on TV during the 1950's.

Taken somewhat more seriously during that decade was the family situation comedy "Father Knows Best," starring Robert Young. Robert Young became a role-model as the ideal father for many families during the Eisenhower Years. He later became beloved as a role model for the ideal family doctor during the 1960's as "Marcus Welby, M.D." Another "father figure" who was highly popular on television during the Eisenhower Years was Danny Thomas. Danny Thomas began his show business career in Detroit, Michigan, as a singer on a local radio station. Soon, he began appearing in various nightclubs around the country as a combination singer, comedian, and master-of-ceremonies. He also appeared on many of the early TV variety shows. But his greatest success in front of the camera came from his starring role in the long-running television situation comedy "Make Room for Daddy" (1953 through 1964). In 1954, Danny Thomas won an Emmy, TV's equivalent of the Oscar, for situation comedy, and "Make Room for Daddy" was soon renamed "The Danny Thomas Show."

While "The Danny Thomas Show" and other hits appeared to adults, teenagers, and children as "family entertainment" during prime-time evening hours coast-to-coast, Saturday mornings and after-school time-slots on local TV stations featured programming designed strictly for kids. Cartoons were king. The old 1930's cartoons "Betty Boop," "Popeye," and "Mighty Mouse" were typical Saturday morning and after-school fare for America's children. TV's "Bozo the Clown," "Howdy Doody," and "Kukla, Fran, and Ollie" were network hits with the juvenile set. And Walt Disney's "The Mickey Mouse Club" on ABC was must viewing after school from 1955 through 1959.

The young at heart of all ages loved 'The Little Rascals" on television almost anytime. Producer Hal Roach's juvenile comedy shorts of the 1930's, originally called the "Our Gang" comedies, starring Spanky McFarland—the fat boy leader of the fun-loving gang of little boys and girls—were a mainstay of many local independent stations. Most viewers seemed to never grow tired of re-runs of such "Little Rascals" comedy classic "shorts" as *Free Eats* and *Spanky* (1932), *Forgotten Babies* and *Bedtime Worries* (1933), *For Pete's Sake, Honkey Donkey*, and *Kentucky Kernels* (1934), *Teacher's Beau* (1935), *Bored of Education* and *General Spanky* (1936).

Even more popular was another series of old Hal Roach's Studio's comedy films, starring Laurel and Hardy. Independent TV stations thrived on Laurel and Hardy re-runs. An entire new generation of Americans learned to love and laugh at the wacky, yet often innocent antics of the daffy, skinny, and easily frightened Stan Laurel, with his funny, high-pitched English accent. And they couldn't help but love his friend and constant companion, the fat, officious, straight man of the comedy duo, Oliver Hardy. Together in films since 1926, Laurel and Hardy became the most successful comedy team in motion picture history. Having made more than one hundred comedy films together from 1926 through 1950, Stan Laurel and Oliver Hardy repeated their earlier success through re-runs of their many Hal Roach-produced movies on local television stations across the country. During the "Happy Days" of the Eisenhower Years, comedy of one sort or another seemed omnipresent on TV.

As the decade of the 1950's progressed, more shows of a comparatively serious bent began to appear. By the mid-1950's, some of the most popular programs on television were weekly quiz shows, including "The $64,000 Question" and "Twenty-One." Audiences were held spellbound as quiz show contestants were asked a myriad of academic questions—and many were answered *correctly*. Some contestants became rather famous. One in particular, a young Ph.D. candidate at Columbia University named Charles Van Doren, became a national Celebrity in 1955 while he was in the process of winning $129,000 on NBC's "$64,000 Question," a huge sum at a time when $100,000 could pay cash for the largest mansion in many American cities. Soon, *Dr.* Van Doren became an academic role model for American youth. But the young Columbia University Assistant Professor's world began to turn upside-down following public statements made in 1958 by a former "$64,000 Question" winner that he *and others* had been given correct answers in advance by the quiz show's producer to boost ratings. Frank Hogen, New York City's District Attorney, and the U.S. House of Representatives began investigating the matter. In 1959, Charles Van

Doren finally admitted he had been "coached" at times. He was fired as a substitute host on NBC's *Today* show, and he resigned his position at Columbia University. And the glamour of the academic quiz shows quickly disappeared.

Far less controversial, but still "cerebral" at times, were several television programs, including the "General Electric Theater" and "The Loretta Young Show." Ronald Reagan, the former MGM motion picture star, hosted and often acted in the "General Electric Theater" from 1954 through 1962. Reagan's "G.E. Theater" offered a variety of serious and well-received dramas. Another famous motion picture star, Loretta Young, retired from films in 1953 to begin a second highly successful career, hosting and often starring in her own drama series, "The Loretta Young Show" on NBC. Loretta Young had won an Oscar for "Best Actress" in 1947 for her performance in the motion picture *The Farmer's Daughter*. Between 1953 and 1960, Miss Young won three of TV's Emmy Awards for "Best Actress in a Television Drama."

Raymond Burr studied at Stanford University, Cal Berkeley, and Columbia before he got his start on radio and on the stage. In 1946, he began playing lead roles in motion pictures, usually as a villain. Luckily for him in 1957, he decided to switch from playing bad guys in movies to a good guy on TV—the lawyer in the popular mystery novel series *Perry Mason*. Raymond Burr became famous as TV's "Perry Mason." His hit show ran from 1957 through 1966.

In 1958, "77 Sunset Strip," starring former Yale student and World War II Purple Heart recipient, Efrem Zimbalist, Jr., burst upon the scene. Zimbalist and the rest of the "hip" cast caused quite a stir amongst younger viewers in general and Corvette lovers in particular. In 1959, three new programs made quite a positive impact upon television viewers: "Rawhide," starring a *real* former Army Special Forces Trooper, Clint Eastwood; "Bonanza," starring movie actor Lorne Greene as "Ben Cartwright," owner of the vast "Ponderosa Ranch;" and the brilliant screenwriter Rod Serling's science fiction and supernatural "Twilight Zone." While each of these new 1959 weekly programs had its funny moments, not one could ever be called a comedy. Times were changing.

And television's network news coverage was expanding. During the late 1940's and early 1950's, veteran radio newsmen led by Edward R. Murrow, Robert Trout, and Eric Sevareid brought their journalistic prestige and no-nonsense styles to television with great success. The quality of their news presentations caused the nightly newscasts on network television to be must viewing for most American families. During the 1950's, the evening news visually preceded each evening's prime-time telecasts of situation comedies, variety shows, and dramas. A few newsmen became television stars, including CBS's Edward R. Murrow, and by the end of the decade, Walter Cronkite.

Edward R. Murrow originally became famous in the United States for his CBS radio broadcasts from London during World War II. Beginning in 1951, as Vice President of CBS News, Murrow adapted radio's informative and often controversial news documentary program "Hear It Now" to "*See It Now*." "See It Now" established CBS News as the leader in television journalism. In 1953, the year Dwight Eisenhower first assumed the Presidency, Edward R. Murrow began interviewing famous people in their homes on his newest show, "Person to Person." Ed Murrow's "See It Now" and "Person to Person" specials, and Walter Cronkite and the "CBS Nightly News," which he always ended with his famous statement, "And that's the way it was," and then he would say the day's date, established CBS News as the decade's leader in television news.[18]

Religion also had its place on television. For many years, the major networks broadcast religious programs on radio. NBC had its "Frontiers of Faith" and CBS had its "Lamp unto My Feet." Television kept the faith as those programs and many others transitioned to TV. Evangelist Billy Graham gained national fame on his ABC television program "Hour of Decision" from 1951 to 1955. And Catholic Bishop Fulton J. Sheen gained national prominence on the DuMont Television Network during the evening with his 'Life is Worth Living" hour. When the DuMont network went bankrupt in 1955, Bishop Sheen renamed his popular program "Mission to the World" and switched to ABC. Meanwhile, many independent television stations across the country broadcast Sunday services live from local churches during the Eisenhower Years. Millions watched.

Thanks to television, loyal sports fans during the Eisenhower Years were often delighted by the opportunity to watch their favorite teams

---

[18] Notables on other networks included John Cameron Swayze, Douglas Edwards, David Brinkley, Chet Huntly, and Lowell Thomas.

from the comfort of their own living rooms. And, by attracting hoards of new fans as well, the hypnotic affect of TV on the growth of sports in America cannot be overemphasized. While radio executives and movie moguls nervously watched their revenues steadily decline with the sale of each new television set, revenues for most professional sports actually grew thanks to network payments for TV "rights" to broadcast events, and an expanding fan base due to greater exposure of major teams. And, contrary to more contemporary times, many so-called "minor sports," like wrestling and roller derby, thrived on local independent stations during the early days of television.

Professional wrestling on television became huge during the 1950's. By President Eisenhower's first year in office, many local TV stations offered live wrestling matches from local arenas featuring muscle men with absurd names like "Gorgeous George," "Baron Leoni," "The Masked Marvel," and "Doctor Doom." They paraded in tights around boxing rings in various auditoriums, boxing arenas, and gymnasiums across the country to the delight of largely female audiences. That the wrestling matches, although often violent and sometimes even dangerous, were *fake* seemed to not deter wrestling fans in the slightest. Pro-wrestling, and its co-ed equivalent on skates—"Roller Derby"—provided escape for a growing portion of the war-weary public. Sports purists might scoff, but there was money to be made in televised mayhem—especially in a more legitimate sport called *boxing*.

In professional boxing, the "Friday Nite Fights" were fast becoming hugely popular with male audiences tuned in to television stations across the nation. Sponsored by such companies as Gillette "Blue Blades," and Pabst "Blue Ribbon" Beer, men and boys were glued to their TV sets at home watching "the fights" on Friday nights. America's boxing promoters were among the first sports entrepreneurs to take full advantage of the new medium of television. As a profitable alternative to small-screen viewing at home (or to "TV blackouts" of major bouts), some promoters offered live, pay-for-view boxing matches televised exclusively to selected movie theatres and projected onto their big screens. During the Eisenhower Years, it was not uncommon for fathers to take their sons to local movie theatres to watch televised prizefights *live*. Especially heavyweight championship fights.

It seems fitting that the first sporting event ever televised in the United States involved America's favorite pastime, *baseball*. On May

17, 1939, the venerable NBC radio sportscaster Bill Stern described the pitch-by-pitch action of a college baseball game from New York City between Princeton and Columbia on live television. By the late 1940's, it was apparent to the major networks and to local broadcasters that sporting events of all kinds—baseball, basketball, football, tennis, track and field, golf, and of course boxing, wrestling, and roller derby—were relatively easy to produce, appealing to the public, and profitable. Manufacturers of products most suited for male consumers, such as razor blades, car tires, beer, cigarettes, cigars, motor oil, and gasoline also soon found televised advertisements before, during, and immediately after TV sports events helped increase the sales of their merchandise. During the Eisenhower Years, televised sports expanded rapidly as revenues generated by TV commercials grew.

No one during the Eisenhower Years was more ingenious than Walt Disney when it came to TV commercials. The Coca-Cola Company hit the jackpot when it aired Walt Disney's first one-hour television special on Christmas Day, 1950—"One Hour in Wonderland." "One Hour in Wonderland" commanded an estimated *ninety percent* of the nation's television audience, and possibly helped sell a gazillion Cokes. But the true test of Disney's commercial genius was to come in 1954, during President Eisenhower's second year in office. What did Mr. Disney do that was so ingenious? Walt Disney (1) persuaded ABC to telecast his new hour-long "Disneyland" show each week coast-to-coast at an enormous sum per episode while *also financing a third of the construction costs* of his new *Disneyland* theme park in Anaheim, California; (2) advertised his *Disneyland* theme park through the content of his "Disneyland" television show at no additional advertising costs; (3) narrated his own television show, retaining full control over the show's content while saving the cost of a well-known host; and (4) filmed portions of each TV episode at Disney Studios *in color* to promote on his black and white TV show, and then edit and later release them as Technicolor motion pictures for theatres across America and around the world, thereby earning additional profits in the millions of dollars.[19] Obviously, Walt Disney was one clever hombre. When "Disneyland" first premiered on

---

[19] Many of the nation's top bankers predicted that Walt Disney's proposed *Disneyland* would fail, and were therefore unwilling to finance even a portion of its construction.

ABC television on October 27, 1954, it was an instant success, with Walt as its smiling host. Walt Disney was the first Hollywood producer and major movie studio executive to embrace television. While most other Hollywood studios refused to let CBS, NBC, or ABC broadcast any of their recent films—and especially not their hits—Disney Studios did just the opposite, and thrived as a result. Beginning on December 15, 1954, the first of three "Davy Crockett" episodes aired on Walt's "Disneyland" TV shows. Within hours, the nation's children were singing the episode's theme song, "Da-vy, . . . Da-vy Croc-ket . . . King of the Wild Frontier." Within months, hundreds of millions of dollars worth of Davy Crockett memorabilia, including "coon-skin" caps, had been sold, not to mention more millions in ticket sales following the Technicolor release of the motion picture *Davy Crockett—King of the Wild Frontier* in 1955. While the *real* Mr. David Crockett hated being called "Davy," and disliked coon-skin caps with a passion, who cared?[20] Disney and Davy—and "Disneyland"—were TV winners.

---

[20] See Michael Wallis' *David Crockett: The Lion of West* (New York: W.W. Norton & Company, 2011).

# CHAPTER 4

# SPORTS

No American President since Theodore Roosevelt was a greater advocate of the importance of sports to the development of a man's character than Dwight Eisenhower. Eisenhower loved athletics, especially football and baseball.[21] And, although his Abilene High School yearbook for the Class of 1909 described young Ike as "*'our best historian and mathematician,*'"[22] Eisenhower was also a jock. When a knee injury during a football game cut short his playing career at West Point, Ike was no longer able to play competitive football or his second love, baseball. He even had to give up boxing due to limitations in his ability to move laterally. And so, for the remainder of his days as a cadet at West Point, he compensated by excelling as the Point's unofficial Junior Varsity Football Coach (the officer in charge of the team knew little about the game) and as a highly proficient poker player. After graduating from West Point and gaining a commission as Second Lieutenant in the Infantry, Ike supplemented his income (with the Army's blessing and encouragement) by serving extra duty as the football coach for a military academy, then a small college, and ultimately at the military base where he was stationed while America prepared for war. After rising to the rank of Lieutenant Colonel during

---

[21] See Eisenhower, *At Ease*, p. 96.
[22] *Ibid*, p. 42.

World War I as commander of a large basic training facility near San Antonio, Texas, following the war *Major* Eisenhower was again assigned extra duty as the football coach for numerous camps during the 1920's.[23] Coach Eisenhower still had a genuine love of football as he entered the White House in 1953. But golf was now his game.

Most Americans during the Fabulous Fifties loved sports. The Great Depression of the 1930's, World War II, and finally the Korean War took their toll on Americans of all ages. Many had experienced little else except poverty, and then war. By 1953, it was high time for some "Happy Days." While Hollywood's motion pictures helped ease the pain of hard times and then war for most Americans, there was only so much time and money people could spend on sitting inside a darkened movie theatre staring at the giant screen. Then came television. By 1953, a majority of Americans had a TV set, offering them an ever-growing variety of programs—including sports—*for free*. As a result, Americans began to embrace spectator sports with more enthusiasm than at any time since the "Golden Age" of the 1920's. With the election of Dwight Eisenhower and the end of the Korean War, 1953 marked the beginning of the "Fabulous Fifties." And sports played a big role in making them "fabulous."

While Dwight Eisenhower had long ago given up playing the young men's games of football and baseball, and the sweet science of boxing, he satisfied his competitive nature through golf. Ike played more golf than any President since William Howard Taft. Some critics claimed he spent enough time on the golf course to turn *professional*. But Ike knew better. He left the professional golf tour in the good hands of players like Jimmy Demaret, Ben Hogan, Sam Snead, and Cary Middlecoff. In 1953, Ben Hogan won three out of the four "Grand Slam" tournaments—The Masters, the U.S. Open, and the British Open. A relative unknown by the name of Walter Burkemo won the PGA Championship that year. Meanwhile, on the women's tour, Betsy Rawls beat out the more famous Babe Zaharias to win the U.S. Women's Open for the second time. While golf had obviously become President Eisenhower's favorite recreational pastime, baseball

---

[23] Nearly all officers were either discharged or reduced in rank following the end of the Great War in November 1918.

was still generally recognized as America's "national pastime," with football a close second.

1953 began with *televised* football games on New Year's Day. By 1953, the major college bowl games had expanded from the lone Rose Bowl, first played in Pasadena, California in 1902, to include the Orange Bowl in Miami (1935), the Sugar Bowl in New Orleans (1935), the Cotton Bowl in Dallas (1937), and the Gator Bowl in Jacksonville, Florida (1946). Each was held on January 1st to welcome in the New Year. In 1953, before the largest crowd of all the bowl games (over 100,000), the University of Southern California Trojans defeated the Wisconsin Badgers 7 to 0 in the Rose Bowl. The Alabama Crimson Tide blasted the Orangemen of Syracuse 61 to 6 in the Orange Bowl. The Georgia Tech Yellow Jackets beat the Rebels of Mississippi 24 to 7 in the Sugar Bowl. The Texas Longhorns shut out the Tennessee Volunteers 16 to 0 in the Cotton Bowl. And the University of Florida Gators slipped by an upstart Tulsa team 14 to 13 in the Gator Bowl. No doubt Coach Eisenhower, America's President-elect, watched several of the games on television with keen interest, as did millions of other sport fans across the land.

Back in 1951, as American G.I.'s were fighting and dying in Korea while President Harry Truman and General Douglas MacArthur were having their highly public argument over how the United States should fight the Communist Chinese ("containment" vs. "victory"), a major "point shaving" scandal broke in college basketball. It was the biggest scandal to rock the American sports scene since "Shoeless" Joe Jackson and his Chicago White Sox teammates threw the Baseball World Series in 1919. At about the same time that President Truman fired General MacArthur in April 1951, and while General Dwight Eisenhower was arriving in Paris to assume command of the newly formed North Atlantic Treaty Organization (NATO), eighteen college basketball players were arrested for taking money from gamblers to "fix" games. Seven of the arrested players were from the City College of New York, which had won both the National Collegiate Athletic Association (NCAA) *and* the National Invitational Tournament (NIT) basketball championships one year earlier. In 1950, both national tournaments were played in the friendly confines of New York City's famous Madison Square Garden. A great deal of money was allegedly won by gamblers "in the know" because certain key players were "on the take." But, according to the New York City District Attorney's office, the seven players from the City College of New York were not the only offenders involved. Eleven players from other college teams were arrested, and charges involving an additional fourteen players were on hold pending further investigation. The District Attorney eventually claimed that, between 1947 and 1951, 86 college basketball games had been "fixed" in 23 cities in 17 states by 32 players from seven universities—the City College of New York, Long Island University, New York University, Manhattan, Toledo, Bradley, and even the legendary coach Adolph Rupp's Kentucky.

But the extent of the University of Kentucky's involvement in the "point shaving" scandal was not fully discovered until after Kentucky won the 1951 NCAA Basketball Championship at the Williams Arena in Minneapolis with a 68 to 58 win over coach Jack Gardner's fine Kansas State team. Kentucky's victory was led by its seven-feet-tall junior all-American Bill Spivey and sophomore Cliff Hagan. Soon, however, Bill Spivey paid dearly for his alleged involvement in the scandal. Spivey never admitted he had cheated, but the potential NBA star was banned from college basketball, and he never played a single minute as a professional.

And so, during President Eisenhower's first days in office, beginning with his Inauguration on Thursday, January 20, 1953, America's college basketball teams and their coaches were under tremendous scrutiny to be squeaky clean. The college basketball scandal of 1951-52 was one of the many reasons for the growing perception by both Protestant fundamentalists and Catholic laymen that 1950's America needed a moral and spiritual rebirth. Soon after Dwight Eisenhower's election in 1952, encouraged by the newly-elected, more conservative Republican majority in both houses of the Eighty-Third Congress, many religious groups, led by the Catholic Knights of Columbus, lobbied Congress to add "under God" to the Pledge of Allegiance. Since 1892, the Pledge of Allegiance had read ". . . one Nation, indivisible, with liberty and justice for all."[24] The Eighty-Third Congress agreed to the addition of

---

[24] The Pledge of Allegiance, written by Francis Bellamy and originally published in *The Youth's Companion* magazine in 1892, was first recited by students at a limited number of public schools on Columbus Day, October 12, 1892. It eventually became America's official pledge by

"under God." And so, since 1954, the Pledge of Allegiance has read ". . . one Nation under God, indivisible . . .", thanks, in no small part, to the college basketball scandal of the early 1950's. Since the "Golden Age of sports" during the 1920's, most Americans have taken their spectator sports *seriously*. The Eisenhower Years were no exception.

The NCAA, college athletics' governing body, continued to keep the sports programs of the basketball scandal-plagued universities under close scrutiny. In the case of the University of Kentucky, the NCAA concluded that Coach Rupp had not been involved with gamblers, but that he had been guilty of violating NCAA rules regarding *recruiting*. As a result of its findings, the NCAA ordered the University of Kentucky's entire 1952-53 season *cancelled*, and the Southeastern Conference (SEC), of which Kentucky was a member, complied. The Kentucky Wildcats, who had won the NCAA Basketball Championship under Coach Rupp in 1948, 1949, 1951, and had a 29 and 3 record in 1952, did not field a team during the 1952-53-basketball season. The banning of Kentucky for an entire season provided one more reason for college basketball programs to be squeaky clean during the Eisenhower Years.

1953's NCAA Basketball Champion was Indiana University. Led by their six-feet-ten-inch-tall center Don Schlundt, and needing a Bob Leonard free throw with just twenty-seven seconds left on the game clock, Coach Branch McCraken's Hoosiers beat Coach Phog Allen's Kansas Jayhawks and their star center B.H. Born at the Municipal Auditorium in Kansas City by the final score of 69 to 68. Indiana University became the first of many schools to win NCAA basketball championships during the Eisenhower Years. Meanwhile, at Madison Square Garden in New York City, second-ranked Seton Hall beat seventh-ranked St. John's 58 to 46 to win the NIT title.

While professional basketball traces its first National Basketball Association (NBA) championship back to the 1946-47 season, roughly one year before Dwight Eisenhower began serving as the President of Columbia University, today's NBA was then called the BAA—the Basketball Association of America. The NBA was officially formed in 1949 when the BAA and the National Basketball League (NBL)

---

Act of Congress on June 22, 1942. Francis Bellamy was a cousin of the famous American socialist Edward Bellamy, who wrote the popular utopian novel, *Looking Backward, in 1888*.

merged following the 1948-49 season. In 1953, during Ike's first year as President, the NBA's Western Division Champion Minneapolis Lakers, led by George Mikan, defeated the Eastern Division Champion New York Nicks four games to one. But frankly, President Eisenhower and most other sports fans in America could hardly wait until the baseball season began. Would those ("damn") Yankees win *again*?

Since the 1935 World Series, when manager Mickey Cochrane's Detroit Tigers of the American League defeated Charlie Grimm's National League Chicago Cubs four games to two, the New York Yankees dominated major league baseball, first under Joe McCarthy, and then under Casey Stengel. New York City's "Bronx Bombers" won the World Series in 1936, 1937, 1938, 1939, 1941, 1943, 1947, 1949, 1950, 1951, and 1952. Would the Yankees win their *fifth* world title in a row in 1953? Very likely.

Following World War II, as peace and prosperity came to America, major league baseball attendance reached an all-time high of 21,300,000 fans in 1948. 1948 was the year that the American Leagues' Cleveland Indians beat the National Leagues' Boston Braves in the World Series, even though the American Leagues' Yankees and the National Leagues' Brooklyn Dodgers, the St. Louis Cardinals, or the New York Giants had been pre-season favorites to win their respective leagues. Competition brought out the fans—over two million in Cleveland alone. By 1949, however, normalcy had returned with the New York Yankees back on top. A lack of competition breeds complacency. Ballpark attendance for most major league teams began to drop. Some blamed television for the drop in attendance—why pay to go to the ballpark when you can watch games at home for free? Others cited decaying stadiums in deteriorating neighborhoods as a cause for the drop. Still others claimed shifts in population from inner cities to the suburbs as a culprit. Ironically, neither the so-called "racial crisis" that fans had been warned about for years if major league baseball became *integrated*, as it finally was in 1947, nor the controversial notion that the increase in the number of night games played would ruin the grand old game, were ever cited as factors for the decline in overall attendance. To the contrary, when President Branch Rickey of the Brooklyn Dodgers broke the "color barrier" in 1947 with second baseman Jackie Robinson (Robinson soon proved he belonged in "The Bigs" by winning Rookie-of-the-Year honors in the National League), and when Cleveland's owner Bill Veeck gave outfielder Larry Doby the opportunity to become the first Black player in the American League, attendance *grew*. So did attendance at night games.

By 1953, one sports fact was clear: New York City dominated major league baseball. New York City had baseball's three greatest young stars playing center field for their respective teams: Mickey Mantle for the Yankees, Willie Mays for the Giants, and Duke Snyder for the Dodgers. Even worse as far as major league "balance" was concerned, from 1947 through 1957, the New York Yankees won a total of ten American League pennants, the Brooklyn Dodgers won *six* National League pennants, and the N.L. Giants won *two*. One city. One decade. *Eighteen pennants*. Little wonder attendance was generally down elsewhere.

In 1953, two long-established baseball franchises moved to greener pastures in pursuit of fans and profits—the Boston Braves of the National League and the St. Louis Browns of the American League. The Boston Braves and the St. Louis Browns, relegated to playing in the shadows of their more successful cross-town rivals, the *Red Sox* and the *Cardinals*, packed up and moved, lock, stock, and barrel. Finishing in seventh place in the National League in 1952, with a record of 64 wins and 89 losses (32 fewer wins than the first-place Dodgers and 28 fewer than the second-place Giants), the Boston Braves became the *Milwaukee* Braves prior to the start of the 1953 season. In 1953, adapting well to their new home at County Stadium, the Milwaukee Braves set club attendance records while finishing in second place behind the Brooklyn Dodgers. The Braves compiled a fine record of 92 wins and 62 losses, thanks in large part to two young pitchers named Warren Spahn and Lou Burdette. A then-unknown rookie outfielder named Henry Aaron would join them in 1954, making the Braves even more competitive. Meanwhile, "Go West, young men" proved to be sound advice for the National League Braves. The *Browns*? They chose to go *East* from St. Louis and then take a short turn *South* to Baltimore. Waiting for their dismal 1953 season to end in St. Louis (at season's end, they trailed the pennant-winning Yankees by forty-five games), the Browns changed their names to the *Orioles*. The Baltimore Orioles began in the fall of 1953 to prepare for their new home debut in the spring of 1954.

Richard T. Stanley

In the fall of 1953, during Eisenhower's first year in office, the question on most baseball fans' minds was, "Would those ("damn") Yankees win again?" Yes. In yet another "cross-town" World Series (as in 1947, 1948, 1951, and 1952), the New York Yankees defeated another New York team, this time the Brooklyn Dodgers, four games to two. But each game *was* exciting, and TV sets were turned on across the country. Most Americans—at least most red-blooded males, including our Commander-in-Chief in the White House—could name the starting lineups of both star-filled teams. For the defending World Champion Yankees, there was Yogi Berra behind the plate, Joe Collins at first, Billy Martin at second, Gil McDougald at third, "The Scooter" Phil Rizzuto at shortstop, and in the outfield, the switch-hitting Mickey Mantle in center, flanked by Hank Bauer and Gene Woodling, with the great veteran Johnny Mise waiting as a backup on the bench. And the Yankees' pitching staff included right-handed throwers Allie Reynolds, Johnny Sain, and Jim McDonald, and lefties Eddie Lopat and Whitey Ford. For the National League Champion Dodgers, there was the equally famous roster of Roy Campanella behind home plate, Gil Hodges at first base, the flashy rookie Jim "Junior" Gilliam at second, Billy Cox at third, "Pee Wee" Reese ("The Little Colonel") at short, Duke Snyder in centerfield, joined in the outfield by Jackie Robinson in left and Carl Farillo in right. The Dodgers' pitching staff included right-handers Carl Erskine, Clem Labine, and Billy Loes, and lefties Preacher Roe and Johnny Padres. Clearly, America's two best baseball teams in 1953 were playing in the World Series. And both were New York teams.

New York may have dominated major league baseball in 1953, but that certainly was not the case with college football. The last Associated Press poll in 1953 had the following college teams ranked in the nation's top ten: (1) Maryland; (2) Notre Dame; (3) Michigan State; (4) Oklahoma; (5) UCLA; (6) Rice; (7) Illinois; (8) Georgia Tech; (9) Iowa; and (10) West Virginia. The closest any New York area team came to the top ten was Coach Red Blaik's Army squad, ranked 14$^{th}$ (7-1-1) at season's end. Former West Point alumnus Dwight Eisenhower was no doubt proud of Coach Blaik's record—especially his 20-7 victory over arch-rival Navy at Philadelphia before 100,000 fans and a national TV audience.

West Point's academic scandal of August 1951 decimated Coach Blaik's 1951 and 1952 teams through no fault of his own, as 37 players were among the 90 cadets who were dismissed in August 1951 for violating West Point's Honor Code against cheating, or for failing to report those who cheated. Ike's own discipline record at West Point—for violations *not* including cheating—had been less than stellar. Cigarettes and stubbornness had nearly been his downfall several times. For President Eisenhower in particular and the Cadet Corps' morale in general, the resurgence of West Point's football team in 1953 was uplifting.

1953 was a transitional year in college football. For years, traditional top ten schools like Notre Dame, Ohio State, and USC rolled over most of their opponents due to their depth of talented players at each position. They substituted throughout games rather freely, keeping their offensive and defensive squads relatively fresh. To less fortunate schools, their teams could look like "thundering herds" as games progressed, battering them with wave after wave of fresh, talented players. Beginning with the 1953 football season, the NCAA Rules Committee, determined to create more "balance" so that dozens of former "also-ran" schools could better compete with the traditional elite teams, instituted the "single platoon" system. In essence, the NCAA's new "single platoon" rule barred substitutions, except for injuries, for an entire quarter of football. *The same eleven players would have to play on both offense and defense for an entire quarter.* As a result, the new "iron man" approach clearly slowed the game down with fatigued players on *both* sides. Elite schools like Notre Dame occasionally countered by faking injuries to substitute fresh players at opportune moments, as in their highly controversial tie with the University of Iowa on November 21st. The resulting 14 to 14 tie saved number-one-ranked Notre Dame from what would very likely have been its only loss of the season, but it clearly cost them fan support and allowed a former also-ran, the University of Maryland, to be crowned as the Associated Press' National Champion of 1953. The "single platoon" rule also allowed players opportunities to achieve records impossible under today's two-platoon system: In 1953, Stanford's quarterback Bobby Garrett led the nation in both *pass completions* and, as Stanford's safety on defense, *interceptions*.

While college football went to the single-platoon system in 1953 in pursuit of "parity," professional football purposely restored unlimited free substitution in 1950 in order to generate more fan excitement and increase ticket sales. Specialization in kicking extra points and field goals, kickoff returns, and other "special teams" efforts on both offense and defense became hallmarks of the National Football League (NFL). For the NFL, the single-platoon system had simply become too old-fashioned. Likewise, NFL teams were among the first to drop the old "single-wing" offense in favor of the more wide-open "T-formation." UCLA's legendary coach, Henry "Red" Sanders, clinging to old-school tradition, still utilized the single-wing offense in 1954 when his Bruins won their first (and only) national championship in football. During the 1950's, NCAA football increasingly became associated with *tradition*; NFL football with *innovation*. Innovation—and the fact that colleges generally played on Saturdays and the pros on Sundays—attracted growing numbers of college football fans to follow both college and pro games on TV, and compare.

In 1950, while President Truman was still sending American G.I.'s to fight in Korea, the Los Angeles Rams became the first NFL team to televise all of their games at home and away (they later televised away games only). Back East, the Washington Redskins soon followed the Rams' lead. By 1951, most NFL teams televised some of their games. And, on December 23, 1951, the NFL Championship Game was televised coast-to-coast (on the DuMont Network) for the first time. The Rams defeated the Cleveland Browns 24 to 17. While the Rams became the 1951 NFL Champions, all NFL teams benefited in the minds of most fans as a result of the exciting, wide-open style of pro football they clearly saw on TV.

By 1953, due in part to the NFL's exciting style of play and their availability on TV, professional football was more popular than ever. Also, there was no concentration of most of the top teams in one area, as was the case with major league baseball. New York won only *one* NFL Championship from 1950 through 1960—the 1956 New York Giants (47 to 7 over the Western Conference Champion Chicago Bears). In 1953, the Western Conference Champion Detroit Lions defeated the Eastern Conference Champion Cleveland Browns 17 to 16 in their December 27th contest in snowy Detroit for the NFL title (the Super Bowl, generally played in a warm weather location, had not yet been invented). In spite of Detroit's narrow victory, the United Press International named Otto Graham, the star quarterback of the

Cleveland Browns, as its 1953 NFL Player of the Year for his stellar play in guiding the Browns to their 11 and 0 regular season record. Photos of Otto Graham, battered and bleeding following victories on the playing field, became commonplace. So too did similar pictures of another popular and gallant champion, Rocky Marcianno.

Rocky Marcianno became the undisputed Heavyweight Champion of the World when he knocked out defending champion Jersey Joe Walcott in the thirteenth round of their fight on September 23, 1952, in Philadelphia. At times, their boxing match looked more like a brawl. While the Champion Walcott, taller, heavier, and a more skilled boxer, tried to fend off the ever-charging 184 pound Marcianno by landing punch after punch, the challenger kept coming like a charging bull. Bloodied about his face, Marcianno simply refused to stop until Walcott finally went down for the count in the 13$^{th}$ round. Rocky Marcianno, battered and bleeding, was the new Heavyweight Champion of the World. Soon, he would become one of the most famous—and feared—heavyweight boxing champions in history. In 1953, during their return match for the title, Marcianno knocked Walcott out in the first round of their May 15$^{th}$ bout in Chicago, ending any speculation whatsoever that his first victory over Walcott may have been a fluke. During Dwight Eisenhower's first year in office, Rocky Marcianno became, in the eyes of many boxing fans, the next Jack Dempsey. And possibly, the greatest heavyweight ever. Who would be the undefeated fighter's next victim? Roland LaStarza. On September 24, 1953, in front of a packed stadium at the old Polo Grounds in New York City, Rocky Marcianno gave LaStarza a punishing beating before the referee mercifully stopped the fight in the 11$^{th}$ round on a "TKO."

In 1953, boxing was extremely popular, and Rocky Marcianno was *the man*. But other weight divisions, especially due to boxing's expanding exposure on television, had their national heroes too. The ageless Archie Moore would successfully defend his World Light Heavyweight Championship title (maximum weight of 175 pounds) against all challengers for nearly *eleven years* (1952 to 1962). In the Middleweight Division (160 pounds or less), Sugar Ray Robinson—pound-for-pound one of the greatest practitioners of the "sweet science" who ever lived—headed a list of national favorites who won and lost the Middleweight Championship (Sugar Ray reclaimed the title a record four times) during the decade of the 1950's, including Jake LaMotta,

Randy Turpin, Carl "Bobo" Olson, Gene Fullmer, and Carmen Basilio. Among Welterweights (147 pounds or less), Sugar Ray Robinson held the World Welterweight title from 1946 until 1951, when he relinquished it to fight for and win the Middleweight Championship. Johnny Bratton soon replaced Sugar Ray as Welterweight Champion only to be defeated later in 1951 by Kid Gavilan. Kid Gavilan, with his famous upper-cut "bolo" punches, successfully defended his Welterweight Championship in numerous nationally televised fights until he was finally defeated by Johnny Saxton in 1954. Johnny Saxton gave way to Tony DeMarco in 1955. DeMarco then lost to Carmen Basilio before the end of the year. Then Johnny Saxton beat Carmen Basilio . . . . needless to say, the Welterweight Division was highly competitive, and a great favorite of boxing fans across the country.[25]

While the Lightweight Division (135 pounds or less) was seldom as popular with most fans during the 1950's as were the heavier divisions, Lightweight Champions such as Ike Williams, James Carter, Lauro Salas, Paddy DeMarco, Wallace "Bud" Smith, and Joe Brown entertained thousands in person and millions via television. And the quickest moving fighters in all divisions, the Featherweights (126 pounds or less), were dominated by four crowd-pleasing champions: Sandy Saddler (1948 to 1940 and 1950 to 1957); Willie Pep (1949 to 1950); Hogan "Kid" Bassey (1957 to 1959); and Davey Moore (1959 to 1963). Viewed as a whole, boxing was big business during the Eisenhower Years.

An even more rapidly growing sports business in American during the Fabulous Fifties was stock car racing. With its roots firmly planted in Southern soil, the National Association for Stock Car Racing (NASCAR) was founded following World War II. During the 1950's, NASCAR's biggest crowds attended races at the Daytona International Speedway in Daytona Beach, Florida, and at the Darlington International Raceway in Darlington, South Carolina. The Heinz Southern 500, the NASCAR circuit's oldest race, was first held in Darlington in 1950 to the delight of thousands of Rebel fans. Drivers such as Herb Thomas,

---

[25] The decade of the 1950's saw the World Welterweight title change hands three more times: Carmen Basilio (1956-57); Virgil Akins (1958); and Don Johnson (1958-60).

Speedy Thompson, and Fireball Roberts helped popularize the sport of stock car racing during the decade of the 1950's.

While stock car racing at Daytona Beach, Florida, dates back to 1936, NASCAR's first Daytona 500 was held in 1959, during President Eisenhower's seventh year in office. Lee Petty, driving a modified Oldsmobile, was the first Daytona 500 Champion, completing two hundred laps around Daytona's two-and-one-half-mile track at an average speed of 135.5 miles per hour—only a fraction slower than the historic and more prestigious Indianapolis 500 that same year.

The Indianapolis 500 has been held every Memorial Day weekend at the famed Indianapolis Motor Speedway since Dwight Eisenhower first received his appointment to attend West Point in the spring of 1911. Long before Ike's first year as President in 1953, the Indianapolis 500 had become America's favorite auto race. Although Ike may have been aware that there was a Heinz Southern 500 race in 1953 (won by Buck Baker), he certainly knew about the Indianapolis 500 that year. Ike, along with millions of his fellow Americans from coast-to-coast, no doubt saluted 1953's Indy Champion Bill Vukovich as the newly declared champ drank the traditional quart of milk in celebration of his victory in Victory Lane before the nation's motion picture and television cameras.

In auto racing, the Indianapolis 500 was America's premier event during the Fabulous Fifties. In thoroughbred horse racing, then as now, the Triple Crown—three majors for three-year-olds run during a six-week's period in May and June each year—ruled supreme. The most famous of all the races, the Kentucky Derby, held at Churchill Downs in Louisville, Kentucky, generally offers the largest purse to the winner. In 1953, Dark Star beat out the favored Native Dancer. Native Dancer finished a disappointing second in the Derby. But Native Dancer soon roared back to victory in the Preakness Stakes at Pimlico Race Course in Baltimore, Maryland, two weeks later. He then went on to win the Belmont Stakes at Belmont Park in Elmont, New York, in early June. Native Dancer had come so close to being the first horse to win the Tripe Crown since Citation won the Derby, the Preakness, and at Belmont in 1948. During the Eisenhower Years, three other thoroughbreds would come as close as Native Dancer to winning the Triple Crown—Nashua (1955), Needles (1956), and Tim Tam (1958), each winning two of their three races. But America would have to wait until 1973 for its next Triple Crown winner, Secretariat.

The pinnacle in thoroughbred horse racing—"The Sport of Kings"—is winning the Triple Crown. In international tennis—another sport with a royal history—it is being victorious at all four "Grand Slam" tournaments: The Australian Open, the French Open, the U.S. Open, and the Wimbledon Championship. As air travel improved, and television coverage of matches increased, interest in international tennis steadily grew during the Eisenhower Years. In 1953, an Australian, Ken Rosewall, won the Australian Open and the French Open. America's Vic Seixas won at Wimbledon, and later lost at the U.S. Open to his fellow countryman Tony Trabert. On the women's side, America had a rare Grand Slam winner. Maureen "Little Mo" Connelly won on the hard surface at the Australian Open in Melbourne in January 1953, on clay at the French Open in Paris in June, on grass at Wimbledon in London that July, and on the hard courts at the U.S. Open at Forrest Hills, New York, that September. A major obstacle to winning a Grand Slam in tennis for even the most talented man or woman is his or her ability to master playing on all three of the very different court surfaces—concrete, clay, and grass. That challenge alone makes winning a Grand Slam in tennis a monumental accomplishment. During Ike's first year in office, "Little Mo" Connelly did just that, to the delight of tennis buffs around the world.

Football fans across the nation might have witnessed one of the greatest Rose Bowl games in the bowl's legendary history on January 1, 1955, giving a grand farewell to an exciting 1954 fall season, had it not been for two facts: A drenching rainstorm and the "No Repeat Rule." Against all odds in Southern California, heavy rains drenched Pasadena that New Year's Day. Even worse, the nation's number-one-ranked UCLA Bruins, the undefeated and untied Champions of the Pacific Coast Conference, were not eligible to play the unbeaten number-two ranked Ohio State Buckeyes and their sensational junior halfback Howard "Hopalong" Cassady to settle the question on the playing field, *Who's number one?* Why? The 1950's No Repeat Rule.

On January 1, 1954, a junior-led UCLA team barely lost to a fine Michigan State squad 28 to 20 at the Rose Bowl. UCLA was destined to field a greatly improved senior—led team in 1954. With 1954 regular season victories over each of their opponents, including conference wins of 72 to 0 over Stanford, 41 to 0 over Oregon, and 34 to 0 over arch rival USC, UCLA was clearly the best team to represent the West Coast against the Big Ten's best squad, Ohio State, in the Rose Bowl on January 1, 1955. Instead, because of the rule that no team could represent its conference for two consecutive years in the Rose Bowl, UCLA's players, including all-Americans Bob Davenport, Jack Ellena, and Jim Salsbury, and their highly talented tailback, Primo Villanueva, were forced to stay at home and watch thrice-beaten USC represent the Pacific Coast Conference on television against Coach Woody Hayes' heavily favored Buckeyes on New Year's Day. The Buckeyes prevailed over USC in the ankle-deep mud by the final score of 20 to 7. Ho-hum.

In college athletics during the mid-1950's, football, with its "single-platoon" system and bowl agreements like the No Repeat Rule, did not have a monopoly on controversy in NCAA sports. Adolph Rupp's University of Kentucky Wildcats, still smarting from the 1951 "point shaving" scandal and the cancellation of their entire 1952-53 season for "recruiting violations," were on the hot seat again in 1954. During the 1953-54 regular season, Kentucky, led by seniors Cliff Hagen, Frank Ramsey, and Lou Tsioropoulos, complied the nation's best record of 25 wins and 0 losses. But Coach Rupp turned down his team's invitation to play in the 1954 NCAA tournament when he learned the NCAA had decided that all three of his star seniors had run out of eligibility at the end of regular season play because each of them had already earned enough credits to graduate and would therefore not be allowed to participate in post-season tournament play. Thus, within months of Ohio State's drubbing of USC's football team by a score of 20 to 7 in the mud at the Rose Bowl instead of a Herculean battle between the nation's two top teams, UCLA and Ohio State, an undefeated Kentucky basketball team sat at home while LaSalle, with a regular season record of 21 and 4, cruised to victory over runner-up Bradley 92 to 76 for the NCAA Championship at Kansas City in the first nationally televised final. Most college basketball experts—as well as most fans—had no doubts about Kentucky's superiority over each of 1954's Final Four in the NCAA tournament—LaSalle, Bradley, Penn State, and USC. Yet, just as Ohio State claimed to be number one following their Rose Bowel victory, so too did LaSalle after their tournament win. Ho-hum.

During the Eisenhower Years, college basketball was by no means simply a period for sour grapes. In fact, the NCAA's future brightened dramatically in 1955 when a Cinderella team from the West Coast, the University of San Francisco Dons, led by their lanky center Bill Russell and their star guard K.C. Jones, began compiling an amazing record of 57 wins and only one loss during the 1954-55 and 1955-56 seasons. USF's only loss during that amazing streak was to Coach John Wooden's UCLA Bruins in Westwood by a score of 47 to 40. Soon, Bill Russell and his teammates went from underdogs to national heroes in the eyes of many basketball fans (and Coach "Red" Auerbach and his Boston Celtics) as the squad from the little-known California association knocked off team after team from the nation's top basketball conferences. There were no doubts about Coach Phil Woolpert's Dons being the best team in college basketball following both the 1955 and 1956 NCAA Championship games. In 1955, USF beat LaSalle 77 to 63 to finish at 28 and 1, and in 1956, USF beat Iowa 83 to 71 to finish 29 and 0. Bill Russell, the Don's center, went on to play professionally and, together with such outstanding teammates as Bob Cousy and Tommy Heinsohn, led the Boston Celtics to an amazing run of eleven NBA Championships in thirteen years (1957, 1959, 1960, 1961, 1962, 1963, 1964, 1965, 1966, 1968, and 1969).

During Ike's tenure as President, college basketball produced many superstars besides Bill Russell, USF's all-American center. Another college center, the Kansas Jayhawks' Wilt Chamberlain, did pretty well for himself both in college and later with the Harlem Globetrotters and then with the NBA. Wilt Chamberlain went on to lead all NBA players in scoring for seven straight seasons, from 1960 through 1966. At forward, there was Tom Gola of LaSalle, Elgin Baylor of Seattle, and Bob Pettit of LSU—all future NBA stars. And at the guard position, Kentucky's Cliff Hagen, Cincinnati's Oscar Robertson, West Virginia's Jerry West, and Furman's Frank Selvy proved their star status was no fluke once they turned professional.

In 1957, the USF Dons, minus Bill Russell, came back down to earth when the University of North Carolina Tar Heels replaced them as national champions with a 32 and 0 win streak of their own. That year, Coach Frank McGuire's Tar Heels, led by forward Lennie Rosenbluth, defeated Kansas and its sensational sophomore center Wilt Chamberlain in triple overtime 54 to 53. Down but not out, the defending champs, USF, beat Michigan State for a very respectable third-place finish.

In 1958, soon after President Eisenhower celebrated the launching of America's first satellite, Explorer I, into space on January 31$^{st}$ from Cape Canaveral, Florida, Coach Adolph Rupp led still another Kentucky team into the NCAA tournament—this time, with no major scandal. Coach Rupp's ninth-ranked Wildcats entered the tournament with a modest regular-season record of 19 and 6; they exited with a 23 and 6 record and another NCAA Basketball Championship following an 84 to 72 victory over runner-up Seattle, while Temple finished third and Kansas State fourth. Meanwhile, the nation's number one and number two ranked teams at the end of the regular 1957-58 season—West Virginia (26 and 1) and Cincinnati (24 and 2)—both lost in the first round of the NCAA tournament, sending sophomore sensations Jerry West (West Virginia) and Oscar Robertson (Cincinnati) home to lick their wounds and look to the future.

1959 witnessed another West Coast team's rise to the top of college basketball. This time, that team was Coach Pete Newell's eleventh-ranked University of California Golden Bears. Led by their center Darrall Imhoff and forward Bill McClintock, Cal defeated West Virginia and tournament MVP Jerry West in a thriller at Louisville, Kentucky, 71 to 70. Cincinnati, led again by Oscar Robertson, finished third. Hometown favorite Louisville finished fourth. Many basketball fans in America's two newest Western states—Alaska, admitted to the Union as our 49$^{th}$ state on January 3, 1959, and Hawaii, admitted as our 50$^{th}$ state on March 18$^{th}$—rejoiced at the news of neighboring Cal's victory. And, of course, fans in the Oakland/San Francisco Bay area were ecstatic. But Cal was to finally run out of luck exactly one year later at the hands of Ohio State and their outstanding center Jerry Lucas in the 1960 championship game of the Final Four in Bear-friendly San Francisco. Cal fans had good reason to be optimistic regarding the Golden Bears' chances of repeating as NCAA champs in front of their hometown fans. Cal had just defeated the junior sensation Oscar Robertson and his Cincinnati teammates in the semifinals 77 to 69. The Associated Press had Cincinnati, with a record of 25 and 1 at the end of the regular season, ranked number one in the nation, with Cal (24 and 1) at number two. AP had Ohio Stat, at 21 and 3, ranked third. Now, Cal, at 28 and 1, was just one more hometown victory away from a repeat championship. Could a fired-up Cal team possibly lose the final game with the Bears' proven senior Darrall Imhoff's solid defensive play against the Buckeyes' explosive but inexperienced sophomore Jerry Lucas? Yes. Ohio State, shooting over sixty-eight percent from the field, shredded Cal's vaunted defense by a final score of 75 to 55. And Cincinnati beat NYU to earn third place.

During the Eisenhower Years, the National Basketball Association (NBA) was still in its infancy. The first "official" NBA Champions were the Minneapolis Lakers at the end of the 1948-49 season, when the Basketball Association of America and the National Basketball League agreed to merge to form the NBA. Television, and the infusion of increasing numbers of former college stars into professional basketball, helped contribute to the NBA's growing popularity during the mid and late 1950's. From 1949 through 1954, the Minneapolis Lakers, led by their center George Mikan, dominated the young NBA. In 1955, Syracuse won the NBA title by defeating the Fort Wayne Pistons. In 1956, it was the Philadelphia Warriors' turn to defeat those same Pistons for the NBA title. Finally, in 1957, "Red" Auerbach's Boston Celtics won their first of many titles to come when they beat the St. Louis Hawks for the championship. In 1958, the Hawks got their revenge over the Celtics four games to two. But in 1959, with rapidly-growing fan interest in the Bill Russell-led Celtics, Boston would go on to win *eight straight NBA Championships.*

Track and field never drew the numbers of fans in the United States that baseball, basketball, or football could claim during the Eisenhower Years. But one monumental track event certainly caught the attention of most Americans, and of sports fans around the world: Dr. Roger Bannister's breaking of the fabled "Four Minute Mile" at a track meet in Oxford, England, on May 6, 1954. For centuries, it had been considered humanly impossible for a man to be able to run a mile race in under four minutes. It was generally assumed that was one barrier to man's athletic progress that would never be broken. Dr. Bannister, a young British physician and competitive runner, believed differently, and he set out to prove that ancient assumption false.

On May 6, 1954, Roger Bannister (later, *Sir* Roger) ran the mile in three minutes, 59.4 seconds, for all the world to see. Dr. Bannister became the first athletic in history to run a mile in less than four minutes. News of his incredible feat resulted in headlines around the world and instant fame for the young Brit. Many distance runners began to reason, "If Bannister can do it, *I can do it.*" One did, less than two months later. Australian John Landy ran the mile in three minutes, 58 seconds flat. Soon, in August 1954, in a heralded race between the world's two fastest distance runners, Roger Bannister defeated John Landy in Vancouver, Canada. *Both men finished the race in under four minutes*, forever crushing the myth of the "Four Minute Mile."

During the 1954 baseball season, the American League's New York Yankees won 103 games; their most regular season wins since 1942. But it wasn't enough to finish first because that same season the red hot Cleveland Indians won an amazing 111 regular season games behind the superb pitching of Bob Lemon (23 and 7), Early Wynn (23 and 11), Mike Garcia (19 and 8), Art Houtteman (15 and 7), and their aging ace, Bob "Rapid Robert" Feller (13 and 3). Their pitching staff was aided by the splendid hitting of their second baseman Bobby Avila (with his .341 batting average), the big bat of their third baseman Al Rosen (a .300 hitter, including 24 home runs), and their slugging center fielder Larry Doby with his 32 home runs and 126 runs batted in. Ecstatic Cleveland fans (and many others who were weary of the Yankees' long-standing dominance) could hardly wait for the World Series to arrive. Surely Cleveland, with its superior pitching, would win. Besides, a National League team had not won a World Series since 1946.

The 1954 National League season was a dogfight between Leo Durocher's New York Giants (97 and 57), Walter Alston's Brooklyn Dodgers (92 and 62), and Charlie Grimm's Milwaukee Braves (89 and 65), with an exhausted Giants team finally coming out on top. Was their pitching staff of Johnny Antonelli (21 and 7), Ruben Gomez (17 and 9), Sal "The Barber" Maglie (14 and 6), Marv Grissom (10 and 7), and Hoyt Wilhelm (12 and 4) any match for the red hot Indians?

The Giants swept the Indians in four straight. The Indians' pitching staff, after breezing through their American League season while giving up an average of only 2.78 runs per game, gave up 21 runs in four World Series games to the Giants. The clutch pinch hitting of Dusty Rhodes, the sterling defensive play and stolen bases by Willie Mays, along with timely hits by Alvin Dark, Hank Thompson, and Don Mueller, plus strong Giants' pitching, steamrollered the bewildered Indians. On TV, it appeared to a surprised nation that the Tribe didn't know what hit 'em. It was also apparent to fans across the country that New York City still dominated major league baseball when it mattered most.

Would 1955 be any different? No. In fact, in 1955, both World Series teams were from New York—the Dodgers and the Yankees. This time, however, the Dodgers would finally come out on top. In 1955, the Brooklyn Dodgers won their first World Series title in franchise history, four games to three, on pitcher Johnny Padres' gutsy 2 to 0 shutout in Yankee Stadium in game seven on October 4th. All of Brooklyn erupted in wild celebration. Their heroes, and especially Duke Snyder with his eight hits, including four home runs and seven RBI's, had finally done it.

During the 1955 regular season, the focus of many baseball fans—especially in the Middle West—had been on the new Kansas City Athletics. Following the end of the 1954 season, the once-proud Philadelphia Athletics who had fallen on hard times since World War II, moved their American League franchise to Kansas City. Suddenly, the St. Louis Cardinals of the National League were no longer the only major league team left west of the Mississippi. Thanks to improvements in air transportations, continuing population growth in the Middle West, and hopes for a better future, the Kansas City Athletics began their first season in 1955. That year, they finished a somewhat respectable sixth in the American League, six games ahead of the Baltimore Orioles (the old St. Louis Browns), and ten games ahead of the Washington Senators. They also gave many of President Eisenhower's old Kansas acquaintances and relatives a local major league team to root for (Ike tended to be a Yankee fan).

In 1956, as President Eisenhower campaigned for re-election, baseball history repeated itself. Except this time the Yankees defeated the Dodgers in the World Series four games to three. Without a doubt, the highlight of the 1956 World Series was Yankee pitcher Don Larsen's "perfect game"—the first World Series no-hitter in history. With the series tied at two games apiece, game five, played in a jam-packed Yankee Stadium on October 8th, began as a pitchers' duel between the Dodgers' Sal Maglie, the winning pitcher in game one, and Larsen. Maglie matched Larsen pitch for pitch through the first three innings. After the Yankees scored a lone run in the fourth, the pitching duel continued. In the home half of the sixth, Mickey Mantle hit a solo home run off Maglie. That was all Don Larsen needed. Don Larsen's perfect game that day—97 total pitches including no hits, no walks, and no Dodger reaching first base—placed him forever in the Pantheon of the Yankees' greatest heroes.

The scrappy Dodgers' Clem Labine responded to Don Larsen's perfect game the following day in game six by pitching a near-perfect four-hit shutout of his own when Jackie Robinson singled in the bottom of the tenth inning off hard-luck Yankee starter Bob Turley on a fly ball misjudged by outfielder Enos Slaughter, allowing the game's only run to cross home plate. But the Yankees weren't to be denied the 1956 World Championship. In game seven in Brooklyn, the Yankees buried the Dodgers in front of their hometown fans by a final score of 9 to 0. The Dodgers lost another hard-fought World Series to their cross-town rivals, the Yankees. But there was no doubt that New York still dominated baseball.

In November 1956, Ike was re-elected in a landslide. Would New York still dominate the 1957 baseball season during President Dwight Eisenhower's fifth year in office? Yes and no.

Yes, because the Yankees won still another American League pennant. No, because they *lost* in the 1957 World Series to the upstart Milwaukee Braves of the National League four games to three. Milwaukee, behind the strong pitching of right-hander Lou Burdette, won games 2, 5, and 7. Lefty Warren Spahn won game 4. Hank Aaron, baseball's newest star, led Milwaukee's offensive attack with eleven hits, including three home runs and seven RBI's. The 1957 Braves beat the perennial American League Champion Yankees, sending the World Baseball Championship out west. Was New York's stranglehold on major league baseball slipping? More than most fans might have imagined. Following the end of the 1957 major league season, the unthinkable happened: Owners Walter O'Malley of the Brooklyn Dodgers and Horace Stoneham of the New York Giants announced they were both *moving their teams from New York to California.*

New York's hold on major league baseball was never the same after both the Dodgers and the Giants left the "Big Apple" and headed west. Prior to 1958, the "City by the Bay"—San Francisco—had long been the home of the Seals of the old Triple-A Pacific Coast League.[26] The

---

[26] For an excellent account of the old Pacific Coast League, see Kevin Nelson's *The Golden Game: The Story of California Baseball* (San Francisco:

"Yankee Clipper" Joe DiMaggio, a native of San Francisco, began his professional career as a star with the San Francisco Seals. And a young Ted Williams, then known as the "Splendid Splinter," began as a skinny home run slugger for the Seals' Coast League rival San Diego Padres. Between San Francisco and San Diego lay Los Angeles, California's largest city and the long-time home of the Coast League's Los Angeles Angels *and* the Hollywood Stars. Bob Lemon, star pitcher for the Cleveland Indians, hailed from Long Beach, just a few miles south of L.A. More major leaguers came from California than any other state. Jackie Robinson had starred in both football and baseball at UCLA. California already had pro-football—the San Francisco 49'ers and the Los Angeles Rams. Why was it taking so long for major league baseball to arrive? Needed advancements in transportation and the will to take risks.

Thanks to the newly-developed jet passenger aircraft and the fortitude of the owners of the Dodgers and the Giants, major league baseball finally became bi-coastal in 1958. As construction hastily began on the new ballparks at Candlestick Point and Chavez Ravine, the Pacific Coast League's Seals and Angels quietly disappeared. To the delight of California baseball fans, their long-standing rivalry was replaced by two of the most successful franchises in major league baseball history—now known as the *San Francisco Giants* and the *Los Angeles Dodgers*. Play ball!

In 1958, the San Francisco Giants, led by Willie Mays, finished third in the National League behind Milwaukee and Pittsburgh, while the aging Dodgers, led by Duke Snyder, Carl Furillo, and Don Zimmer, finished seventh, two games ahead of the last-place Phillies. In the American League, the Yankees, now New York City's only team, finished in first place, again. After losing the first three games of the 1958 World Series to Milwaukee, the Yankees came roaring back to win four straight. The 1958 New York Yankees—Hank Bauer, Yogi Berra, Andy Carey, Elston Howard, Tony Kubek, Mickey Mantle, Gil McDougald, Bill Skowron, and pitchers Bob Turley, Don Larsen, Whitey Ford, and Ryne Duren—became the first team since the 1925 Pittsburgh Pirates beat the Washington Senators to win the World Series after losing three of the first four games. New Yorkers were still devastated by the loss of

---

California Historical Society Press, 2004).

the Dodgers and the Giants, but, where it counted most, their Yankees were World Champions again in 1958.

But not for long. 1959 was an off-year for manager Casey Steingel's Yankees, who, at 79 wins and 75 losses, finished third in the American League, fifteen games behind the Chicago White Sox, who won the pennant for the first time since the infamous "Black Sox Scandal" rocked baseball in 1919. In the National League, the Los Angeles Dodgers, doormats during much of the 1958 season, surprised everyone—including many of their most loyal fans—by winning the National League pennant in the last week of regular season play. Their arch rival, the San Francisco Giants, spent most of the season in first place while construction workers raced to complete their new Candlestick Park stadium in time for the 1959 World Series. When the rag-tag Dodgers—not the heavily favored Giants—finally clinched the pennant, headlines in Los Angeles screamed, "**CANDLESTICK PARK IS COLD AND DARK: THE GIANTS ARE IN THIRD PLACE!**"

How did the Los Angeles Dodgers leap from seventh place in the National League in 1958 to World Champions in only their second season in Los Angeles in 1959? Coliseum "Moon Shots" over the high chain link fence in a shortened left field by the former St. Louis Cardinals' outfielder, Wally Moon; a .308 batting average, including 23 home runs by their veteran left-handed slugger, Duke Snyder—in spite of the deepest right field fence in baseball; excellent play by infielders Norm Larker, Charlie Neal, and Jim Gilliam; and the outstanding pitching of Don Drysdale, Sandy Koufax, and Johnny Padres, and an excellent reliever named Larry Sherry.

Against all odds (Don Drysdale and Sandy Koufax were still in the early phases of their fabulous pitching careers), the rag-tag 1959 Dodgers replaced the Giants as the darlings of the National League during the last few days of the season. Next, they faced the heavily-favored Chicago White Sox in the World Series. The 1959 Chicago White Sox had outstanding offensive and defensive players in their lineup, including Luis Aparicio at shortstop, Nellie Fox at second, Jim Landis in the outfield, and the slugging Ted Kluszewski at first. Odds-makers in Las Vegas had the White Sox as heavy favorites over the Dodgers. Six games later, Las Vegas odds-makers took it in the shorts, losing big-time. The Dodgers, playing on their temporary home field in the

Los Angeles Memorial Coliseum with over 92,000 screaming fans in attendance during games three, four, and five, won the series in game six in Chicago with a 9 to 3 victory, powered by two-run home runs by both Duke Snyder and Wally Moon. The powerful Chicago White Sox won only one of the three games played on their home field. Again, Chicago fans—Cub fans and White Sox fans alike—would have to settle for that old battle cry: "Wait 'till next year!" Back on the West Coast, there was joy in mudville... and *Hollywood*!

The arrival of fall is that time of year that many American relish most because it marks the beginning of football season. Dwight Eisenhower, the one-time West Point player and coach, was no exception. The 1955 college football season began on Friday night, September 16th, in the Los Angeles Memorial Coliseum when Texas A & M, coached by the up-and-coming Bear Bryant (who would later lead Alabama to several national championships) met the old veteran "Red" Saunders' UCLA Bruins. UCLA won 21 to 0 in spite of the fact that A & M included among its talented players three future "All-Pro" NFL players—halfback John David Crow, fullback Jack Pardee, and end Gene Stallings. As a result, on the 19th of September, the Associated Press ranked UCLA's football team number one in the nation. But 1955 would prove to be a season of surprises. The University of Maryland was named the number one team in the nation the very next week when the Terrapins upset the Bruins 7 to 0 on September 24th. Far more surprising—in fact, *shocking*—was the result of the Hawaii-Nebraska game in Lincoln that same day. Still smarting from their 1954 50 to 0 shellacking by the Cornhuskers in front of their homefolks in Honolulu, the University of Hawaii beat Nebraska 6 to 0 *in Lincoln* on the 24th of September. For the nation as a whole, however, the greatest shock of all that day was the news that, while on vacation in Denver, Colorado, President Eisenhower suffered a heart attack.

News of President Eisenhower's heart attack surprised the nation. Ike had always projected an image of robust health in public. Few Americans were aware that Ike had suffered for years from bouts of ileitis, or that he had just recently kicked his long-time habit of smoking four packs of cigarettes per day. Fortunately for the nation, President Eisenhower soon recovered from his "mild" heart attack. Most Americans were fully aware that Ike's young and ambitious Vice President, Richard Nixon, hoped to become President one day.

Following Ike's heart attack, one of the nation's most popular "sick jokes" had the ambitious Vice President Nixon greeting President Eisenhower at the entrance to the White House during his return from the hospital by saying, "We're all glad to have you back home, Mr. President. *Can I race you up the stairs?*"

By Saturday, October 1st, President Eisenhower was feeling much better, especially after he learned that, on that afternoon, his Army team had drubbed Penn State 35 to 6. On November 26th, Ike felt fully recovered after Army beat Navy 14 to 6 in Philadelphia. And, no doubt like football fans across the country, he saw Vanderbilt beat Auburn 25 to 13 on television from the Gator Bowl on December 31st. On January 2, 1956, TV's across the nation were first tuned in to the Orange Bowl from Miami (Oklahoma 20, Maryland 6), next, to the broadcast of the Sugar Bowl from New Orleans (Georgia Tech 7, Pittsburgh 0), then, to the Cotton Bowl from Dallas (Mississippi 14, Texas Christian 13), and finally, to the Rose Bowl from Pasadena (Michigan State 17, UCLA 14). By late evening, most red-blooded American males, including the President of the United States, were reeling from overdosing on college football.

Professional football was still growing in popularity in 1955. While the Cleveland Indians still fielded good baseball teams (they finished a close second to the New York Yankees in the American League pennant races in both 1955 and 1956), the National Football League's Cleveland Browns were the pride of Ohio during much of the 1950's. The Cleveland Browns won the old American Conference championship in 1950, 1951, and 1952, and the new Eastern Conference championship in 1953, 1954, 1955, and 1957. The Browns won the NFL Championship, played at the end of each season during the last week in December, a total of three times during the Fabulous Fifties—in 1950 over the Los Angeles Rams, in 1954 over the Detroit Lions, and in 1955 over the Rams again.

Other dominant NFL teams during the decade of the 1950's included the Rams (NFL Champs in 1951), the Lions (NFL Champs in 1952, 1953, and 1957), the New York Giants (NFL Champs in 1956), and the Baltimore Colts (NFL Champs in 1958 and 1959). Such stars as Bob Waterfield, quarterback of the Rams, Otto Garham, quarterback for the Browns, Cleveland's phenomenal running back Jim Brown, Johnny Unitas, the young quarterback for the Baltimore Colts,

Dick "Night Train" Lane, defensive back for the Detroit Lions, and Y.A. Tittle, quarterback for the New York Giants, all became household names during the Eisenhower Years.

Back to college football. College football still had a much larger overall following than the pros during the 1950's. By 1955, Coach Bud Wilkinson was fast becoming a legend at Oklahoma. With a 40 to 0 victory over Notre Dame *in South Bend*, a 45 to 0 drubbing of arch rival Texas, 66 points scored against Kansas State, and 67 points on Missouri, Wilkinson's "Sooners," with a record of ten wins and no losses, became the undisputed National Champions of college football for 1956. The Sooners also set an all-time win streak of forty straight games, besting the old record of thirty-nine victories in a row set in 1914 by the Washington Huskies. But, like UCLA at the end of its 1954 national championship season, Oklahoma's 1956 championship team was "bowl-ineligible" due to the NCAA's *No Repeat Rule*. So once again, the nation's best college football team spent New Year's Day watching their lesser peers play on TV: In the Orange Bowl, Colorado beat Clemson 27 to 21; in the Sugar Bow, it was Baylor over Tennessee 13 to 7; at the Cotton Bowl in Dallas, Texas Christian University edged Syracuse 28 to 27; and, in the Rose Bowl in Pasadena, Iowa beat Oregon State 35 to 19.

For all but Sooner fans, the highlight of the 1957 college football season was Notre Dame's stunning 7 to 0 upset of number-one-ranked Oklahoma on November 16th in Norman, ending their 47-game win streak before a national television audience. The heavily-favored Sooners were held to a scoreless tie on their home field by the Fighting Irish through the first three quarters of the defensive contest. For Sooner fans, the game was all the more frustrating because their all-time win streak of 47 games in a row was at stake, and because Notre Dame, after winning their first four games of the season, had just lost to Navy (20 to 6) and to Michigan State (34 to 6). Their frustration turned to despair when Irish halfback Dick Lynch scored a fourth quarter touchdown for the game's only points.

But Oklahoma's fans fared better than the Cornhuskers' followers in Lincoln, Nebraska. Nebraska's football team began the 1957 season with two straight losses—34 to 12 at the hands of the Washington State Cougars, and even worse, a 42 to 0 woopin' by the Black Knights of Army. Meanwhile, Coach Woody Hayes went ballistic after his highly-touted Ohio State Buckeyes were upset by Texas Christian on September 24th by a score of 18 to 14. And Coach Bear Bryant of Texas A & M—highly successful with the Aggies—resolved to leave A & M and restore the football program at his alma mater, Alabama, following 'Bama's 40 to 0 loss to Auburn in Birmingham on November 30th.

Meanwhile, on the West Coast, there was little joy in Trojan Land. 1957 was the worst year in the University of Southern California's storied football history. USC ended their dismal season with a 1 and 9 record following their loss to Notre Dame in the snow at South Bend, Indiana, on November 30th, 40 to 12.

On New Year's Day 1958, while the losing bowl teams and their fans were disappointed, there were no big surprises or upsets: Favored Oklahoma defeated Duke 48 to 21 in the Orange Bowl; a strong Mississippi team swamped Texas 39 to 7 in the Sugar Bowl; Navy out-scored Rice 20 to 7 in the Cotton Bowl; and Ohio State edged Oregon 10 to 7 in the Rose Bowl.

While President Eisenhower was disappointed by Army's 14 to 0 loss to Navy in November 1957 in their traditional battle in Philadelphia, 1958 was a splendid year for his alma mater. In 1958, Army not only defeated Navy 22 to 6, they also beat Notre Dame 14 to 2, Penn State 26 to 0, and South Carolina 45 to 8. The only blemish on their undefeated season was their 14 to 14 tie with a very good Pittsburgh team on October 25th. At season's end, Army was ranked as the third-best team in the nation by the Associated Press (LSU and Iowa were ranked first and second), and their star halfback, Pete Dawkins, won the 1958 Heisman Trophy as the nation's best college football player. Ike was proud of both Pete and West Point. Army's Pete Dawkins, by winning the coveted Heisman Trophy, joined the highly exclusive football fraternity of Heisman winners during the Eisenhower Years, including Johnny Lattner (Notre Dame, 1953), Alan Ameche (Wisconsin, 1954), Howard "Hopalong" Cassidy (Ohio State, 1955), Paul Hornung (Notre Dame, 1956), and John David Crow (Texas A & M, 1957).

1958 was a year for the games between traditional rivals. On October 4th, Michigan battled to a 12 to 12 tie with Michigan State, while on October 18th, Georgia tied Auburn 7 to 7, and Florida tied Vanderbilt 6 to 6. Later that season, other ties between traditional rivals included West Virginia vs. Penn State (14 to 14), Purdue vs. Indiana

(15 to 15), Missouri vs. Kansas (13 to 13), and USC vs. UCLA (15 to 15). There was even a tie in the Cotton Bowl on New Year's Day to begin 1959: Texas Christian and Air Force battled to a scoreless finish. Except for the Rose Bowl and Orange Bowl games, in which Iowa beat Cal 35 to 12 in Pasadena and Oklahoma defeated Syracuse 21 to 6 in Miami, the other major season-ending bowl games were also nearly scoreless. On December 27, 1958, Mississippi edged Florida 7 to 3 in the Gator Bowl, while in the Sugar Bowl on January 1, 1959, LSU squeaked by Clemson by the score of 7 to 0.

If 1958 was the year of the tie in college football, 1959 was the year of the Orangemen from Syracuse University. Led by halfback Ernie Davis, fullback Art Baker, and tackle John Brown, the 1959 Syracuse team went undefeated (11 and 0), were named national champions by both the Associated Press and the United Press International, and finished first in the nation in both total offense and defense. Meanwhile, President Eisenhower's favorite team, Army, was headed in the opposite direction. Army had gone undefeated in 1958, and had finished third in the nation, ahead of such perennial powerhouses as Auburn, Oklahoma, Ohio State, and Notre Dame. Not so in 1959.

While the 1959 Army football team managed to tie the Air Force Academy's squad in their first-ever meeting on October 31st in New York City 13 to 13, they were later bombed by arch rival Navy on November 28th in Philadelphia due to the heroics of a young midshipman named Joe Bellino. The final score? Navy 43, Army 12. As Commander-in-Chief of *all* the nation's armed forces, President Eisenhower was publicly cordial. But privately, Ike was seething over his alma mater's worst defeat in the sixty years of Army-Navy football.

Army was not alone in its sudden decline. Except for USC's 7 to 0 win over Wisconsin in the 1952 Rose Bowl game, the Middle West's Big Ten Conference football teams had won twelve of the last thirteen Rose Bowls prior to January 1, 1960. As a result, except for UCLA's National Championship team of 1954, Pacific Coast teams came to be viewed by football fans and sports writers alike as generally inferior to their Big Ten counterparts. That is, until a one-eyed junior quarterback for the underdog University of Washington Huskies named Bob Schloredt led his team to a 44 to 8 shellacking of the Big Ten's champion Wisconsin Badgers before 100,000 screaming fans in Pasadena and millions more on national television. Bob Schloredt and his purple-and-gold-clad teammates became instant heroes to West Coast football fans from Seattle to San Diego. And their head coach, Jim Owens, would soon become a coaching legend in the Pacific Northwest. With one game, the tide turned. The Rose Bowl, once considered the domain of Big Ten teams, soon became an annual playground for whoever represented the West Coast on New Year's Day. Twenty of the next twenty-seven Rose Bowl games would be won by West Coast teams.

The 1960 Rose Bowl was certainly a turning point for West Coast football. That November, eleven months later, a new President was elected to replace Dwight D. Eisenhower—John F. Kennedy. Indeed, change was in the air.

# Chapter 5

# MUSIC

By the end of the 1920's, America's musical gift to the world of "hot jazz" established the United States as the world's leader in popular music. During the Great Depression of the 1930's, American ballads helped soothe Depression-weary souls at home and aboard. Such American melodies as "Body and Soul" (1930), "Mood Indigo" (1931), "Star Dust," "Night and Day," and "April in Paris" (1932), "Smoke Gets in Your Eyes" and "Stormy Weather" (1933), and the hauntingly beautiful "Blue Moon" (1934), made American music—jazz *and* ballads—popular world-wide. But America's songwriters and musicians weren't finished innovating. By 1936, the "swing era" of the big bands had arrived. America's "swing" music with its big sound and up-beat rhythms swept the country, changing musical tastes and dancing styles across America, and eventually, around the world.

By 1936, Benny Goodman with his clarinet, Harry James with his trumpet, and Tommy Dorsey with his trombone led their respective dance bands to staggering heights at live concerts and in dance halls, on the radio, and through phonograph record sales. The record business became a big-time American industry in spite of an otherwise rocky economy. Soon, rival bands led by Artie Shaw, Gene Krupa, "Count" Basie, Louis Armstrong, Jack Teagarden, and Glenn Miller wowed audiences and "jitterbug" dancers across the nation with their "in the groove" and "boogie-woogie" music. And a young band singer named

Frank Sinatra, first as a vocalist with the Harry James Orchestra, and then as the lead singer for Tommy Dorsey's Band, became the idol of "bobbysoxers" everywhere.

Then came the war in Europe and the sudden fall of France to Hitler's Nazis, inspiring the hauntingly beautiful and plaintive "The Last Time I Saw Paris" (1940). Soon after the United States entered the war, American composer Irving Berlin wrote his classic ode to America's troops overseas who were likely to be dreaming in foxholes somewhere of being back home for a "White Christmas" (1942). Singer Bing Crosby recorded "White Christmas" for the entire world to enjoy for years to come. Meanwhile, the dynamic duo of Rogers and Hammerstein wrote and then produced their rousing musical "Oklahoma!" Their Broadway show set all-time attendance records in New York, and soon, Americans at home and abroad were singing "Oh, What a Beautiful Mornin'," and "People Will Say Were in Love" as World War II raged on. Many Americans also sang other popular tunes of the time, such as "Praise the Lord and Pass the Ammunition" and "Comin' in on a Wing and a Prayer." America's prayers were eventually answered as the war in Europe and then Asia finally ended in 1945, and most of America's fighting men and women returned home.

1946 was celebrated with such new Broadway musical hits as Irving Berlin's lighthearted Western comedy "Annie Get Your Gun," and Lerner and Loewe's "Brigadoon." And Walt Disney Studios in Hollywood contributed their highly popular, up-beat song from their motion picture *Song of the South*, "Zip-a-dee-do-dah." In 1948, Americans seemed happy when they sang "All I Want for Christmas Is My Two Front Teeth," and when they went to the polls that November and chose the feisty underdog Harry S. Truman over the more urbane favorite Thomas E. Dewey for President of the United States. Then, in 1949, Rodgers and Hammerstein's marvelous musical "South Pacific" first opened to raves on Broadway. Soon, the world was singing their songs: "Bali Ha'i," "Some Enchanted Evening," "So In Love," and "I'm in Love with a Wonderful Guy." The stage was set for the Fabulous Fifties. America set the tone for the "Jazz Age" of the 1920's, the soothing ballads of the early 1930's, and the "Swing Era" of the late 1930's and 1940's. What new innovation would American music contribute to the world next? *Rock 'n' roll.*

Rock' n' roll began during the early 1950's as an amalgam of America's popular country-and-Western music, traditional folk music, and the "blues" music of Southern Blacks. Best identified by its heavily accentuated beat and its repetition of simple phrases, 1950's rock 'n' roll usually featured electronically amplified instruments—especially guitars—and gyrating vocalists. Early pioneers such as Les Paul and Mary Ford mastered the use of the electric (or "steel") guitar, while Elvis Presley popularized the art of singing while gyrating his hips to the delight of his female fans. While a young lad from Hoboken, New Jersey, named Frank Sinatra drove female "bobbysoxers" (and their moms) to swoon to his singing during the early 1940's, most parents approved because Sinatra sang *their* songs in his unique, yet traditional style. Most of Sinatra's songs had been popular ballads since the early 1930's. He simply sang them better. By contrast, Elvis Presley represented a musical—and *sexual*—revolution.

Elvis Presley was born in 1935 in Tupelo, Mississippi, while Col. Dwight Eisenhower was serving as an aide to General Douglas MacArthur in the Philippines. In 1948, as General Eisenhower was leaving Paris as the Supreme Commander of NATO to become President of Columbia University in New York City, thirteen-year-old Elvis Presley moved to Memphis, Tennessee, with his parents. Who knew then that Dwight D. Eisenhower would soon become the first Republican President since Herbert Hoover and Elvis Presley, movie theatre usher turned truck driver, would be hailed as "The King of Rock 'n' roll"?

After briefly touring parts of the South as "The Hillbilly Cat," Elvis Presley began recording songs for a Memphis record company, Sun Records. In 1954, at the tender age of nineteen, Elvis made his first "hit" records, including "That's All Right" and "Blue Moon of Kentucky." Signed by RCA Records in 1955 at the age of twenty, Elvis Presley skyrocketed to stardom with several singles, including "Mystery Train," "I'm Left, You're Right, She's Gone," and "I Forgot to Remember." Then, in 1956, Elvis Presley struck it rich as "The King of Rock 'n' roll" with "Love Me Tender," "Hound Dog," "Blue Suede Shoes," "Don't Be Cruel," "Heartbreak Hotel," "Blue Moon," and "Tutti Frutti." Elvis also flew to Hollywood to star in the first of his thirty-three motion pictures, *Love Me Tender*. Elvis had gone from a poor hillbilly to a multimillionaire in less than twenty-four months. Not even the great Frank Sinatra had become as rich and famous so fast.

But Elvis Presley was not invited to attend President Eisenhower's second Inauguration following Ike's landslide re-election that November. Why? Ike, like most other Americans during the mid-1950's, was anything but a revolutionary. And Elvis' suggestive songs and his bump-and-grind singing style was nothing short of a revolution in the show business world of popular music. Besides, Ike was not pleased when he learned that "O Solo Mio" and "Army Blue," two of his favorite songs, had been "adapted" by Elvis as "It's Now or Never" and "Love Me Tender." Most parents and the vast majority of clergy saw Elvis' highly suggestive on-stage gyrations as threats to America's "standards of sexual decency."

Adult America's momentary antipathy towards Elvis Presley wasn't because he was not likeable. Or because he lacked talent. And it wasn't because he treated his mamma poorly. He certainly didn't. Simply put, his music and style were too unconventional to be easily accepted. To be sure, Elvis Presley was by no means the only rock 'n' roller of the Fabulous Fifties. Fats Domino ("Blueberry Hill"), Lloyd Price ("Lawdy Miss Clawdy"), Bill Haley and His Comets ("Rock Around the Clock" and "Shake, Rattle and Roll"), Little Richard ("Tutti Fruitti" and "Long Tall Sally"), Chuck Berry ("Roll Over Beethoven"), Jerry Lee Lewis ("Whole Lot of Shakin' Going On" and "Great Balls of Fire"), and Buddy Holly ("Peggy Sue") were also vastly popular with America's youth. But none of those recording artists reached the pinnacle of sexual debauchery that Elvis "The King" had so rapidly achieved in the eyes of the general public. And so, during most of the Eisenhower Years, Elvis Presley was viewed by many citizens of our fair land as a threat to American morals. Even TV producers seeking profits by televising Elvis Presley's performances refused to allow their cameras to focus on Elvis in concert below the waist. To get the *full Elvis* during the Eisenhower Years, one had to pay to attend his concerts or see his movies. And "depraved" Americans did both in droves.

Regardless of one's opinion of Elvis Presley in particular, or rock 'n' roll in general, any review of American music during the 1950's would be grossly inadequate if it did not include the spectacular range of other highly creative forms of popular music during the fabulous decade. America during the 1950's was awash in song. And Elvis

Presley certainly wasn't America's only pop music "King" during the Eisenhower Years.

Nat "King" Cole's 1950 recording of "Mona Lisa" had become a romantic classic by Ike's first year in office, as had his 1951 rendition of "Too Young." Young and old alike loved his soothing, romantic style, and his popularity lasted throughout the 1950's. In 1953, Miss Peggy Lee was one of America's leading female vocalists with such hit recordings as "Black Coffee," "My Heart Belongs to Daddy," "I Didn't Know What Time It Was," "I've Got You Under My Skin," and "Love Me or Leave Me." To most Americans, Peggy Lee's voice was sultry and sexy, and her tempo was "cool."

Many other hits of 1953 were not nearly as "cool" as Peggy Lee's, but songs such as "Doggie in the Window" and "Baubles, Bangles, and Beads" were as popular as they were corny. That same year, Hank Williams won the country music world's praise with his classic recording of "Your Cheatin' Heart," a group called "The Orioles" broke many a teenager's heart with "Crying in the Chapel," and Duke Ellington charmed the socks off of jazz sophisticates everywhere with his rendition of "Take The "A" Train." And three of the most beautiful and soulful songs ever written were big hits in 1953—"Ebb Tide," "Stranger in Paradise," and "I Love Paris."

1954 proved to be another good year for lovers of traditional pop music in America. Frank Sinatra reemerged fresh and full of song following the resurrection of his show business career when he won the Oscar for "Best Supporting Actor" for his dramatic performance in the 1953 Academy Award winning motion picture, *From Here to Eternity*. In 1954, Sinatra had four of the nation's "Top Twenty" song hits: "Get Happy," "Just One of Those Things," "All of Me," and "I'm Gonna Sit Right Down and Write Myself a Letter." To his fans everywhere, "ol' Blue eyes" was back!

Other popular mainstream songs of 1954 included "Hernando's Hideaway," "Mister Sandman," "Young at Heart," "Three Coins in the Fountain," "Goodnight Sweetheart," and "Hey, There." For the more rock-oriented, there was Ray Charles' "I've Got a Woman," "Earth Angel" by The Penguins, "Sh-Boom" by The Cords, "Pledging My Love" by Johnny Ace, and "Sincerely" by The Moonglows. And for the regular folks, there were marvelous singers like Pat Boone, Rosemary Clooney, Perry Como, Bing Crosby, Vic Damone, Doris Day, Eddie

Fisher, Frankie Lane, Julie London, Tony Martin, and Johnny Ray, who sang their favorite "standards."

In 1955, the United States of America was still comprised of a total of forty-eight states (Alaska and Hawaii were not admitted to the Union until 1959), the Federal minimum wage was raised from 75¢ to 90¢ per hour, New York was still our most populas state, much of the South was still segregated, the U.S. Senate recognized the sovereignty of the new Republic of West Germany on April Fool's Day, and President Eisenhower suffered a "mild" heart attack while vacationing in Denver, Colorado, in late September. Meanwhile, hard-core baseball fans and musical comedy aficionados had at least one thing they could all share in common in 1955—appreciation of the new hit Broadway show by Adler and Ross called "Damn Yankees." "Damn Yankees" was the first of a marvelous series of new hit Broadway musicals introduced during the mid and late 1950's. Eventually, each of these Broadway productions—"My Fair Lady" (1956), "West Side Story" (1957), "The Music Man" (1957), "Flower Drum Song" (1958), "The Sound of Music" (1959), and "Gypsy" (1959)—would tour the country, spreading "culture" across the land.

In 1955, American "culture" also included Mercury Record's two big hits, "Only You" and "The Great Pretender" by a group called The Platters, Tennessee Ernie Ford's "Sixteen Tons," "Why Do Fools Fall in Love" by The Teenagers, and Julie London's plaintive "Cry Me A River." Fats Domino was back in the limelight with "Ain't It A Shame." Johnny Cash skirted the dark side of life with "Folsom Prison Blues." Much of America was singing "The Yellow Rose of Texas" with conductor Mitch Miller. And kids everywhere were singing the praises of America's "King of the Wild Frontier" as seen through the eyes of Fess Parker and Walt Disney while sporting coon-skin caps and mouthing the words to "The Ballad of Davy Crockett." (Never mind that, in real life, the former Congressman and Alamo hero disliked coon-skin caps and hated to be called "Davy.")

And what about Frank Sinatra? 1955 was a banner year for Mr. Sinatra. He starred in five films that year—*Young at Heart*, *Not as a Stranger*, *Guys and Dolls*, *The Tender Trap*, and was nominated for an Oscar as Best Actor for his dramatic performance as a drug addict in *The Man with the Golden Arm*. He also recorded numerous hit songs, including "Love And Marriage," "In the Wee Small Hours of The

Morning," "Mood Indigo," "It Never Entered My Mind," "What Is This Thing Called Love?" "I'll Be Around," and "I Get Along Without You Very Well."

1955 also saw other artists, and heard other songs. Chief among 1955's remaining hits was the beautiful yet haunting "Love Is a Many-Splendored Thing," the coquettish "Whatever Lola Wants," and that teen classic, "Rock Around the Clock."

1956 was a year for big instrumental recordings, with the theme song from the Hollywood motion picture *Around the World in 80 Days* being the name of one of the year's most popular tunes. Another example was the very popular "Poor People of Paris." On Broadway, Alan Jay Lerner and Frederick Loewe's original production of the musical "My Fair Lady" opened to rave reviews. Soon, most of America was singing along with Julie Andrews, "I Could Have Danced All Night." Billie Holiday's album "Lady Sings the Blues" was a tremendous hit, Miles Davis' "Birth of The Cool" album sold well, and Frank Sinatra's album "Songs for Swingin' Lovers" was solid gold. Doris Day had a highly popular hit song in "Que Sera, Sera," and Gene Vincent made teenagers happy from coast to coast with "Be-Bop-A-Lula." But two of the biggest winners of 1956 were Dwight D. Eisenhower and Elvis Presley. Why them? Because Ike was reelected President in a landslide in spite of the fact that the Democrats carried both houses of Congress, and Elvis was named the number one recording artist of 1956 despite all the opposition to his bump-and-grind delivery.

Two of the greatest Broadway musicals ever written, Leonard Bernstein's "West Side Story" and Meredith Wilson's "The Music Man," both premiered in sold-out theatres in New York City during 1957. Soon, "Tonight" and "Maria" from "West Side Story" and "Seventy-Six Trombones" from "The Music Man" could be heard again and again on radio and television throughout the nation and around the world. But the omnipresent Elvis Presley was still number one in record sales thanks to his latest smash hits, "Jailhouse Rock" and "All Shook Up."

To be sure, the stream of new pop music hits from other recording artists during 1957 was nearly endless. Nat "King" Cole was right behind Elvis in record sales with his classic renditions of "When I Fall In Love," "Route 66," and "Stardust." A young Paul Anka became a star with "Diana." Bo Diddley did "Bo Diddley." Johnny Cash sang "I Walk The Line" while riding "The Rock Island Line." Danny and The

Juniors were "At The Hop." Chuck Berry went to "School Days." Bill Haley And His Comets claimed they could "Rock Around The Clock." Buddy Holly promised he would "Not Fade Away." Carl Perkins bragged that "Everybody's Trying to Be My Baby," while Little Richard extolled the virtues of "Long Tall Sally" and "Tutti Frutti." Jerry Lee Lewis observed "A Whole Lot of Shakin' Going On," followed by "Great Balls of Fire." Even Bugs and Germs got into the act when Buddy Holly and The Crickets chirped "That'll Be The Day" and Huey Smith and The Clowns warned their fans about the "Rocking Pneumonia and the Boogie Woogie Flu." Also, in a slightly more traditional mode, numerous artists sang about "Love Letters in the Sand." While there were those who claimed at the time that Ike and his administration were old-fashioned and "up-tight," the same certainly could not be said regarding 1957's pop music.

The popular music world of 1958 was a little less wild and wooly. Rogers and Hammerstein's new hit Broadway show "Flower Drum Song" was more low-key than 1957's "West Side Story" or "The Music Man." And, while two of 1958's most popular songs, "The Purple People Eater" and the "Chipmunk Song" were certainly not traditional in nature, other popular songs that year included such mellow melodies as "Chanson d'amour," "Volare," "Catch a Falling Star," and "A Certain Smile." Bobby Darin did get wild with his "Splish Splash," but Frank Sinatra countered with "Only The Lonely" and "What's New?"

The Everly Brothers were quite popular during 1958. Two of their biggest hits that year were "Bye Bye Love" and "Wake Up Little Susie." As usual, Chuck Berry made the "Top Twenty" charts with his "Rock and Roll Music," "Reeling' And Rockin'," and "Sweet Little Sixteen." And Tommy Edwards summed up life in 1958 with "It's All In The Game."

It can be argued that 1959 was the year of Ray Charles. Elvis Presley was in the Army after being drafted. Frank Sinatra was busy making movies. And Buddy Holly was dead at the age of twenty-two following his tragic February 3rd plane crash, leaving Ray Charles to sing his heart out. Ray Charles contributed a flood of hit songs, including "What'd I Say?," "What Kind of Man Are You?," "Let The Good Times Roll," "Rockhouse," "It Had To Be You," and "Come Rain or Come Shine." His voice could be heard most everywhere—on car radios, coming from department store sound systems, café and bar jukeboxes . . . . But

1959 was also the year for two great new Broadway musicals—Richard Rogers' "The Sound of Music" and Julie Styne's "Gypsy." Soon, Broadway singing star Ethel Merman's booming voice could be heard singing "Everything's Coming Up Roses" from "Gypsy" in just about every nook and cranny in America. Likewise, it seemed that every hill and dell in the land echoed with "The Sound of Music," or other songs from that popular show.

Unfortunately for many of the nation's top disc jockeys who played rock 'n' roll records on their radio shows, 1959 was also the year of the great "Payola Scandal." By 1959, the rock 'n' roll music business had grown so exponentially since the early 1950's that nearly two hundred new and different 45 r.p.m. records were being produced and distributed *each week* by a growing number of competing companies in America. Obviously, the more copies a new record sold, the greater the profit. Just as obvious, a disc jockey could only play a limited number of records each hour he was on the air. Also obvious, the more times a particular record was played during a popular program, the greater the likelihood it would become a "hit." Hence, the stage was set for a widespread scheme that came to be called "payola." Simply put, "payola" was a code word for pay for play—record companies *paid* so disc jockeys *played*. For the record business and big-time radio hosts, it was a win-win scheme until a recently unemployed and disgruntled disc jockey from Boston blew the whistle before a Congressional subcommittee looking into allegations of wrongdoing in radio's rock 'n' roll programming.

The original target of the investigation by the United States House of Representatives' subcommittee was television's quiz show scandal involving Charles Van Doren and NBC's "The $64,000 Question." However, once Dr. Van Doren admitted under oath that he had been secretly "coached" by the hit TV show's producer while he was winning over a hundred thousand dollars as a contestant on the program, the House Special Subcommittee on Legislative Oversight shifted its attention to alleged wrongdoing in popular teenage-oriented radio programs specializing in rock 'n' roll music. The committee soon discovered that "payola" was a common business practice unique to the music world of rock 'n' roll. The committee soon concluded that most of rock 'n' roll's hit records had become so due to "bribes"—money or gifts paid by record companies or distributors to key disc jockeys in large-market areas to "plug" certain songs by praising them and playing them on the air again and again.

While America's leading disc jockey of the day, Dick Clark, was not found in violation of any specific laws, ABC's teenage idol and host of "American Bandstand" was ordered by the radio and television network to sell all of his considerable shares of stock in various music publishing and record companies to eliminate any possible conflict of interest concerns. Many other leading disc jockeys were not so fortunate. Some were summarily fired by their employers. Others were later indicted under the new Federal anti-payola law passed in 1960. Meanwhile, most of America's teenagers continued to listen to rock 'n' roll on the radio and buy their favorite 45 r.p.m. recordings at record stores across the country.

In reality, throughout the Eisenhower Years, rock 'n' roll was the target of many conservative parent and religious groups and liberal as well as conservative devotees of "classical" music and opera long before the Congressional subcommittee sprang into action in 1959. Even in the nation's mainstream publications, rock 'n' roll music was often put down or simply dismissed as "inferior." To many Americans, rock 'n' roll was a passing teenage fad, not something that would endure the test of time. For example, one of the nation's leading encyclopedia yearbooks for 1959 spent nearly its entire three-page section on "Music" covering the latest symphony orchestra concerts, classical recitals, operas, and ballet performances. According to *The New Funk & Wagnalls Encyclopedia Yearbook for 1959*, Russia's visiting Bolshoi Ballet captured the hearts of most New Yorkers with their splendid rendition of *Romeo and Juliet*. Meanwhile, the New York Philharmonic Symphony Orchestra conducted by Leonard Bernstein greatly impressed audiences during its grand European tour. In America, stars of the regular recital season included violinist Jasha Heifetz and pianist Beveridge Webster. And Swedish soprano Brigit Nillson wowed audiences with her performance of "Isolde" at the Metropolitan Opera House in New York City. Only in its last paragraph on page 214 did the article even mention "popular music." Quoting *Funk & Wagnalls*,

> "The news in popular music, as the payola scandals indicated, was that nothing in radio and television was not for sale, at a price. For the past few years the price was met,

and so we have enjoyed the phenomenon known as rock 'n' roll. Perhaps the only healthy thing to come out of the whole affair has been the strong suggestion that rock 'n' roll was not, in fact, a popular fad at all, but rather a put-up job, and an illegally put-up one at that."

# CHAPTER 6

# BUSINESS

Radio and television were not the only sectors of America's business community that were the subjects of scandal during the Eisenhower Years. In fact, Ike's own White House Chief of Staff came under close scrutiny during the spring of 1958 for alleged wrongdoing involving Federal agencies and the manufacture by one of his friends of "wool" coats containing less-expensive *nylon*.

During much of man's past, those institutions which most required some sort of organization were the military, the church, and the landed estates. And of these, historically speaking, the military seems to have been the most organized. The line-and-staff organizational structures of most businesses, governmental agencies, and schools in America during the 1950's were remarkably similar to the chain-of-command established by Philip of Macedonia for his armies more than 2,000 years earlier. In essence, history's first professional managers were military men.

Dwight D. Eisenhower was an astute manager and organizer. As chief of staff of huge, *successful* military organizations—from the development, training, and deployment of the D-day invasion force during World War II to the daily operations of NATO in defense of Western Europe against the threat of the Soviet Union—Ike recognized that the most successful managers, military or civilian, choose the best and brightest to assist them. Delegation of authority and clear lines of accountability are essential to minimizing duplication of effort, avoiding chaos, and preventing failure. Every chief executive, military or civilian, needs a trusted second-in-command. Eisenhower knew this because he had lived both roles, from being General Douglas MacArthur's chief aide, to his position as the Commander of all Allied Forces in Europe. For his first six years as President, Eisenhower delegated enormous power to his White House Chief of Staff, Sherman Adams, so he could concentrate on major issues and still have time for an occasional round of golf.

By design, President Eisenhower was the public face of his administration (with a good deal of help from his trusted Press Secretary, James Hagerty) and the nation's chief decision-maker, while Sherman Adams acted as his chief gate-keeper and traffic cop outside the Oval Office. During the first six years of Ike's Presidency, Sherman Adams was America's *de facto* assistant president. The former Governor of New Hampshire was President Eisenhower's closest and most trusted aide. True to his New England roots, Sherman Adams was a Yankee workaholic who was often stern, curt, and directive. But to Eisenhower, Adams was the perfect White House Chief of Staff—he got things *done*. Then came the spring of 1958.

Sherman Adams' fall from power came swiftly. Rumors began to circulate across the nation's capital that Sherman Adams had improperly used his enormous influence to gain "preferential treatment" for his wealthy Boston friend, Bernard Goldfine, from the Federal Trade Commission (FTC) and the Securities and Exchange Commission (SEC). As rumor had it, one of Mr. Goldfine's companies was caught manufacturing coats labeled natural "wool" that actually contained much cheaper, synthetic *nylon*. Rumors claimed that Goldfine had rewarded Adams with gifts of expensive vicuña coats and vacation trips in exchange for "favors" from the FTC and the SEC. Adams flatly denied the allegations, and President Eisenhower privately defended his Chief of Staff. But the political pot continued to boil. Both Congressional Democrats and Adams' enemies within his own party smelled blood in the water, and, like so many sharks, closed in for the kill. During the summer of 1958, Democratic Congressman Oren Harris of Arkansas, Chairman of the House Subcommittee on Legislative Oversight, began investigating Bernard Goldfine's relations with the FTC, the SEC, and Sherman Adams. Sherman Adams volunteered to appear before Harris' subcommittee.

Sherman Adams testified under oath before the House Subcommittee on Legislative Oversight that he had committed no illegal acts, and that his long-term friendship with Bernard Goldfine had not caused him to use undo influence with any government agency. His only possible mistake had been "poor judgment" in accepting gifts of friendship. The subcommittee exonerated Sherman Adams of any criminal wrongdoing, but cited a belligerent Goldfine for "Contempt of Congress." And the Internal Revenue Service soon investigated Mr. Goldfine for income tax evasion. Meanwhile, new rumors circulated regarding Sherman Adams' alleged use of his position of influence in return for more than a million dollars' worth of various 'bribes" from other "friends." The growing scandal of the "Sherman Adams Affair" became a political liability to both the President in particular, and to all Republicans in general. To avert a complete political disaster to Republicans in the November 1958 mid-term Congressional elections, and to avoid further damage to President Eisenhower's personal reputation, Sherman Adams resigned as Ike's Chief of Staff on September 22, 1958. Accepting his loyal friend and trusted aide's resignation was, according to Ike, the saddest moment of his Presidency. Ike defended Adams to the end. Like that other West Pointer in the White House—Ulysses S. Grant—Ike could be loyal to a fault.

Dwight Eisenhower's entire career prior to his elevation to the Presidency, except for his relatively brief tenure as President of Columbia University, was devoted to military service. But Ike never lost sight of the fact that *private enterprise*—not the Federal government—was the engine that drove America's economy. Eisenhower, like President Calvin Coolidge before him, believed that the national government—and its President—should befriend America's business community by staying out of its way. On February 6, 1953, in one of his first executive orders as President, Ike abolished all Federal controls on wages in an effort to stimulate the economy. Many of these government controls on wages had been in effect since the early days of FDR's "New Deal." Many others had been instituted during World War II.

In an effort to reduce the Federal government's control over America's petroleum deposits, President Eisenhower signed the Tidelands Act on

May 22, 1953. The Tidelands Act returned to the states the rights to submerged and reclaimed lands within their boundaries, thus ending the tidelands oil deposits controversy that began when President Franklin D. Roosevelt brought those lands under Federal control in 1937. The economies of California, Louisiana, Texas, and other coastal states with large oil deposits were immediately stimulated.

Following the end of World War II, the United States was the only nation with its business community undamaged by the ravages of war. By war's end, the United States had become the greatest industrial complex in the history of the world. It can be argued that it was America's great industrial might and agricultural prowess that ultimately won World War II.

Nazi Germany and Imperial Japan, both great industrial powers in 1939, lay totally devastated by 1945. Great Britain, although "victorious," was exhausted, broke, and pressured by major parts of her vast global empire to grant each independence. Much of France, Italy, and the rest of Western Europe had been reduced to rubble. China was embroiled in civil war. And an industrially primitive Soviet Union was preoccupied with directing her economic resources to the Red Army's occupation and control of her newly acquired Western empire of twice-conquered Eastern European nations. Much of Eastern Europe, already devastated by war, was imprisoned behind the Soviet Union's "Iron Curtain"—Communist Russia's defensive "buffer" against Western capitalism. Simply put, these geopolitical realities left the United States of America with a de facto monopoly of most of the world's manufacturing might. To put America's position in a global perspective regarding the consumption of goods, according to United Nations' statistics in 1953, the United States contained only six percent of the world's total population, but it had 60% of all the world's automobiles, 58% of all telephones, 75% of all radio sets, and 34% of all railroads.

In 1953, General Motors was the world's largest manufacturer of automobiles. United States Steel was the world's greatest producer of steel. General Electric made more appliances than any other corporation in the world. DuPont led the world in the production of chemical products. Boeing and Douglas Aircraft manufactured most of the world's commercial aircraft. American Telephone & Telegraph was the world's leader in communications technology. Exxon Mobil and Texaco were world leaders in the oil business. International Business Machines was the world's leading manufacturer of typewriters and calculators. RCA was the world's leading brand of radios, TV's, and phonographs. Processed food products from Armour, Kraft, General Foods, and General Mills could be found on dinner tables not only in America but in many other parts of the world. Procter & Gamble's products kept much of the world clean. Americans and most foreigners drove on Goodyear or Firestone tires. People the world over used Eastman Kodak film to take family pictures. And the sports world primarily depended on Wilson products *made in the U.S.A.* President Eisenhower and his Secretary of Commerce, Sinclair Weeks, were determined to assist American businesses in maintaining their world supremacy.

Long before 1953, American business was given a giant boost by such visionary entrepreneurs as Alexander Graham Bell (American Telephone & Telegraph), Andrew Carnegie (United States Steel), Donald Douglas (Douglas Aircraft Company), James Duke (American Tobacco Company), Thomas Edison (The Edison Companies), Harvey Firestone (Firestone Tire & Rubber), Henry Ford (Ford Motor Company), Charles Goodyear (Goodyear Tire & Rubber), E.H. Harriman (New York Central, Union Pacific, and Southern Pacific railroads), William Randolph Hearst (Hearst Publications), James Hill (Great Northern Railroad), Howard Hughes (Hughes Tool Company, RKO Studios, Trans World Airlines, and Hughes Aircraft Company), J.P. Morgan (J.P. Morgan & Company, investment bankers), John Pemberton (*Coca-Cola*), John D. Rockefeller (Standard Oil), Gustavus Swift (Swift & Company, meat packers), George Westinghouse (Westinghouse Corporation, air brakes and appliances), Frederick Weyerhauser (Weyerhauser & Company, forest products), and a host of others. The huge organizations they founded and developed during the late $19^{th}$ and early $20^{th}$ Century in America required the employment of professional managers—men who could put sound business theories into practical use—to help these giant enterprises continue to grow and prosper.

By the dawn of the $20^{th}$ Century, the stream of immigrants crossing the Atlantic Ocean from Europe to America in search of economic opportunity had expanded from a river to a veritable flood in spite of objections from various groups, including organized labor. Cheap, untrained labor became abundant. Charles Darwin's theory concerning the survival of the fittest and Herbert Spencer's notions about superior and inferior human traits also crossed the Atlantic. As a result of these factors, coupled with an extraordinary supply of America's own natural resources, innovative entrepreneurs with practical vision, and a general "hands-off" policy toward business on the part of government, private enterprise thrived under professional managers who made every effort to answer this fundamental business question: *How can the needs of the organization and each individual within it be satisfied to the benefit of both?*

History shows us that every age develops an organizational form and a management style appropriate to the time. For early 20$^{th}$ Century America, Frederick Winslow Taylor and his "scientific management" became the organizational form and style for most businesses. For centuries, the so-called "man problem" was handled in numerous ways, including the apprentice system for skilled trades and low-volume manufacturing. In the apprentice system, experienced craftsmen worked along side less skilled apprentices, teaching them the necessary skills to complete an entire process or create an entire product. But high-volume assembly lines such as Henry Ford's automobile factories changed all that. Under Henry Ford's manufacturing model, for example, an assembly line *manager* assigned *specific, well-defined,* and *different tasks* to the employees under his supervision. The ultimate result, a Model "T" Ford, was the product of no one individual or small group. It was the product of a large "team" effort. Enter Frederick Winslow Taylor.

Frederick Winslow Taylor, the father of "scientific management," sincerely believed that the answer to the problems of modern business—and especially manufacturing—was the scientific planning of work, task by task. Taylor was largely responsible for making management a recognized profession. His two major works, *Shop Management* and *The Principles of Scientific Management*, both published in 1911, quickly became highly influential in the United States, and soon spread to the rest of the industrialized world.

Frederick Winslow Taylor's "task system," with its goal of producing high profits *and* high wages, was based on six principles:

- There is always *one best way* to do a task.
- Accurate *time-studies* are indispensable.

- Workers should *not* plan their own work; that is the task of managers.
- Workers should *not* decide which production methods to use; that is best left to managers.
- Workers must receive *bonuses for exceeding quotas*.
- Strict on-the-job *discipline* must be maintained.

Taylor believed that his "task system" was essential because the average person prefers to be directed, wishes to avoid responsibility, has relatively little ambition, and wants security above all. According to Taylor, people are inherently self-centered and indifferent to organizational needs. Most dislike work and will avoid it if they can. Hence, professional managers must define each employee's work in specific detail and closely monitor their performance of assigned tasks. During the Eisenhower Years, many managers adhered to these same assumptions about the nature of their subordinates.

One of Newton's laws of motion states that for every action there is an opposite and equal reaction. Translated into social science terminology, we get the pendulum theory of history. The Taylorists pictured management as the science of supervising impersonal, well-oiled machines. The next generation of management theorists, led by Elton Mayo, Fritz J. Roethlisberger, and William J. Dickerson, had strong inclinations to throw away the supervisor's whip and hang lace curtains on his subordinates' machines. Certainly the extremes of scientific management—including timing a worker's performance using a stop watch to determine future work quotas—caused a rather predictable reaction: the "human relations" movement.

The powerful influence upon American society of a relatively new field of study—psychology—was increasingly felt during the late 1920's and early 1930's. During the early 1930's, while the shock and suffering of the Great Depression rocked the business world, Elton Mayo and his associates, Fritz J. Roethlisberger and William J. Dickerson, conducted their now famous, "Hawthorne Experiments" at the giant Hawthorne plant of American Telephone & Telegraph's subsidiary, Western Electric, in Chicago. Results of the Hawthorne experiments were initially popularized in Mayo's book, *The Human Problems of an Industrial Civilization*, first published in 1933. According to Mayo and his colleagues, the more "democratic" managers were, the better the production levels of their subordinates. This emphasis on the superiority of a "democratic" management style and the importance of "human relations" in the work place was in direct conflict with the principles of "scientific management," but it was more in tune with the changing tenor of the times.

The hardships of the Great Depression filled many Americans with feelings of fear and uncertainty. Some choose to seek economic "protection" through government "entitlements." Others sought job protection through labor unions. For many Americans, entrepreneurship and *individualism* lost popular favor to survival and *cooperativism*.

During the "Roaring '20's," the average workweek for Americans was a ten-hour day, six days per week (generally, Monday through Saturday). Unemployment was low; prosperity was widespread. Then came the Great Depression and, in March 1933, President Franklin D. Roosevelt's "New Deal." Growing pressure from organized labor and just plain folks to create a more communal society by "sharing the wealth" helped the recently-elected F.D.R. and his New Dealers in the Federal government take a much greater role in regulating businesses, including the establishment of the eight-hour work day and the five-day work week. According to the new "social engineers" in Washington, D.C., the five-day work week and eight-hour day would employ *three* people to do the work of *two*, with the added bonus that workers would have twenty more hours per week of leisure time. Unemployment would be reduced by the hiring of additional help, workers would be happier and healthier, and the newly-shared wealth would stimulate the economy at little or no extra cost.

Meanwhile, Depression-era motion pictures and popular literature often portrayed bankers and businessmen as oppressors, and workers as the oppressed. To many Americans, the same people and corporations that had been symbols of what was best about our free-enterprise system during the prosperous 1920's, such as the Ford Motor Company and its popular founder Henry Ford, became targets of derision by organized labor and many other folks during the dark days of the Depression. Bankers and other business managers were often portrayed as "bad guys." Bluntly put, many managers were pressured to be more "democratic," or else.

Following World War II and America's return to more prosperous times, public attitudes toward business began to change again. So too did theories about how America's businesses should be run. Eclectic management theorists began taking the "best" tenets of the "human relations" and "scientific management" models and blended them into a new synthesis of "best practices." Known as "The Revisionists," many agreed with certain aspects of Taylor's "task system" while also siding with Mayo's "humanists" that workers can be motivated to do their best to achieve goals to which they are committed. They generally agreed with Taylor that most workers are like children waiting to be led, but they also agreed with Mayo that good "human relations" between a supervisor and his subordinates is a key to the success or failure of any organization. Some had come to the conclusion that the best boss is a "benevolent" dictator—a scientific manager with human relations skills.

The primary focus of Dwight D. Eisenhower's Presidency was foreign policy due to his personal philosophy of limited governmental involvement in domestic issues and the major demands of the Cold War abroad. Whenever possible, Ike attempted to keep the Federal government out of the way of American business during his administration. During his first months in office, President Eisenhower issued an executive order that abolished all Federal controls on wages in specified industries, and he pressed Congress to return control of all Federal coastal tidelands to the states. As a result of Ike's actions, the Federal minimum wage in 1953 remained at 75¢ per hour, but specific corporations that once had rates of pay set by bureaucrats in Washington, D.C., were free to determine their own pay levels in negotiations with organized labor. In addition, control of off-shore drilling for oil was placed in the hands of state legislatures and local governmental units, increasing revenues for both.

President Eisenhower's management style was a blend of "scientific management" and "human relations." Ike was masterful at maintaining a positive public image of himself as someone the average American could *trust*. "I Like IKE!" wasn't simply a political slogan. It was an expression of genuine feelings amongst most Americans—ideological friends *and* foes. Ike had *credibility*, an essential "human relations" trait for successful managers at any level.

Maintaining Ike's credibility was not simply left to chance. From the beginning, while Eisenhower had no desire to establish himself as an *activist* President in the public's eye, he was very active behind-the-scenes in maintaining his positive public persona. Robert Montgomery, the long-established movie star and former President of the Screen Actors' Guild, served as his personal choice as Special Consultant to the President on TV and Public Communications. In addition, Ike enlisted the help of New York City's leading advertising agency, Batten, Barton, Durstine, and Osborn, to conduct *weekly* public opinion polls to keep the President informed regarding John Q. Public's take on current issues, policies, and trends. And Ike quickly established the Office of Congressional Relations to promote improved communication between the White House and Congress. He appointed General Wilton B. Persons, who was one of the Army's chief liaison officers with the Congress during World War II, to promote the administration's legislative programs in the friendliest of ways. Simply put, Ike had built his highly successful military career on his keen organizational skills and his knack for establishing and maintaining good "human relations." He was not about to change as President.

As President, Ike also maintained his eye for detail. The "scientific management" side of him was apparent to White House insiders in the way he held his Cabinet members—the chief managers of each major Federal department—responsible for crafting policy and measuring results. From the beginning, Ike involved the members of his Cabinet more than most previous Presidents—certainly more than F.D.R. had—in the nation's governance. Ike scheduled weekly meetings of his full Cabinet, and made it clear to each Secretary that the information they shared and the recommendations they made regarding their respective departments were important to him. Ike made every effort to listen to each Secretary regarding their issues and possible solutions. He was no micromanager, but he expected his subordinates to examine every detail of each proposal before they made their recommendations to him for his final approval. Ike *delegated*, held his managers *accountable*, and acted as his administration's "benevolent" dictator by offering a "guiding hand" when he deemed it necessary. In essence, Ike called the shots like a good CEO should.

America had many successful CEO's in private business during the Eisenhower Years. But, unlike the inventor/entrepreneurs of the early 20th Century—Bell, Edison, Firestone, Ford, Goodyear, Rockefeller—these professional managers were not well-known to the general public. But the names of the corporations they headed certainly were. In 1955,

Fortune magazine issued its first annual list of America's "Fortune 500" corporations, each listed on the New York Stock Exchange. The top ten American corporations in 1955, according to their reported revenues in the millions of dollars, were: (1) General Motors; (2) Exxon Mobil; (3) United States Steel; (4) General Electric; (5) Esmark; (6) Chrysler; (7) Armour; (8) Gulf Oil; (9) Mobil Oil; and (10) DuPont Chemicals.[27] Other well-known corporations on Fortune's 1955 list included Bethlehem Steel, 12th; CBS, 13th; Texaco, 14th; Shell Oil, 16th; Kraft Foods, 17th; Goodyear Tire & Rubber, 19th; RCA Victor, 23rd; Firestone Tire & Rubber, 25th; Douglas Aircraft, 26th; Proctor & Gamble, 27th; Republic Steel, 28th; General Foods, 31st; Wilson Sporting Goods, 37th; Eastman Kodak, 43rd; General Mills, 56th; International Business Machines, 61st; American Motors, 76th; Ralston Purina, 77th; Nabisco Brands, 82nd; Campbell Soup, 88th; Pillsbury, 90th; Singer, 91st; Hormel Foods, 92nd; Carnation, 95th; Reynolds Metals, 97th; and American Standard, 100th. The names of most of these corporations—and many of the products they produced—were as well known to most Americans during the mid-1950's as were the names of their next-door neighbors. Corporate America was an integral part of daily life in the United States during the Eisenhower Years.

Our thirtieth President, Calvin Coolidge, proudly presided over America's greatest period of economic prosperity prior to the Eisenhower Years, the "Roaring Twenties." President Coolidge, the acknowledged guru of "Coolidge Prosperity," made the most memorable statement of his Presidency during a gathering of the American Society of Newspaper Editors in January 1925 when he declared to his audience, "The business of America is business." During his own Presidency, Dwight Eisenhower made no such memorable statements regarding business.[28] But actions Ike took early in his first term proved he was in full agreement with Mr. Coolidge. Ike recommended and eventually signed into law two bills, one authorizing construction of *The St. Lawrence Seaway*, and another, the building of a *National Highway System*. These two massive government-sponsored projects eventually did more to benefit business in America by improving our nation's

---

[27] Ford Motor Company was not listed because it was still family-owned.

[28] Except for his warning about the "military-industrial complex" during his Farewell Address.

transportation system than any Federal legislation since the completion in 1869 of President Lincoln's dream of a trans-continental railroad.

In an attempt to improve the economies of both the United States and Canada, our neighbor to the north, President Eisenhower signed a bill passed by Congress on May 13, 1954, that authorized joint Canadian-U.S. construction of the St. Lawrence Seaway. Today, the St. Lawrence Seaway connects Montreal and Lake Ontario in the east to Lake Erie, Lake Huron, Lake Michigan, and ultimately, Lake Superior in the west. Begun in 1954 and opened in 1959, the St. Lawrence Seaway is one of the world's largest and most important inland navigation systems. From early April to late November, the St. Lawrence Seaway provides a continuous channel for large cargo ships at great economic benefit to both Canada and the United States.

In July 1954, President Eisenhower requested that the governors of each state study the needs of their highway systems, including roadways, bridges, tunnels, and drainage. In September, he appointed General Lucias D. Clay to head the President's Advisory Committee on a National Highway Program to work with the nation's governors to prepare a plan of action for submission to Congress. Federal, state, and local governments would share in the management and costs of planning and constructing a national highway system. With the findings of his Advisory Committee in hand, President Eisenhower sent his message regarding the recommended National Highway Program to Congress on February 22, 1955. In his message, Eisenhower pointed out that the "Three million three hundred and sixty-six thousand miles of road, traveled by 58 million motor vehicles . . . is inadequate for the Nation's growing needs." The newly—elected Eighty-fourth Congress (1955-57) had a slight majority of Democrats in both Houses, but Ike won their support with a strong bi-partisan appeal. Eisenhower argued that a modern national highway system would result in (1) *fewer deaths and injuries* caused by unsafe roads; (2) *reduced operating costs* for family and commercial vehicles as the result of a network of more modern and efficient routes; (3) *improved evacuation routes* in the event of an atomic attack; and (4) *fewer traffic jams* on the nation's streets and highways. For the future good of the nation, Ike reasoned, an improved national highway system simply made sense. On June 30, 1956, the Congress of the United States authorized the expenditure of *thirty-three billion dollars* for Eisenhower's National Highway Program.

The greatest highway construction program in American history was about to begin.

While President Eisenhower was pushing to improve our nation's transportation system for the good of all Americans, another far more subtle transformation of America had already begun. According to sociologist Vance Packard, the author of the best-selling book, *The Status Seekers*, "Big Business, Big Government, Big Labor, Big Education"—all products of modern technology and our nation's growing prosperity—were causing American society to become *more* stratified, rather than less so.[29]

A highly popular notion during the 1950's was that America, unlike Europe and the rest of the world, was rapidly becoming the most "classless society" in history. Another widely-accepted belief was that America was evolving into "one vast middle class." Some American businessmen—especially those involved in new home construction, sales, and advertising—knew better, Packard pointed out. Why else would businessmen in a variety of fields—not just home construction—spend large sums of money on studies of American social class behavior and *buying habits*? And why would they advertise their products accordingly if America was not a nation of "status seekers"?

During the 1950's, the construction industry across America—especially in areas adjacent to large cities such as Los Angeles—experienced an unprecedented boom in new home building and sales. In some areas, entire communities were created within a few months, such as Lakewood, California. "The Lakewood Plan," a first for its time, is a prime example of the newly-found cooperation between private business and local and state governments during the Eisenhower Years. According to the pattern first established by "The Lakewood Plan," entire new communities could be set up at relatively low cost by contracting out with the county and nearby school districts such essential services as police, fire, and schools on a fee-for-services basis. The success of "The Lakewood Plan" sparked a revolution in suburban California, and soon, across certain parts of America in the business of creating new communities.

---

[29] Vance Packard, *The Status Seekers* (New York: David McKay, Co., 1959).

Business and income go hand in hand. And if "The business of America is business," as President Coolidge believed, then a person's occupation and income can be viewed as major indicators of his or her social status within our society, which brings us to the thorny issue of "social class." Unfortunately, Karl Marx, the father of communism, has given the term "social class" a bad reputation. For Marx viewed history as one long and bloody struggle between the "ruling class" and the "working class." Marx's solution? Murder the ruling class—the *owners and their managers*—and thereby create a "classless society"—a so-called "workers' paradise." What Karl Marx failed to understand and Mikhail Gorbachev eventually learned the hard way when the Soviet Union suddenly collapsed underneath his feet on a cold Christmas day, no modern society can exist without social classes and differences in responsibility, expertise, and income. Such disparity is as natural as the sun rising in the east. America's noble goal of equality of *opportunity* should never be confused with equality of *condition*. The fact that America was not a "classless society," or simply "one vast middle class" during the 1950's is no sin. Free-enterprise, with a little boost from the tax-payers now and then, made the United States great. During the Eisenhower Years, Ike and the Congress gave business an occasional boost, but it was business, not government, that drove the engine of America's economy. It was private ownership of the means of production, distribution, and exchange of goods—*capitalism*—that flourished during the Fabulous Fifties.

During the 1950's, the income and social status of Americans varied considerably. According to Vance Packard and his book *The Status Seekers*, the relative social status of Americans could be measured by four basic yardsticks in descending order of importance: (1) occupation; (2) education; (3) source of income; and (4) kind of home. At the top of America's social ladder, or upper class, were major executives of large corporations, leading medical specialists, and partners in top law firms, most of whom had advanced university degrees, whose annual income was mostly from inherited wealth or investments and savings, and who owned at least two homes, both with fashionable addresses. Their reported net annual incomes tended to range from a high of $200,000 (although a few made substantially more) to a low of $37,000. Throughout his eight years in office, President Eisenhower's annual salary was $100,000. When Richard Nixon became Vice President in

1953, his salary was $30,000 per year; in March 1955, it was raised to $35,000. If monetary compensation is the only factor considered, it remains obvious that during the 1950's, when the Federal minimum wage was finally increased to $1.00 per hour in August 1955, America was certainly not a "classless society."

According to U.S. Department of Labor statistics for 1957, most electricians and plumbers made over $110 per week, or over $5,720 per year. Automobile assembly line workers averaged $100 to $110 per week. Workers on aircraft assembly lines made $90 to $100 a week. Public school teachers averaged $80 to $100 per week, or approximately $4,000 per year (unless they also taught summer school). Meat packers made approximately $80 to $90 weekly. Bakers, carpet makers, and sawmill workers, $70 to $80 per week. Grocery store clerks, bank tellers, and telephone switchboard operators averaged $60 to $70 per week. Seafood packers, $50 to $60 a week. Department store clerks and hotel workers averaged $40 to $50 per week. The minimum wage remained at $1.00 per hour. Full-time workers paid at the minimum wage rate generally earned $2,000 per year minus social security and payroll withholding taxes.

Most wages for Americans in various occupations during the Eisenhower Years were extremely low by today's standards. Yet Americans were enjoying high employment rates and general prosperity. Were prices equally low? During most of the Fabulous Fifties, the price of a new "tract" home in the rapidly developing suburbs of America's largest cities averaged $9,000 to $15,000. "Fancy" homes in "fashionable" residential areas generally cost from $25,000 to $50,000. Most Americans bought their new cars from one of America's "Big Three" automobile manufacturers: General Motors, Ford Motor Company, or Chrysler Corporation. A brand-new Chevrolet, Ford, or Plymouth cost an average of $2,000 to $2,500, depending on the model and "accessories" selected, such as automatic transmission, radio, white-wall tires, air conditioning, carpets, etc. A new Pontiac (GM), Mercury (Ford), or Dodge (Chrysler), generally carried a price tag around $2,800. If one wished to step up to a new Oldsmobile or Buick (both made by GM), or a DeSoto (Chrysler), approximately $3,600 was the asking price. For top-of-the-line automobiles such as Cadillacs, Lincolns and Lincoln Continentals, or Chryslers and Chrysler Imperials, the price shot up to a starting amount of $5,100 to a high of over $14,000 for a Cadillac El Dorado Brougham.

Brooks Brothers was a famous name in quality men's suits during the 1950's. A Brooks Brothers suit could be purchased on sale for as low at $35. A dinner for four, complete with soup, salad, and dessert, could cost as little as $7.80 plus tip at a family restaurant in the suburbs of most cities, while two adults could dine at a ritzy café in the city for $10 to $12, not counting cocktails, tip, or valet parking. Even attending college away from home was a relative bargain when compared to today's prices.

In 1985, when Ronald Reagan occupied the White House, tuition plus room and board at Harvard University cost $13,775 for the year.[30] At Yale that same year, the total was $12,980. At Wellesley, $11,970. At Smith, $11,901. Princeton, $12,910. Notre Dame, $8,700. Stanford, $12,839. And USC, $11,970. Today, their annual costs generally range from $40,000 to $60,000 per year. In 1957, tuition plus room and board at these same private schools cost approximately $1,500 to $2,500. At Stanford University, tuition for the 1957-58 academic year was $1,005, and room and board was $750. According to the *Stanford University Bulletin*, "A realistic estimate of expenses for Stanford freshmen is about $2,250 for the year. This includes tuition, room and board, books and supplies, laundry and cleaning, and recreational expenses."[31] And state universities in 1957 averaged about $1,100 to $1,350 for room and board plus tuition. Obviously, even when considering increases in the annual cost-of-living index, a college education was a relative bargain during the Eisenhower Years.

---

[30] *Barron's Profiles of American Colleges* (New York: Barron's Educational Services, Inc., 1985).

[31] *Stanford University Bulletin*, series 9, No. 79, October 1, 1957, p. 31.

# CHAPTER 7

# EDUCATION

Colleges and universities, both public and private, experienced an unprecedented period of rapid growth following the end of World War II. And growth rates were even more spectacular for our nation's elementary and secondary schools. Why? Following the return of millions of American G.I.'s from Europe and Asia after the end of the War, nature took its course and a "baby-boom" began. With the Great Depression and history's bloodiest war behind them (and educational and economic incentives provided by President Truman's "G.I. Bill"), most veterans and former defense workers were ready to settle down, get married, raise families, and lead normal, peaceful lives. Birth rates soared. State compulsory attendance laws were followed. And, by the early 1950's, many of America's existing public schools became overcrowded, especially in America's rapidly growing urban and suburban areas. Huge clusters of newly-built housing "tracts," especially in areas such as Los Angeles and Orange Counties in California, became *cities* almost overnight, requiring instant police, fire, water, electricity, and sanitation services, roads, street lights, and traffic signals, telephone services, parks and playgrounds, *and schools*.

The *Constitution of the United States* contains no direct reference to schools. Our Founding Fathers believed that education could best be guided by the states and their local communities. Of our Founding Fathers, Thomas Jefferson stands out as the greatest champion of a well-education citizenry. Jefferson—the founder of the Library of Congress and the father of the University of Virginia—fervently believed that only an "enlightened" society was capable of genuine self-government. While he was fluent in Greek, Latin, and French, and was an aristocrat by birth and education, he consistently encouraged *public* education for all children of the Republic, under local control, as the best way to protect and perpetuate liberty. He especially emphasized the importance of elementary schools, where America's young would be instructed in reading, writing, and arithmetic.

Schools in America have always reflected America's society. In 1789, the United States adopted a *federal* system of government, meaning that the national government had those powers enumerated in the *Constitution*, and the states, or the people, had all the rest. The *Constitution* does not mention schools. Therefore, since its earliest days in America, public education was *decentralized*, and schools were under *local* and *popular* control. By adopting a federal form of government and decentralized systems for schools, America's early citizens turned away from the Old World ways of Europe in politics *and* education. Unlike the European model of the centralization of education in the hands of the official state church, or the national government led by an emperor, king, or queen, schools in America became the *democratic* products of their local communities, and, to some degree, the state.

Massachusetts was a leading state in the early development of America's public schools. Boston High School became the first public high school in the United States when it opened in 1821. Massachusetts was the first state to offer a free public education for all children in 1827, although it took many years for the law to become reality for all the Bay State's children. In 1845, as many Americans braced for a possible war with Mexico over the disputed Texas border, Horace Mann, the leader of the Massachusetts State School Board, vigorously advocated a wide range of public school innovations and reforms, including better school facilities and teaching aids, higher standards for the training, examination, and selection of teachers, and an expanded curriculum. Horace Mann faced a daunting task, since, even in his "progressive" Massachusetts, many schools were actually abandoned log cabins with no toilet facilities and no chalkboards. Often, teachers had no formal training, few were college graduates, and many of them had been selected solely for their potential disciplinary skills. Some schools even lacked textbooks. Still, Mann pushed on. Meanwhile, Henry Barnard, following Massachusetts' lead, attempted similar reforms in Connecticut and Rhode Island. By the War of 1846, the "Common School" movement in America was rapidly gaining momentum.

As early as 1834, following publication of the English translation of the *State of Public Education in Prussia*, many Americans began to favor compulsory school attendance based on the German model. Eventually, compulsory school attendance laws requiring that every child must attend a public or private school were adopted by most states after the Civil War. But such laws were not to be found in all the states until 1918, at about the same time that a twenty-eight-year-old Lieutenant Colonel named Dwight Eisenhower was busy training troops for combat in France at Camp Colt, near Gettysburg, Pennsylvania.

As late as 1918, American public schools were not close to the level of complexity that they exhibit today. But the engine of democracy was certainly present in most schools across the land, thanks in large part to *McGuffey's Readers*. Philosophy Professor William Homes McGuffey's *Eclectic Series Readers* for grades one through eight became the "Bible" of America's schools from just before the Civil War to the end of World War I. Originating in Ohio, McGuffey's *Readers* contained far more than lessons on spelling, grammar, and punctuation. His *Readers* introduced the youth of America to the best in English and American literature while emphasizing the importance of such American values as the rewards of hard works, sobriety, thrift, modesty, the "Golden Rule," the importance of family, and loyalty to country. Frankly patriotic, McGuffey's *Reader* promoted national pride.

World War I brought profound changes in American education in the form of "intelligence tests" and "placement." Following the publication of Lewis M. Terman's *The Measurement of Intelligence* in 1916, I.Q. tests soon became common in public and private school placement and admissions across the country. However, the first I.Q. tests were *not* mass produced for public and private schools, but for admission to *Army* schools. When President Woodrow Wilson suddenly commanded our relatively tiny, peacetime Army to prepare for its entrance into the Great War on the battlefields of France by recruiting, organizing, and training over one million men in a matter of months, Army brass recognized the value of the I.Q. test as a quick, inexpensive, and "objective" means of classifying men. Men who tested at or above a certain I.Q. score were classified as "officer material." Those who tested below a certain score were relegated to the ranks of "enlisted men." Those who scored really low were deemed "unfit for military service." The I.Q. test therefore was first widely used as a cheap, quick, and relatively accurate way to process millions of men (along with a physical exam) during a short period of time into three groups, two of which were vital to the war effort.

When Dwight Eisenhower graduated from Abilene High School in 1909, his senior class had nine boys and twenty-five girls.[32] A ratio of two or more female students to each male student in America's *public* high schools during the 19th and early 20th Centuries was not uncommon. After all, full-time employment awaited most males once they reached the age of twelve if they wished to work and be on their own, while females were encouraged to attend school until graduation or marriage. In the male-dominated world of work, an eighth-grade education met or exceeded the educational prerequisite for most jobs during the 19th and early 20th Centuries. That Ike and three of his five brothers, Earl, Edgar, and Milton, all graduated from high school *and* college speaks volumes about the aspirations of their hard-working, relatively poor, yet knowledgeable parents, David and Ida Eisenhower.[33] All the Eisenhowers practiced those values so dear to *McGuffey's Readers*—hard work, sobriety, thrift, modesty, the "Golden Rule," the importance of family, patriotism, *and education.*

Adolescence is a cultural invention. In 1909, most American males who had reached the age of twelve or thirteen were not viewed as adolescents or "teenagers"; they were seen as job-ready young adults! In rural America and in much of Europe, such ceremonies as the Christian "Confirmation," held at about age twelve or thirteen, were originally puberty rites marking an individual's official entry into adulthood. America's early compulsory education laws rarely went beyond elementary school age. Shakespeare's Juliet was only fourteen. It should be noted that during colonial times in America, and even into the 19th Century, many young people got married at age twelve or thirteen. During the decade between Ike's graduation from high

---

[32] See Dwight D. Eisenhower, *At Ease*, p. 99.
[33] After graduating from high school, Ike's brother Arthur became a banker, and brother Roy worked as a druggist.

school in 1909 and his promotion to Lieutenant Colonel in 1918, as America prepared for the war effort by rapidly becoming the factory for the forces of democracy against the Kaiser's armies, America became the world's leader in manufacturing and technology. Manufacturing and technology required more training and education. Thus, high schools became more important than ever. And that relatively new age classification known as "teenagers"—old enough for sex but lacking in many necessary work skills—was born. What to do? Keep teenagers at home and in school.

During the 1920's and 30's, a number of educators and psychologists greatly influenced schools in America, including John Dewey, Franklin Bobbitt, G. Stanley Hall, Jesse B. Sears, and George S. Counts. John Dewey, in his book *Democracy in Education*, first published in 1916, emphasized "learning by doing." According to Dewey, education is most effective when learning is "hands-on" and part of a practical "social process," including group projects. While Dewey gained fame during his many years as a professor at Columbia University, many of his theories were based on his earlier work with elementary students at his laboratory school at the University of Chicago. John Dewey's influence was greatest at the elementary school level.

Meanwhile, Franklin Bobbitt, in his book *The Curriculum*, first published in 1918, strongly emphasized the need for vocational education at the high school level to better prepare students for the world of work. Soon, most larger high schools across the country expanded their traditional academic curriculum, including Latin, algebra, ancient history, and English, by adding such "electives" as wood shop, metal shop, auto shop, mechanical drawing, typing, business math, bookkeeping, shorthand, and home economics. Such schools came to be known as "comprehensive" high schools, and became the educational model for grades nine through twelve for America's secondary schools.

An increasing number of public school districts in the United States during the 1920's and 30's also began to focus on the findings of prominent psychologist G. Stanley Hall's landmark publication, *Adolescence*, which first appeared in 1904. Hall's psychological study furnished the philosophical basis for the junior high school movement. In essence, the movement argued for the need to provide a *transitional* school to help young students bridge the gap between pre-puberty and the emotional upheaval of early adolescence. Many public school districts began to adopt a plan first utilized in Berkeley, California, for transitional, "junior high" schools. Under the "Berkeley Plan," elementary schools included Kindergarten and Grades 1 through 6. Junior high schools embraced students in Grades 7 through 9. Senior high schools, Grades 10 through 12.

In 1928, as "Coolidge Prosperity" was nearing its zenith, Jesse B. Sears, in his book *The School Survey*, urged public schools to survey their communities through "needs assessment" questionnaires—especially local businesses—in order to adapt their curriculum to the needs of the local society. According to both Jesse B. Sears and Franklin Bobbitt, the main purpose of schools was to serve the interests of society through the process of "social adaptation"—to go with the needs of the time.

During the Great Depression of the 1930's, some "progressive" educators argued that public schools should go *beyond* assuring social stability by transmitting traditional American values and culture. Professor George S. Counts of Columbia University's Teachers College, in his 1932 book, *Dare the School Build a New Social Order?*, claimed that public schools should lead in the "social reconstruction" of American society. John Dewey, his aging colleague at Columbia, agreed. These and other "social reconstructionists" believed that the main purpose of schools was to motivate ("indoctrinate") students to improve society by emphasizing controversial issues and arriving at new solutions to society's problems, much like the newly-elected President Franklin D. Roosevelt was attempting to do with his "New Deal."

Over the years, not all educators agreed with Sears and Bobbitt's belief that the main purpose of schools was to adapt to the vocational needs of the local community, nor did they agree with Counts and Dewey that the main purpose of schools was to reform American society. In 1945, at the end of World War II, Harvard University President James B. Conant, a former Harvard chemistry professor, took exception to the growing importance of vocational education and efforts to indoctrinate students in order to transform society. In the Harvard Report, *General Education in a Free Society*, published in 1945, Conant and others claimed that the main purpose of schools is to foster the intellectual growth of students in those subjects most worthy of study. According to the *Harvard Report*, some subjects are more important than others, and all children should be introduced to math, science, literature, philosophy, and history. To President Conant and other academicians, schools at the high school and university levels should prepare students for life by stressing the great ideas of mankind though discussion, analysis, and comparison. In full agreement with Harvard's Conant was the President of the University of Chicago, Robert M. Hutchins. Hutchins, together with the noted philosopher Mortimer Adler, published *Great Books of the Western World* in 1952. Conant followed with his own book, *The Conflict in Education in a Democratic Society* in 1953, which emphasized the need for students to read the great books. In 1953, Dwight D. Eisenhower, a former professional colleague of Hutchins and Conant while President of Columbia University, and who had a keen interest in and an amazing knowledge of the great figures of the ancient world, became President of the United States.

President Eisenhower fully appreciated the importance of public education. After all, Abilene High School and West Point—both publicly-supported schools—had given him the opportunity to begin his long upwardly mobile journey that eventually led him to the position of Supreme Commander of all Allies Forces in Europe during World War II, and ultimately, the Presidency. Ike was a proud product of America's public schools. He was also an advocate for the continuance of local control. But, as a strategic thinker on a grand scale, Ike could visualize situations in which Federal assistance to local schools and universities could benefit local communities *and* the nation as a whole. In 1953, the United States faced a growing crisis of transportation gridlock due to its outdated system of highways, bridges, and roads. A similar crisis was looming over our nation's various public school systems, especially in our most rapidly growing areas, as a result of the post-war "baby boom." Ike's first move was to give education status in his Cabinet. On April 1, 1953, with Senate approval, Eisenhower added the newly created Cabinet position of Secretary of Health, Education, and Welfare, with Oveta Culp Hobby as its first Secretary. Mrs. Hobby was married to a former Democratic governor of Texas. A staunch advocate of the Women's Army Corps (WAC) during World War II, she and her husband ran the *Houston Post*, and, during the 1952 Presidential campaign, she helped spearhead the "Democrats for Eisenhower."[34]

---

[34] See Jim Newton's *Eisenhower: The White House Years*, p. 88.

As the nation's first Secretary of Health, Education, and Welfare, Oveta Culp Hobby's greatest contribution during her three years as Secretary was her active sponsorship of the development and trials of Dr. Jonas Salk's anti-polio vaccine, which was finally approved for public use in April 1955. Soon, hundred of thousands of children were being vaccinated against the dreaded disease of infantile paralysis that killed or crippled so many Americans each year. A cure for polio had finally been found in the "Salk Vaccine."

On May 17, 1954, Chief Justice Earl Warren, a former Republican governor of California and an Eisenhower appointee, presided over the unanimous decision by the United States Supreme Court in the case of *Brown v. Board of Education of Topeka*. *Brown v. Board of Education* overturned an earlier Supreme Court ruling on the matter of segregated schools in *Plessy v. Ferguson* (1896) by declaring "separate but equal" schools *unconstitutional*. The Warren Court's most famous decision eventually transformed American society. But in 1954, it was met with both hostility and growing resistance in the segregationist South.

In 1896, a landmark case in the realm of "Civil Rights," *Plessy v. Ferguson*, came before the United States Supreme Court. In 1890, the Louisiana State Legislature passed a law that required "separate but equal" accommodations on all passenger trains originating from or passing through Louisiana: Whites were to ride in *white* cars; Blacks ("Negroes") were to ride in *colored* cars. In 1892, a Black man named Homer Plessy refused to ride in a *colored* car. He was arrested, and brought before Judge John H. Ferguson of the Criminal Court of New Orleans. Judge Ferguson upheld the Louisiana law by finding Plessy guilty. Plessy's defense had argued that Plessy had not broken any law because Louisiana's "social segregation" statute regarding "separate but equal" facilities on the basis of race was in violation of the 13th and 14th Amendments to the *Constitution of the United States*. Ferguson's "guilty" verdict was appealed (and upheld) all the way to the United States Supreme Court. In 1896, the Supreme Court, with only one justice dissenting, ruled in favor of the Louisiana law, stating that, "If the civil and political right of both races be equal, one cannot be inferior to the other civilly or politically. If one race be inferior to the other socially, the Constitution of the United States cannot put them upon the same plane." Hence, "separate" but equal laws are constitutional.

*Plessy v. Ferguson* encouraged a rash of "segregation" laws to be passed throughout the "Solid South" of the old Confederacy regarding public accommodations following the Supreme Court's 1896 decision. Some Northern communities passed such laws as well. Soon, segregated trains, *public schools*, public swimming pools and water fountains, and even court house entrances became commonplace south of the old Mason-Dixon line. As far west as California, some rural public school districts with no Black populations created "separate but equal" schools for Whites and *Mexicans*.

In one of the ironies of American history, the lone Supreme Court dissenter in *Plessy v. Ferguson* was Justice John Marshall Harlan, *a former slave-owner from Kentucky*. According to Justice Harlan in 1896, "I am of the opinion that the statute of Louisiana is inconsistent with the personal liberty of citizens, white and black, in that state, and hostile to both the spirit and letter of the Constitution of the United States . . ." Some fifty-four years later, Justice Harlan's argument finally won out when the Supreme Court, led by Chief Justice Earl Warren, reversed *Plessy v. Ferguson* by ruling that "separate but equal" social segregation was *unconstitutional* in *Brown v. Board of Education* on May 17, 1954.

Opposition to *Brown v. Board of Education* included claims that the Warren Court's decision violated "states' rights" and the concept of local control, especially in education. By 1956, several Southern states, including Arkansas, Georgia, Mississippi, and Virginia had passed additional segregation legislation in direct defiance of *Brown v. Board of Education*. In Arkansas, public schools remained segregated. In Georgia, it became a *felony* for any school official to spend tax money on racially-mixed schools. In Mississippi, it became a crime for any organization to sue for desegregation in the state's courts. And in Virginia, some public schools were simply closed to *all* students. It was as if these Southern states were saying, "Justice Warren has made his decision. Now let him try to enforce it!" And so the culture war *Civil Rights vs. Segregation* was born.

Events that unfolded in September 1957 during the start of the new school year at Central High School in Little Rock, Arkansas, brought this new culture war, *Civil Rights vs. Segregation*, to the attention of the entire nation on black and white television. All across America, people began to take sides. For several turbulent weeks, Little Rock's Central High School became a primary focus of the nation's news media. When several young Black students with encouragement from the NAACP attempted to attend Central High School, many local Whites resisted, including many students, some faculty, and even the Governor of Arkansas, Orville Faubus. Governor Faubus called out the Arkansas National Guard to "maintain order" in the capital city of Little Rock. Governor Faubus gave specific orders to his National Guard troops to "block" the Black students from entering Central High School to enroll for classes. When a Federal district court judge ordered the state's National Guard troops withdrawn, angry pro-segregation mobs, joined by local elected officials (including the police chief and the county sheriff), blocked the doors to Little Rock's main high school, preventing the Black students from entering. By then, the national news media's coverage of Dr. Martin Luther King, Jr. and his civil rights marchers had shifted from Montgomery, Alabama, to Little Rock, Arkansas, with the media's latest emphasis on the struggle to integrate public schools in the South.

Back on December 1, 1955, Rosa Parks, a Black resident of Montgomery, Alabama—the original capital of the Confederacy—demonstrated the courage to defy the Southern custom that Blacks only sat at the *back* of municipal busses in the "colored section." For her courage and act of civil disobedience, she was arrested and jailed. Outraged, local Black leaders responded by organizing protests and boycotting Montgomery's city bus line. This was the first such organized "Civil Rights" protest to gain national attention in the post-*Brown v. Board of Education* era.

What happened at Little Rock more than a year later, however, greatly increased the nation's interest in the Civil Rights Movement, as photographs and TV pictures of angry policemen holding clubs and snarling dogs on leashes to prevent the integration of Central High School shamed much of the North and West into sympathizing with the Black students, while enraging many in the South against the Blacks. With Little Rock Central High School, civil rights and states' rights collided head-on in a manner and to a degree not seen since the pre-Civil War days when slave owners became pitted against abolitionists.

In fairness to the people of Little Rock, it should be noted that less than a week after the Supreme Court announced its decision in *Brown v. Board of Education* in 1954, Little Rock's own board of education began making plans to comply with the court's ruling, agreeing to integrate its schools in an orderly manner over the coming years. Their plan was soon approved by a local Federal judge. It was the Arkansas State Legislature, not the city's elected school board, who immediately opposed any effort to integrate Little Rock's schools. It should also be noted that it was the mayor of Little Rock, Woodrow Wilson Mann who, on September 23, 1957, cabled President Eisenhower with an urgent request to rush Federal troops to Central High School "within several hours" to protect the lives of the Black students attempting to enroll there and "restore peace and order." Mayor Mann knew he could not depend on Governor Faubus, the Arkansas National Guard, or his own police department to do so. President Eisenhower acted swiftly.

Just after midnight on September 24, 1957, President Eisenhower briefly conferred with Attorney General Herbert Brownell, Jr. and General Maxwell Taylor and then ordered a contingent of highly-trained regular Army troops from the 101$^{st}$ Airborne Division to Little Rock, Arkansas ASAP. Their mission? *To integrate Central High School as Federal law required.* That evening, President Eisenhower addressed the nation on national television to explain the reason for his action: To restore "the image of America and all of its parts as one nation, indivisible, with liberty and justice for all."

During the 1957-58 school year, the U.S. Office of Education estimated that America's public school enrollment for all forty-eight states and the District of Columbia was a total of 33,508,814. Of those thirty-three-and-one-half-million pupils, approximately 23,804,621, or 71% were enrolled at the elementary level, and some 9,704,193, or 29%, were secondary students. For that same year, there were approximately 1,329,551 public school teachers who earned an average annual salary of $4,520. The average amount of tax dollars for the year in support of students and their schools (known by insiders as "ADA") was $320 per pupil. Of that amount, an average of 55.8% came from local sources such as property taxes, 40.6% came from state revenues, and 3.6% came from the Federal government. In an effort to keep up with the nation's "baby boom," approximately 69,000 additional classrooms—some new construction, some "temporary portables" or "bungalows"—were utilized across the country during the 1957-58 school year at an extra cost to the taxpayers of nearly three billion dollars, or approximately 25% of all state and local capital budgets.

The ten leading states in estimated public elementary school enrollment during the 1957-58 school year were: #1, California (1,975,000); #2 New York (1,650,000); #3 Texas (1,462,761); #4 Ohio (1,300,000); #5 Illinois (1,260,000); #6 Pennsylvania (1,168,084); #7 Michigan (990,000); #8 Indiana (715,000); #9 New Jersey (711,000); and #10 Georgia (705,000). Because numbers often translate into dollars, and textbooks are expensive to develop, most major educational publishers focused on these states during the development of their textbooks and other curriculum materials, especially for materials designed for use with students in Grades One through Eight. For example, the adoption of a particular textbook or series of texts by a large school district such as Los Angeles Unified School District could mean *millions* of dollars for the lucky publisher selected. Textbooks were big business. And competition among publishing companies and their "sales reps" was often fierce.

A great deal of money in book sales was also available at the secondary level. But at the high school level in particular, academic course offerings were increasingly being dictated by the "subjects most worthy of study" to meet the admissions requirements of the major colleges and universities. The recommended preparatory curriculum for the average "college-bound" student (as opposed to "vocational education" students taking "shop classes" and basic classes to meet the minimum local academic requirements for high school graduation) became more uniform—at least by course titles—across the country as guidance counselors continued to utilize I.Q. test results and results from standardized tests in reading and math for placing their "brighter" students on college-prep "tracks." "Ability grouping" according to test results was commonplace. The typical comprehensive high school in America during the Eisenhower Years placed its students in one of three tracks on the basis of academic "ability": The College-prep track, the Vocational track, or Special Education. As in the military's mass I.Q. testing during World War I, each student was either College-prep ("officer material"), Vocational ("enlisted man"), or Special Education ("unfit for military service"). Little wonder that the first track was more prestigious in most school communities than the rest.

One of the most prestigious universities in the United States—at least on the West Coast—is Stanford. To be considered for admission to Stanford University as a freshman during the 1957-58 school year, each applicant was required to have satisfactorily completed the following minimum course requirements during their high school years:

- English—4 years
- Mathematics—2 years
- Foreign Language—3 years (ancient or modern)
- Biology, Botany, Physiology, or Zoology—1 year
- American History—1 year
- European or World History—1 year[35]

As a former President of Columbia, one of the most prestigious universities on the East Coast, Dwight Eisenhower fully recognized the importance of education. Education had been his ticket out of Abilene to see the world. President Eisenhower wished to see his good fortune replicated by many deserving members of the latest generation of Americans. But many of America's most rapidly growing school districts were financially overwhelmed by obsolete facilities and rising costs. So, while he understood that Federal aid to education was an unpopular concept for many of his fellow citizens, he recommended Federal aid for America's school to meet the crisis. On January 6, 1955, during his third "State of the Union Address" to Congress, Eisenhower advocated an expanded program of Federal support for the nation's public elementary and secondary schools. Soon thereafter, the *Report of the President's Committee for the White House Conference on Education* was released, and Ike proposed that the Congress spend two billion dollars on a national school aid program. But Federal aid to education, a highly controversial issue during the 1950's in a nation with a long history of *local control* of public schools, was put on hold by the Congress—*until Russia launched its "Sputnik" satellite in October 1957.*

*Astronautics*—the science of constructing vehicles for travel in space beyond the earth's atmosphere—began with such futuristic science fiction writers as France's Jules Verne (*A Trip to the Moon*, 1865), and England's own H.G. Wells (*The War of the Worlds*, 1898, and *The First Men on the Moon*, 1901). Fantasies regarding space travel were further popularized in America by comic books, comic strips, and science

---

[35] *Stanford University Bulletin*, 1957, p. 39.

fiction movies featuring such popular heroes as Buck Rogers and Flash Gordon. Even television got into the act early on with space-travel shows such as "Space Patrol." But when Dwight D. Eisenhower first became President in 1953, space travel and going to the moon and back were still considered by the American public as strictly *science fiction*—some day, but not soon. On October 4, 1957, that pedestrian notion was suddenly shattered when the Soviet Union proudly boasted that *they* had successfully launched *Sputnik 1, the world's first space satellite*, in orbit around the earth. Americans were shocked. Three scathing questions were asked by the American press: (1) How could a relatively backward and oppressive society like Russia be the *first* to propel a satellite into space orbit?; (2) why wasn't the *United States* the first to do so?; and (3) what did President Eisenhower and the Congress plan to do about it? The "Space Age" had been launched, and the *astronautics race* between the world's two superpowers—the U.S.S.R. and the United States—was on.

America's first response to Russia's space challenge came just three months after the launch of Sputnik 1 with the successful launching of *Explorer 1*, America's first space satellite, from Cape Canaveral, Florida. *Explorer 1* was the brainchild of Wernher von Braun and a host of his lesser-known colleagues who were feverously working on developing the Army's space exploration and rocket warfare capabilities. Wernher von Braun was the brilliant young Nazi engineer who helped design the deadly V-2 rockets that bombarded England from their launching pads in France during World War II. At war's end, von Braun, fearing capture by the Soviets, sought out the U.S. Army and offered his expertise in rocketry in exchange for relocation to America. Far more loyal to his passion for rocketry than his Nazi past, von Braun soon became the public face of America's astronautical endeavors. By the late-1950's, the three most famous scientists in America were Dr. Jonas Salk (polio vaccine), Admiral Hyman G. Rickover (atomic submarines), and Wernher von Braun (rockets).

On December 17, 1957, the United States made its first successful test firing of an intercontinental ballistic missile, the *Atlas*, from Cape Canaveral, Florida. Soon thereafter, on January 31, 1958, *Explorer 1*, America's first satellite, was also successfully launched from Cape Canaveral. Nevertheless, public dismay over Russia being first into space caused a political firestorm that resulted in the rapid passage by the Congress of the National Aeronautics and Space Act of 1958. The National Aeronautics and Space Act created the National Aeronautics and Space Administration (NASA) to coordinate the nation's peaceful pursuit of space exploration separate from the military. The military would continue to work on aeronautic weapons systems while NASA would focus on peaceful space travel and exploration. Meanwhile, speculation in the news media and elsewhere that the Soviet Union was exceeding the United States in the education of engineers, mathematicians, and scientists for both industry and teaching caused much criticism of America's public schools at all levels—K-12 and college. As a result, new incentives were called for to entice young people to pursue careers in math and science. On September 2, 1958, President Eisenhower signed the National Defense Education Act, designed to increase the number of students pursuing careers in science, mathematics, and engineering by granting student loans and academic fellowships. Did it help? Just eleven years later, American astronauts Neil Armstrong and Edwin Aldrin, Jr., *walked on the moon.*

# CHAPTER 8

# LITERATURE

As a young boy growing up in Abilene, Kansas, Ike Eisenhower was a voracious reader. As a West Point cadet, he readily absorbed minute details of major historical battles, from the triumph of an eighteen-year-old Alexander the Great at the Battle of Chaeronea to the legendary Robert E. Lee's paramount blunder of his otherwise brilliant career when he ordered General Pickett to charge the center of the Union line along Cemetery Ridge during the Battle of Gettysburg. As the Lieutenant Colonel and training camp commander during the peak of World War I, Eisenhower utilized author Frederick Winslow Taylor's *Principles of Scientific Management* by emphasizing to the camp's young recruits, *There is always one best way to do a task.*

During the 1920's, *Major* Eisenhower (nearly all the officers who remained in the Regular Army following the Great War were reduced in rank as the size of our military shrank from millions to thousands) was mentored by his commanding officer, General Fox Conner, while serving as his aide in Panama. General Conner had Major Eisenhower read a wide range of literature from his personal library. Conner's motive? To broaden Ike's already promising aptitude to successfully organize and command armies of men. Under Conner's tutelage, Ike studied Plato and his *Republic*, William Shakespeare's tragedies, including *Richard II, Henry VI, Othello, King Lear, Hamlet,* and *Macbeth,* Cornelius Tacitus' historical works on the psychological make ups of ancient Rome's leaders, German General Karl von Clausewitz's three-volume military science classic, *On War*, Friedrich Wilhelm Nietzsche's "superman" philosophy in *The Joyful Wisdom, Beyond Good and Evil, On the Genealogy of Morals*, and *The Will to Power*, American Civil War General Phil Sheridan's *On Proper Conduct of War*, and General Ulysses S. Grant's classic *Personal Memoirs*.

Under the cordial yet challenging tutelage of Major Eisenhower's Mississippi-born commander, General Lee Conner, Ike learned from U.S. Grant to "Find out where your enemy is. Get at him as soon as you can. Strike him as hard as you can." From Phil Sheridan's confiscatory sweep through the Shenandoah Valley just prior to Lee's surrender at Appomattox, Ike learned that the best way to shorten a war and thus *save* lives was to assure that "the people must be left with nothing but their eyes to weep with." From studying the philosopher Nietzsche and his concept of the "superman," General Conner helped Ike to better understanding the thinking of a rising star in Europe, Adolf Hitler, and his "super race" followers. Only through superior force could Hitler, or someone else like him, be stopped. While Ike (and General Conner) objected to Nietzsche's abandonment of morality, both embraced the teachings of another German, General Karl von Clausewiz, who believed that a nation's military should provide its political leaders with such superior weaponry, military tactics, flexibility, and covert intelligence that war could be *prevented*. Clausewiz's main theme? Destroy the enemy's *will to fight* so that he chooses *not to.*

From Tacitus, Major Eisenhower gained insights into the psychological profiles of successful and unsuccessful Roman leaders. Ditto Shakespeare. And from Plato's *Republic* and his concept that the "ideal state" is made up of three classes: The merchant class, the military class, and the political class—the "Philosopher-Kings," Ike's firm belief in the American system of civilian control of the military, as clearly stated in Articles I and II of the *Constitution* and endorsed by both Plato *and* Clausewiz, was reinforced. During their tour of duty together in the steaming jungles of Panama during the 1920's, there is little doubt that neither Fox Conner nor Dwight Eisenhower ever pictured himself as a future American President. But both would probably have agreed with the following statement: If a member of the American military should one day in the future become President of the United States, he should have the *knowledge* of a philosopher-king.

From the early years of the Republic, American authors have produced a rich and varied literature. Early on, Washington Irving turned the superstitions and tall tales of his native Hudson River Valley in New York into the immortal story of Rip van Winkle, and the unforgettable legend of Ichabod Crane and his terrifying encounter with the Headless Horseman. Creating excitement about America's primitive and endless frontier was the forté of James Fenimore Cooper. While Washington Irving's stories about the Dutch settlers in upstate New York were popular in America and England, James Fenimore Cooper became synonymous with frontier America both at home and throughout Europe with his gripping series of "leather stocking" novels, including *The Last of the Mohicans* (1826), *The Pathfinder* (1840), and *The Deerslayer* (1841). Cooper was America's first novelist to gain international fame. Harvard's Henry Wadsworth Longfellow became America's favorite poet in an age when poetry was truly popular with regular folks. Thousands of Americans, both young and old, could recite from memory lines from his moralistic and patriotic poems on historic American themes, such as "The Village Blacksmith" (1841), "The Song of Hiawatha" (1855), "The Courtship of Miles Standish" (1858), and "Paul Revere's Ride" (1863).

In the prestigious twenty-seven volume set of *The Harvard Classics*, only two volumes are exclusively devoted to American authors: One to Richard Henry Dana, and the other to Ralph Waldo Emerson. Richard Henry Dana's classic *Two Years Before the Mast* was first published in 1844. Dana's account of the . . . brig Pilgrim on her voyage from Boston round Cape Horn to the Western coast of North America" became an instant best seller and was widely read in both the United States and Europe by scholars and common folks alike. Ralph Waldo Emerson's famous volume of *Essays*, containing such philosophical tomes as "History," "Self-Reliance," "Friendship," and "Heroism" was first published in 1841. While scholars at home and abroad pointed to Emerson's *transcendentalism* and uttered their praises, common folks considered his message of *self-reliance* and his belief that there is *nobility in all men* and in *all work*—that all human beings are *important*—reinforced their natural optimism and reaffirmed their love-affair with American democracy.

Henry David Thoreau's essay on "Civil Disobedience" (1849) and his book *Walden* (1854) greatly influenced generations of people in

America and abroad. From the abolition of slavery movement during the mid-19th Century to Mahatma Gandhi's "nonviolent" revolution in India against British colonial rule during the 20th Century, and Dr. Martin Luther King, Jr.'s civil rights marches through the American South during the late 1950's and early 1960's, Thoreau's principles of civil disobedience provided their primary rationale for nonviolent protesting as the best means to ultimately achieve victory.

Back to fiction. Nathaniel Hawthorne and Herman Melville wrote classic novels that remain required reading in many literature classrooms to this day: Hawthorne's *The Scarlet Letter* (1850) and Melville's *Moby Dick* (1851). And Edgar Allan Poe introduced Americans to the detective story with his widely popular "The Murders in the Rue Morgue" (1841). But no American storyteller of the 19th Century was more widely read and beloved than Samuel Langhorne Clemens, who wrote under the pseudonym Mark Twain. Mark Twain's novels about antebellum life in the South on and along the Mississippi River, *The Adventures of Tom Sawyer* (1876) and *The Adventures of Huckleberry Finn* (1884), revealed small-town American life and values to a fascinated world.

The early 20th Century in American literature was an era of reform. Following Stephen Crane's *The Red Badge of Courage* (1895), an anti-war novel describing in vivid detail the horrors of battle during the American Civil War, Frank Norris exposed the stranglehold the Southern Pacific Railroad had over California's economy and politics in *The Octopus* (1901), and Upton Sinclair railed about the filth and vermin in Chicago's giant meat-packing plants in *The Jungle* (1906). Both books led to major "progressive" reforms of their intended targets.

During the decade of the 1920's—the "Jazz Age"—many of America's leading authors rebelled against the status quo. Sinclair Lewis made a fortune as a writer by satirizing American society, novel by novel, beginning with his put down of small-town life in *Main Street* (1920). Next, the former Yale student explored the emptiness of a businessman's world in *Babbitt* (1922), dishonesty in the medical profession in *Arrowsmith* (1925), and greed and womanizing by an evangelical preacher in *Elmer Gantry* (1927). Sinclair Lewis refused the Pulitzer Prize for *Arrowsmith*, but accepted the Nobel Prize for Literature in 1930, the first American author to be so honored.

But two American authors who proved to be more romantic and lasting symbols of the "Roaring Twenties" were F. Scott Fitzgerald and Ernest Hemingway. F. Scott Fitzgerald's short stories, such as "The Rich Boy" (1926) and his novels, including *This Side of Paradise* (1920), *The Beautiful and Damned* (1922), and *The Great Gatsby* (1925), were international best-sellers. Many of his readers followed newspaper and magazine reports of his lavish personal life-style in Paris, Italy, and on the French Riviera as much as they read his books and short stories about high society and the rich. Meanwhile, Ernest Hemingway, an equally charismatic personality, wrote about the exploits of war-disillusioned young people in Paris, Spain, and Italy in *The Sun Also Rises* (1926) and *A Farewell to Arms* (1929). Ernest Hemingway became the fictional laureate of "The Lost Generation" and a romantic symbol for his fans on both sides of the Atlantic. In short, within a relatively brief time span, these two talented men had not only become famous American authors—they had become *international celebrities*.

During the Great Depression of the 1930's, John Steinbeck's novels about life in California—especially in Monterey and the Salinas Valley—made him America's foremost young novelist of the New Deal era. John Steinbeck's popularity began with *Tortilla Flat* (1935), his colorful and earthy novel about the *paisanos* of Monterey. His far more disturbing "strike" book, *In Dubious Battle* (1936), proved less popular. But his brief novel *Of Mice and Men* (1937) became a huge hit, only to be surpassed by his greatest and most controversial work, *The Grapes of Wrath* (1939), which was later awarded the Pulitzer Prize for fiction.

While F. Scott Fitzgerald died in Hollywood in 1940 while writing for a motion picture studio, Ernest Hemingway and John Steinbeck continued to thrive as famous American authors of international status throughout World War II and into the Eisenhower Years. It was their legacy, and the works of those American writers who came before them, that set the stage for American literature during the Fabulous Fifties.

Why did Americans continue to read novels during the Fabulous Fifties? The answer is simple: Because they *liked* them. Novels gave people pleasure and excitement without painful, real-like consequences. And so demand for new novels was ever-present, and the numbers of popular novelists during the Eisenhower Years seemed endless, including Ray Bradbury (*Fahrenheit 451*), Eugene L. Burdick (*The Ugly American*), Taylor Caldwell (*Never Victorious, Never Defeated* and *Dear and Glorious Physician*), Thomas B. Costain (*The Silver Chalice, The Tonine,* and *Below the Salt*), James Gould Cozzens (*By Love Possessed*), Patrick Dennis (*Auntie Mame*), Lloyd C. Douglas (*The Robe*), Allen Drury (*Advise and Consent*), Daphne du Maurier (*The Parasites, My Cousin Rachel, Mary Anne,* and *The Scapegoat*), Edna Feber (*Giant*), Ernest K. Gann (*The High and the Mighty*), Joseph Heller (*Catch-22*), Ernest Hemingway (*Across the River and into the Trees* and *The Old Man and the Sea*), John Hersey (*The Wall* and *A Single Pebble*), Mac Hyman (*No Time for Sergeants*), Evan Hunter (*The Blackboard Jungle*), James Jones (*From Here to Eternity*), MacKinlay Kantor (*Andersonville*), Frances Parkinson Keyes (*Joy Street, Steamboat Gothic, The Royal Box, Blue Camellia,* and *Victorine*), D.H. Lawrence (*Lady Chatterley's Lover*), Grace Metalious (*Peyton Place*), James A. Michener (*Hawaii*), Vladimir Nabokov (*Lolita*), Edwin O'Connor (*The Last Hurrah*), John O'Hara (*From the Terrace* and *The Family Party*), Boris Pasternak (*Doctor Zhivago*), Ayn Rand (*Atlas Shrugged*), Harold Robbins (*Never Love a Stranger, The Pirate, The Adventurers, A Stone for Danny Fisher,* and *The Dream Merchants*), Kenneth Roberts (*Boon Island*), Henry Morton Robinson (*The Cardinal*), Robert Ruark (*Poor No More*), J.D. Salinger (*The Catcher in the Rye*), Budd Schulberg (*The Disenchanted*), Annemarie Selinko (*Désirée*), Nevil Shute (*On the Beach*), John Steinbeck (*East of Eden* and *Sweet Thursday*), Kay Thompson (*Eloise* and *Eloise at Christmastime*), Morton Thompson (*Not as a Stranger*), Robert Traver (*Anatomy of a Murder*), Leon M. Uris (*Exodus*), Sloan Wilson (*The Man in the Gray Flannel Suit*), Kathleen Winsor (*Star Money*), Herman Wouk (*The Cane Mutiny* and *Marjorie Morningstar*), and Frank Yerby (*Floodtide, A Woman Called Fancy, The Saracen Blade, Benton's Row, Captain Rebel,* and *Fairoaks*). So many novels, so little time . . .

Few Presidents in our nation's history were more avid readers than Dwight Eisenhower. During his eight years in the White House, and later at his farm in Gettysburg, Ike always kept a bookcase filled with historical biographies and Western novels near his bed. Ike regularly read to relax before falling asleep at night. As a young boy growing up in Abilene, Kansas, his favorite books were histories of ancient Greece, Rome, and Carthage. The greatest of the Carthaginian Generals, Hannibal, was Ike's boyhood hero. Other boyhood favorites included Julius Caesar, Pericles, Socrates, Themistocles, Miltiados, and Leonidas.[36] He also loved to read about ancient Egypt, Assyria, and Persia. As Ike was about to enter high school, he also came to appreciate European history—especially the exploits of Frederick the Great, Napoleon Bonaparte, and Gustavus Adolphus. His favorite American hero was George Washington. Ike, even as an adult, never tired of reading about General Washington's exploits at Princeton, Trenton, or Valley Forge.

While still a young boy, however, Ike, the precocious roughneck, dared to enjoy a wide range of fiction as well. He loved *The White Company* (1890), an historical romance, and *The Adventures of Sherlock Holmes* (1892) by Sir Arthur Conan Doyle, the short stories of O. Henry, such as "The Gift of the Magi," most of Rudyard Kipling's works, including *The Jungle Book* (1894) and *Captains Courageous* (1897), and Mark Twain's *A Connecticut Yankee in King Arthur's Court* (1889). But as a career officer in the United States Army, as President of Columbia University, and finally, as President of the United States, Dwight Eisenhower often found relaxation by reading his favorite nighttime fiction: Novels of the Old West.

Because Zane Grey was such a prolific and popular author of novels about the Old West, there can be little doubt that Dwight Eisenhower read many of his books over the years. Zane Grey's best-known novel, *Riders of the Purple Sage*, was first published in 1912, when Ike was a young cadet at West Point. Although Grey died in 1939 after writing more than ninety books and becoming one of America's first millionaire authors, *Riders of the Purple Sage* was still in print when Eisenhower entered the White House as President in 1953. And many of Zane Grey's Westerns published posthumously, included *Wyoming* (1953), *Lost Pueblo* (1954), *Black Mesa* (1955), *Stranger from the Tonto* (1956), *The Fugitive Trail* (1957), *Arizona Clan* (1958), and *Horse Heaven Hill* (1959) no doubt found their way to Ike's bedroom bookcase in the White House.

Ike also read many of the so-called "pulp" Westerns written by other popular authors of that genre during his Army career, including books by Max Brand and Ernest Haycox. Ike was familiar with Clarence E. Mulford's original Hopalong Cassidy novels. And he no doubt read many of the more recently written Westerns by one of the 1950's most

---

[36] See *At Ease*, p. 39.

popular writers, Louis L'Amour. Certainly, copies of Louis L'Amour's *Hondo* (1953), *Showdown at Yellow Butte* (1953), *Crossfire Trail* (1954), *Guns of the Timberlands* (1955), *Silver Canyon* (1956), *Last Stand at Papago Wells* (1957), *Radigan* (1958), and *The First Fast Draw* (1959) found their way to his bedside.

Ike was not alone in his love of paperback Westerns. Millions of Americans were similarly addicted. During the 1950's, F.W. Woolworth Company was America's favorite "dime store" chain. Nearly every city and hamlet in the United States had at least one Woolworth's store. And in each Woolworth's store one could find rows of paperback Westerns for sale for as little as 35¢ a copy along side such soft-cover mainstream blockbusters as Grace Metalious' *Peyton Place*, Ernest Hemingway's *The Old Man and the Sea*, Vladimir Nabokov's *Lolita*, and Harold Robbin's *The Dream Merchants*, each for under one dollar. Most drug stores, liquor stores, and markets throughout America also sold paperback books. During the 1950's, paperback books were big business—making literature available at low prices to all but the poorest Americans. Ike, forever thrifty, had a large collection of paperbacks.

Not all literature is fiction, of course. Dwight D. Eisenhower became a best-selling author in his own right following the publication in 1948 of *Crusade in Europe*, his epic account of the Allied struggle against Nazi Germany during World War II. Soon after Eisenhower resigned as President of Columbia University to resume his military career as Commander of NATO in Europe, Rachel Carson helped launch what later came to be called the "Environmental Movement" with her highly popular scientific work, *The Sea Around Us*, first published in 1951. In 1952, while Americans chanting "I Like IKE!" were making political waves across the land, one of America's most popular non-fiction books was a Biblical study entitled *A Man Called Peter*, by Catherine Marshall. In 1953, Ike's first year as President, America's top two non-fiction best-selling books were *The Holy Bible, Revised Standard Version*, and *The Power of Positive Thinking* by Norman Vincent Peale. In 1954, the nation's top non-fiction read was *But We Were Born Free* by Elmer Davis. In 1955, it was Anne Morrow Lindbergh's poetic and thought-provoking *Gift From the Sea*, with its calming message to "Simplify . . ." 1956 saw a number of best-sellers on the nation's non-fiction lists, including *The Search for Bridey Murphy* by Morey Bernstein, *The Birth of Britain* by Winston Churchill, *Arthritis and Common Sense* by Dale Alexander, *Eisenhower: The Inside Story* by Robert J. Donovan, and *The Nun's Story* by Kathryn Hulme. *The F.B.I. Story* by Donald Whitehead led the non-fiction lists in 1957, together with *Day of Infamy* by Walter Lord, *The Day Christ Died* by Jim Bishop, *The Hidden Persuaders* by Vance Packard, and *Baruch: My Own Story* by Bernanrd Baruch. 1958 began with *Please Don't Eat the Daisies* by Jean Kerr, followed by *Masters of Deceit* by F.B.I. Director J. Edgar Hoover, *Inside Russia Today* by John Gunther, *Only in America* by Harry Golden, and the adventures of the *Aku Aku* by Thor Heyerdahl. Alexander King's uninhibited, provocative, and wickedly humorous memoir, *Mine Enemy Grows Older*, topped the non-fiction charts in 1959, followed by Vance Packard's perspicacious *For 2¢ Plain*, and Moss Hart's autobiographical *Act One*. 1960, President Eisenhower's last year in office, saw Alexander King return with his second wacky, autobiographical gem, *May This House Be Safe from Tigers*. That same year, prior to the dawn of J.F.K.'s "New Frontier," Joy Adamson gained admiration for her leonine friends with *Born Free*. Vance Packard published his third blockbuster sociological study in just four years, *The Waste Makers*. And William Shirer, an eyewitness to Adolf Hitler's Germany, produced one of the finest historical accounts of all time, *The Rise and Fall of the Third Reich*.

Just as all literature is not fiction, not all non-fiction literature is found in books. Magazines and newspapers are also important sources of American literature. Magazines and newspapers were especially popular with Americans during the Fabulous Fifties. By 1957, thirty-eight American magazines regularly sold more than one million copies an issue. And six magazines, the *Reader's Digest, Life,* the *Ladies' Home Journal, Look,* the *Saturday Evening Post,* and *TV Guide* had a circulation of over five million copies an issue. Other popular magazines of the day included *Time, Newsweek, U.S. News & World Report, Sports Illustrated, Esquire, Playboy, The New Yorker, Coronet, Redbook, Saturday Review, Argosy, Ebony, Holiday, True, Popular Mechanics, Popular Science, Field and Stream,* and *Family Circle*.

At the beginning of 1957, there were approximately 1,760 daily newspapers in the United States, with an average cost to the customer of a little over five cents per copy. People in many cities had several prominent dailies from which to choose. Among America's most influential newspapers were *The New York Times,* the *New York Post,* the

*New York Herald-Tribune*, the *Wall Street Journal*, the *Boston Globe*, the *Christian Science Monitor*, the *Washington Post*, the *Washington Times*, the *Baltimore Sun*, the *Miami Daily News*, the *Atlanta Constitution*, the *Chicago Tribune*, the *Chicago Sun-Times*, the *Detroit Free Press*, the *St. Louis Post-Dispatch*, the *Kansas City Star*, the *Milwaukee Journal*, the *Des Moines Register and Tribune*, the *Dallas Morning News, the Houston Chronicle, the Denver Post, the Seattle Times*, the Portland *Oregon News Journal*, the *San Francisco Examiner*, the *Los Angeles Examiner*, the *Los Angeles Times*, and the *San Diego Union*. America's daily newspapers had a total estimated circulation of nearly forty-eight million copies per day, and earned approximately two billion and fifty-nine million dollars in advertising revenue for the fiscal year 1956-57.

Advertising was the life blood of America's newspapers and magazines, helping keep subscription costs and newsstand prices low. Advertising space in publications was based primarily upon circulation totals. The more magazines or newspapers a particular publication sold, the higher the rates for advertising in that publication became. Some magazine and newspaper publishers represented vast, and often diversified financial empires, such as the Hearst Corporation, or the less-known but very powerful Chandler family, owners of the *Los Angeles Times*. The Chandlers had extensive real estate holdings in several states, controlled the Santa Fe Railroad, owned Los Angeles television station KTTV, and assumed control of the Long Beach-based Buffums' Department Store chain through marriage. And they helped Eisenhower's Vice President, Richard M. Nixon, get elected to Congress in 1946 when he was a young, relatively unknown Navy veteran and Duke Law School graduate from Whittier, California.

In 1831, following his famous visit to America, the French Aristocrat Alexis de Tocqueville observed in his classic *Democracy in America* that, in the United States, the "periodical press is still, after the people, the first of powers."[37] Tocqueville surely would have been pleased to have his statement regarding the power of a free press validated time and again nearly one hundred and fifty years later, as in the case of Ike's Vice President, Richard Nixon. The *Los Angeles Times* that had once actively supported Nixon in his election to the House in 1946 and to

---

[37] Alexis de Tocqueville, *Democracy in America* (Chicago: The University of Chicago Press, 2000), p. 178.

the Senate in 1950 (and as Ike's running mate in 1952 and 1956), came to oppose him during his 1962 bid for the governorship of California. Nixon lost badly. And Tocqueville certainly would have admired the power that a free press in America still possessed if he had known that two lowly "beat" reporters for the *Washington Post*, Bob Woodward and Carl Bernstein, would cause the downward slide of the most powerful man in the world, *President* Nixon, as a result of their "Watergate" articles during 1972, 73, and 74, and their best-selling book, *All the President's Men*.[38] President Richard M. Nixon resigned on August 9, 1974, the first President in American history to do so. The power of the press?

---

[38] Carl Bernstein and Bob Woodward, *All the President's Men* (New York: Simon and Schuster, 1974).

# CHAPTER 9

# CONCLUSION

1956 was an Olympic year. The 26th Summer Olympic Games were held in Melbourne, Australia, from November 22nd to December 8th—summertime "Down Under." For the first time since Adolf Hitler hosted the 1936 Summer Olympics in Berlin, the United States' team finished in second place, this time behind the team from the Soviet Union. As was the case with Hitler's 1936 Berlin games, during the 1956 Olympics in Melbourne, geopolitics overshadowed the athletes on and off the field of play. Ideology was centermost. Cold War propaganda divided the Olympics' participants into two basic camps: Pro-West and pro-Communist.

The modern Olympic Games began in Athens, Greece, in 1896 as the brainchild of the French educator Pierre de Coubertin and his friends to promote international goodwill among the world's youth by reviving the ancient Greek tradition of holding an athletic festival every four years. With good intentions of easing the world's political discord, the 1936 Olympics had the opposite effect. The 1940 and 1944 Olympics were both cancelled as the direct result of a world at war, as had been the case in 1916 with the cancellation of the Olympics due to World War I. As hope springs eternal, so too does the desire to hold the Olympics competition amongst nations. The Olympic Games resumed in 1948. Held in war-weary London from July 29th to August 14th, the 1948 Summer Olympics went rather well. But the geopolitical reality of the Free World vs. Global Communism was an undeniable presence at the games in light of the recent and ongoing necessity of the Berlin "Air Lift." An "Iron Curtain" had already corralled most of the people of Eastern Europe into a "workers' paradise" within the Soviet orbit. Was another war—this time fought with nuclear weapons—on the horizon?

The 1952 Summer Olympic Games were held in Helsinki, Finland. The ideological differences between the major competing nations was even more apparent: War or no war, which system was more likely to dominate the entire world in the future—*U.S.A.-style capitalism or U.S.S.R.-style communism*? In 1952, that blunt question went far beyond any mere Summer Olympics. And it certainly was a major theme of the 1952 Presidential election campaign. A campaign that Dwight D. Eisenhower won in a landslide. For four years, President Eisenhower managed to guide America's ship of state safely through dangerous international waters while promoting economic prosperity at home. 1956 presented new challenges. It was another Olympic year. And, far more important to most Americans, it was another Presidential election year. The all-important question of who would prevail in the future, the U.S.A. or the U.S.S.R., still hung in the air like a giant lead balloon. Was President Eisenhower deserving of another four years in the White House? According to the voters, "Yes."

"I Like IKE!" was the winning slogan again in 1956. For some time after his landslide election of 1952, President Eisenhower planned to serve only one term. Within his first few years in office, Ike had accomplished most of this administration's goals: Ending the Korean War with honor (1953); abolishing Federal wage limits on American industry (1953); returning control of tidelands oil deposits to the coastal states (1953); abolishing the Communist Party in the United States (1954); beginning construction on the St. Lawrence Seaway (1954); reducing the size of the military and cutting defense costs while establishing a successful peace strategy of threatening to use America's nuclear stockade in "massive retaliation" if necessary (1954); welcoming a *united* West Germany into the family of nations *and NATO* (1955); and launching a gigantic interstate highway system while promoting prosperity and a budget surplus (1955-56). But even Eisenhower was not immune to *Potomac Fever*—he finally decided to run again in early 1956.

By the time President Eisenhower decided to run again, Adlai E. Stevenson, the former Governor of Illinois and his Democratic opponent in 1952, had already thrown his hat in the ring, vowing to win this time. Two other Democrats were serious contenders for their party's Presidential nomination—Senator Estes Kefauver of Tennessee and Governor Averell Harriman of New York. At the Democratic National Convention that August in Chicago, Stevenson was picked on the first ballot. Estes Kefauver (who survived a strong challenge from the young Senator from Massachusetts, John F. Kennedy, was chosen to be his Vice-Presidential running mate. From the start, with *Eisenhower* in the race, Democratic leaders knew their chance of winning the Presidency in November was slim. But they also realized they had a good chance of retaining their majority in both houses of Congress.

Later that August in San Francisco, the Republicans nominated Dwight D. Eisenhower to run again for President by acclamation. "*I like IKE!*" was born again. Due to some questions about the sixty-six-year-old President's health (Ike suffered a "mild" heart attack in September 1955, and had surgery for *ileitis*—inflammation of the small intestine—in June 1956), the Republican delegates decided upon Ike's young, ambitious, and capable Vice President, Richard M. Nixon, as his running mate again (just in case . . .)[39]

The Election of 1956 was primarily a foregone conclusion—Ike would win a second term. All the polls said so. Ike was running a strong campaign based on "Peace, Prosperity, and Progress." Nevertheless, Stevenson ran a strenuous, all-out campaign, pushing his progressive social programs for a "New America." During the last weeks of the campaign, foreign news stole the headlines: Russian tanks crushed a democratic revolt in Hungary, while Egypt's President Gamal Abdel Nasser seized the Suez Canal. Who could best handle America's foreign policy? Prosperity at home plus Ike's proven expertise abroad *increased* his probability of winning. And win he did, by an even greater margin than his landslide victory in 1952. Stevenson carried only seven states—Alabama, Arkansas, Georgia, Mississippi, Missouri, North Carolina, and South Carolina. Ike carried all the remaining *forty-one states*

---

[39] President Eisenhower's *ileo-transverse colostomy* involved removal of the inflamed portion of his small bowel and joining the normal bowel above it to the transverse colon).

(457 Electoral votes to 73). Eisenhower-Nixon's popular vote majority over Stevenson-Kefauver was nearly *ten million*. While the Republicans claimed an overwhelming victory for their *party*, the victory was truly *Ike's*. Both Houses of Congress, in spite of Eisenhower's overwhelming popularity with the voters and his political "coattails," remained in the hands of the Democrats. For the Republicans, "I Like IKE!" had even surpassed their winning 1920's slogan, "Keep Cool with Coolidge." Dwight D. Eisenhower, the President from West Point, had become the most popular Republican of the 20$^{th}$ Century.

In his handling of the Suez Crisis in 1956-57, President Eisenhower, with help from the Dulles Brothers at State and the CIA, forced Great Britain, France, and Israel to back down from their military invasion of Egypt and their ultimate goal of wrestling the Suez Canal from Egyptian control. Many Europeans and Americans alike soon began to fear that a small UN "peacekeeping force" would be insufficient to protect the Canal Zone from potential communist infiltration and the eventual seizure of this most vital international waterway. After all, the Soviets had already begun to finance the construction of Egypt's Aswan High Dam on the Nile River. Might the Suez Canal soon fall behind a Middle East version of Eastern Europe's Iron Curtain? To allay such fears, President Eisenhower submitted a foreign policy proposal to a Joint Session of Congress on January 5, 1957, that soon came to be known as "The Eisenhower Doctrine." President Eisenhower requested Congressional approval for American military and financial aid, *at his discretion*, to *any* country in the Middle East that required assistance to fight "Communist aggression." By a Joint Resolution on March 7, 1957, Congress granted President Eisenhower broad powers for the defense of the entire Middle East. The Russians blinked, and the Suez Canal remained free to the ships of all nations at little cost to the American taxpayers.

While Dwight D. Eisenhower remained one of the most beloved and popular Presidents in American history during his tenure in office (he continued to appeal to many Democrats and Independents, as well as most Republicans), he too had his critics. Ironically, the most vociferous and adamant critics of Ike personally, and of his administration generally, were of the ultra-conservative Right rather than the ultra-liberal Left. As a *Republican* President, Eisenhower, in a similar manner that had befallen Teddy Roosevelt years earlier, increasingly became the ideological target of the conservative wing of his own party. A rising young Republican Senator from Arizona named Barry Goldwater frequently spoke out against Ike's "too liberal policies," both foreign and domestic. But Senator Goldwater never called President Eisenhower a *communist*. The John Birch Society *did*.

The John Birch Society was founded by a wealthy and successful Massachusetts entrepreneur named Robert Welch. Mr. Welch established the John Birch Society in Indiana at a meeting in 1958 with ten other influential and like-minded Americans who firmly believed that the United States Government had fallen under the covert control of the international communist conspiracy. The Society rapidly grew. They dedicated themselves to the memory of John Birch, a Baptist missionary who had been killed by Chinese Communists in 1945, and to the eradication of communism in American society. The John Birch Society vowed to discover, expose, and destroy the careers of all "dedicated, conscious agents of the communist conspiracy." The "agents of the communist conspiracy" they planned to destroy included *President Eisenhower, Chief Justice Earl Warren, Secretary of State John Foster Dulles, and his brother, CIA Director Allen Dulles*, Republicans all. For years, the John Birch Society influenced American political opinion through its numerous publications, essay contests, and other activities. "Birchers" were both feared due to their wealth and influence and ridiculed because of their extremist views, especially the assertion that Eisenhower was a *communist*.

No doubt members of the John Birch Society had a major "*I told you so!*" moment when Ed Sullivan introduced a young Cuban radical named Fidel Castro as "The George Washington of Cuba!" to the vast coast-to-coast audience of his highly popular CBS Television show from New York City, *The Ed Sullivan Show*, on a Sunday evening in mid-1959. At the time, Sullivan was sincere in his praise of Castro. As it soon turned out, he was also gravely mistaken.

Born the son of a wealthy and influential Cuban family in 1927, Fidel Castro received his law degree from the University of Havana in 1950. The twenty-three-year-old lawyer turned revolutionary soon after Colonel Fulgencio Batista seized power in 1952. In 1953, Fidel Castro was jailed for having led the July 26th uprising against Batista. In 1955, Castro was released from prison, and he fled Cuba. Castro returned to Cuba in 1956, and settled in the Sierra Maestra Region of Oriente Province with one burning desire—to overthrow Batista. Fidel Castro called his growing socialist revolutionary force "The 26th of July Movement." The Eisenhower Administration remained highly skeptical of Castro and his merry band of bearded guerrilla-fighters lurking in the mountains of the Sierra Maestra, but many "informed" Americans came to view Castro as a moderate socialist who could "save" Cuba. On January 1, 1959, to the surprise of many, and against major odds, Fidel Castro and his socialist revolutionaries captured Havana, and Fulgencio Batista fled Cuba. Within months, Cuba became a communist state, causing many members of its "ruling class" to flee to Florida.

\* \* \* \* \* \*

William Howard Taft was President when the last of the contiguous "Forty-eight States"—Arizona—was admitted to the Union on February 14, 1912. From 1912 on, America was often referred to as the "Great Forty-eight." Many Americans never dreamed that there would ever be a *forty-ninth* state. They were wrong. Alaska became America's forty-ninth state on January 3, 1959. And Eisenhower became the first President since Taft to welcome a new state into the Union.

European interest in Alaska dates back to a Russian expedition commanded by Vitrus Bering, who explored Alaska's southern coast in 1741. Bering's exploits are memorialized by the "Bering Sea" and the "Bering Straight." But of greatest immediate significance was the rush of Russian fur traders (*promshleniki*) that his pioneering expedition triggered upon his return to Russia with a shipload of otter skins. While Alaska was later found to be rich in gold, copper, coal, oil, natural gas, silver, and, of course, salmon, the fur trade created Alaska's first fortunes. Sitka, founded by Aleksandr Baranov, became Russia's main fortress and headquarters for its fur trade. Alaska remained under Russian control until after the end of the American Civil War.

Abraham Lincoln's able and farsighted Secretary of State, William H. Seward, had long had his eyes on Alaska for its strategic potential, and for its vast and largely unexplored natural resources. But first, there was a war to win—the *Civil War*. When the war ended, and the Union had been preserved, Seward—still Secretary of State, but now serving at the pleasure of President Andrew Johnson—revisited his dream of one day obtaining Alaska for the United States. In one of the great ironies of history, Seward pulled off one of the greatest land heists in the history of the world—*the purchase of Alaska for a mere seven million dollars*—on March 30, 1867. His *reward?* During the remainder of his life, his greatest single triumph—the purchase of Alaska—was widely *ridiculed* as *"Seward's Folly."*

By 1959, "Seward's Folly" had become recognized as one of America's greatest assets. Despite its small population of fewer than five hundred thousand people *total*, it seemed high time for statehood. Alaska had become strategically vital to the defense of the United States during the early days of the Cold War due to its close proximity to the Soviet Union. America's Defense Department set up a series of Distant Early Warning radar stations, or "dew stations," in America's "Last Frontier."

Prior to the Japanese attack on Pearl Harbor, Honolulu, Hawaii, had long been one of the United States Navy's favorite duty stations. Since President William McKinley and the Congress annexed Hawaii as an American territory on July 6, 1898, the Hawaiian Islands played a major role in America's defense of the Pacific. Eventually, Pearl Harbor became the home of America's Pacific Fleet. Long before World War II, many of Hawaii's residents called for statehood, including Hawaii's first territorial governor, Sanford B. Dole (as in *Dole Pineapple*). But due to Hawaii's large Japanese population, its vast distance from the American mainland, and the increasing militancy of its labor unions, Congress chose to delay statehood for Hawaii. The most compelling *public* rationale for denying statehood for Hawaii was the incontrovertible fact that Hawaii was so far away from the "Forty-eight States." With the acceptance of "far away" Alaska's bid for statehood on January 3, 1959, however, the argument for denying Hawaii statehood because it was not *contiguous* to the rest of the United States *collapsed*. Besides, by 1959, Hawaii had shed its reputation as simply the land of pineapple, sugar, and sailors—Hawaii had become a major tourist mecca for the *American public*. "Aloha" had become part of America's vernacular. With more than twice the population of Alaska—and with all those cute "hula" girls in little grass skirts—how could Congress continue to deny their pleas for statehood? And so, on March 18, 1959, the Congress and President Eisenhower made Hawaii—the "Paradise of the Pacific"—America's fiftieth state.

Sometime during the early days of President Eisenhower's first term in office, Ike ordered Allen Dulles, Director of the Central Intelligence Agency (CIA), to conduct a wide variety of covert operations, including maintaining on-the-ground "operatives" (spies) behind the Iron Curtain and air surveillance (more spies) high above the Soviet Union. In a *de jure* world such "espionage" is *illegal*; in a *de facto* world, spying is a necessary and universally practiced *art*. Its *raison d'etre*? National defense. Its *creed*? *Don't get caught*! Its greatest *critics*? *Naïve idealists*.

America has long tended to be an *idealistic* nation. Most Americans sincerely believe in the value of the Golden Rule: *Do unto others as you would have them do unto you.* Who wants to be *spied* upon? And so, when news of the "U-2 Affair" first became public on May 5, 1960, many Americans were shocked—an American *spy plane* had been shot down over the Soviet Union, and the Russians were demanding an apology. Many in the United States asked, "America has *spies*?" (While many others declared, "Thank God we've been doing *something*!")

Francis Gary Powers suddenly became America's best-known pilot (and the Soviet Union's most publicized prisoner). On May 7, 1960, Soviet Premier Nikita Khrushchev announced to the world that an American U-2 "spy plane" had been shot down by Soviet defenders deep inside Russia, near Sverdlovsk, and that its pilot, Francis Gary Powers, a former U.S. Air Force officer now working for the CIA, had admitted to spying on the Soviet people *in violation of international law*. In public, Khrushchev was righteously furious. In private, he was embarrassed that the Soviets had been unable to *prevent* (and for a long while were *unaware of*) U-2 flights over Russia.

When the story first broke on May 5th, the National Aeronautics and Space Administration (NASA) formally announced to the public that a "weather research plane" from Turkey was missing, denying any existence of so-called "spy planes." Following Premier Khrushchev's charges two days later regarding "aggressive acts" and "illegal espionage" on the part of the Eisenhower Administration, Secretary of State Christian A. Herter (who had replaced the recently deceased John Foster Dulles) confirmed that U-2 flights were regularly conducted at an altitude of twelve miles above the Soviet Union in order to prevent "a surprise attack" on the United States and its Western Allies. Ike soon went one step further, publicly admitting that he had ordered the flights. Lockheed Aircraft Corporation built the U-2s, and CIA pilots flew them over their reconnaissance targets, using extremely powerful cameras to photograph detailed objects on the ground below for national defense purposes.[40]

Pilot Powers was soon found guilty of espionage in a Moscow court and sentenced to ten years in a Russian prison (he was released early). Meanwhile, in the United States, many Americans apparently learned for the first time that (1) the American government sanctioned covert operations against other nations, including *spying*, and (2) that America's leaders sometimes *lied* when "national security" was at stake. The U-2 Affair caused a widening creditability gap between Federal officials and the general public in America that has continued ever since. Since The U-2 Affair, government pronouncements are often followed by the question, "Is that the *real* story?"

By 1960, the growing importance of Presidential primaries in American politics demonstrated the evolution of two significant changes in how the major parties choose their presidential candidates: (1) *Profound increases in the costs of running for office* (as fellow Democrat Hubert Humphrey discovered in West Virginia when he was overwhelmed by the avalanche of Kennedy dollars), and (2) *the concomitant decline in the importance of the national conventions in the actual selection process* for the top of the ticket. By 1960, presidential primaries had nearly reduced the quadrennial national party conventions of both the Democrats and the Republicans to rubber stamp status—mere obligatory party referendums on the "People's choices." This was certainly true of the campaign of 1960 prior to the major party conventions. Realistically, both Richard M. Nixon and John F. Kennedy won the nominations to head the tickets of their respective parties by winning in various key state primaries *prior to convention time*. On July 11th, when the Democratic National Convention began at the new Sports Arena adjacent to the University of Southern California campus near downtown Los Angeles, John Kennedy had the nomination in the bag. Only the TV audience was truly uncertain of the ultimate outcome. Kennedy's main obstacles during the primary campaign had been two: (1) Minnesota Senator Hubert Humphrey, and (2) the fact that he was a Roman Catholic (if elected President, would he be subservient to the Pope in Rome?).

---

[40] The CIA's cameras were so powerful, they could pick up the license plates of parked cars.

Kennedy proved he could beat the more-liberal Hubert Humphrey in Humphrey's own mid-Western backyard when he defeated him in Wisconsin's Democratic Primary. And JFK proved a Catholic candidate could win in the predominately Protestant South when he came out on top in West Virginia. With the momentum of these and other primary victories (and a huge "war chest" of dollars from his dad, the former bootlegger, Hollywood mogul, and Ambassador to Great Britain, Joseph P. Kennedy), JFK was poised to accept the nomination of his party on the first ballot in Los Angeles. So too was Richard M. Nixon in Chicago. While Vice President Nixon had no Daddy Warbucks for a father (he grew up *poor*), he had begun his political career with the financial backing of a number of wealthy Californians, including the owner/publisher of the powerful *Los Angeles Times*, Norman Chandler. Since he first became Vice President, "Tricky Dick" had been scheming for this opportunity. Over eight years, he had built up substantial party support, including a sizeable "war chest." Dick Nixon was poised for his party's nomination on the first ballot in Chicago.

For the national television audience, the Democratic National Convention that met in Los Angeles on July 11, 1960, was high drama. There were enthusiastic demonstrations and speeches for Hubert Humphrey of Minnesota and Lyndon Johnson of Texas, as well as those favoring John Kennedy of Massachusetts. Would the one-time "play boy" of the United States Senate and the Pulitzer Prize winning author of *Profiles in Courage* win the nomination? Yes. On the first ballot.

John F. Kennedy proved to be far more politically expedient than even his loyal brother Bobby would have liked. Soon after accepting his party's nomination for President, JFK chose Lyndon Johnson—one of his chief political rivals and a *Southerner*—for his Vice Presidential running mate. Frankly put, Kennedy had long been closer to *Nixon* than he had been to his own party's majority leader in the Senate, LBJ. There was no love lost between the two Democrats. But Kennedy needed the *South* to get elected. Johnson could deliver the South, so JFK thought. And so Kennedy selected *him*. Simple as that. For the Dems, it was JFK and LBJ.

When the Republicans later met in Chicago on July 25th, the nation watched with interest to see if anyone would dare to stand in the way of the ambitious, determined, and sometimes "ruthless" Dick Nixon. Nixon had a reputation for pulling no punches in past political campaigns, especially during his early days in California. There were some half-hearted attempts to oppose him at the Chicago convention, but Nixon was selected on the first ballot *as planned*.

Less politically expedient than Kennedy had been in his choice for V.P., but nevertheless practical, the small-town poor boy from Whittier, California, Richard Nixon, selected the aristocratic "blue blood" Ivy Leaguer from Massachusetts, Senator Henry Cabot Lodge (of *the* Lodge family), to secure the Eastern vote. For the G.O.P., it was Nixon and Lodge.

For the Battle of 1960, both tickets were *balanced*: Kennedy ("new money") and Johnson (the Democrat's Horatio Alger) vs. Nixon (the Republican's Horatio Alger) and Lodge ("old money"). Let the better slate win! And so it was Kennedy-Johnson vs. Nixon-Lodge in the Election of 1960. Kennedy emphasized his "New Frontier;" Nixon claimed "Experience Counts!" Both parties waged vigorous, clean campaigns *on the issues*. In the end, Kennedy's "New Frontier" beat Nixon's "Experience Counts!" by the slimmest margin in the total popular vote since the Election of 1888 (when Benjamin Harrison defeated Grover Cleveland). Many political pundits to this day claim that Kennedy's "upset" victory over Nixon was due to his "winning" the first of four *nationally televised* debates between the two candidates. Nixon was the more experienced debater of the two, and was expected by many pundits to "win," even though the topic of the first debate was *domestic* issues (Nixon's special forte was *foreign affairs*). On September 26th, an estimated seventy million Americans tuned in to the first-ever Presidential debate on live television. On TV, Nixon, who refused to wear makeup that night, looked sinister with his five o'clock shadow and his menacing facial expressions. By contrast, Kennedy looked like the handsome young Harvard graduate turned Senator who made the ladies' hearts flutter and many men wish they could share good cigars and fine Scotch with. Kennedy came off more *likeable*. His answer to each question was brief, positive, and to the point, while Nixon gave more elaborate, detailed answers primarily directed at Kennedy instead of at the TV cameras. To a majority of listeners on radio, Nixon had clearly won at the conclusion of the first debate. But to the larger and more important TV audience, Kennedy had held his own against Nixon on his knowledge of substantive matters, and he had certainly looked *healthier* and more *likeable* than his opponent, giving additional credence to Kennedy's call for "a new generation of leadership . . . a *New Frontier.*"

Nixon gave the campaign his best shot, becoming the first Presidential candidate in history to visit *all fifty states*. As the campaign progressed, the race grew so close that both President Eisenhower (who had planned to remain aloof) and former President Truman (originally lukewarm toward JFK) entered the frey on behalf of their parties' candidates. Near the end of the campaign, the ever-popular Eisenhower gave major speeches on Nixon's behalf in the key states of New York, Ohio, and Pennsylvania (Nixon later carried Ohio, and barely lost in New York and Pennsylvania). Meanwhile, Truman helped Kennedy carry Missouri and Illinois.

In 1960, the "Solid South" was *not solid*: Florida, Kentucky, Oklahoma, Tennessee, and Virginia chose *Nixon*. Nixon also won all of the Western states except Nevada and New Mexico. The *popular* vote was so close that the final margin of national victory was only 115,000 votes. But the Electoral College was stacked for Kennedy, 303 to 219 (a shift of a few thousand votes in Illinois and Texas would have elected Nixon). While there were accusations from some Republicans (and the news media) of widespread voter fraud in Mayor Richard Daley's Chicago and in various parts of Texas and in other Democratic strongholds, Richard Nixon graciously conceded the election, and John Kennedy became our President-elect. To the surprise of many, the "New Nixon" refused to contest the outcome. Perhaps the "Old Nixon," many supporters lamented, would have won. Who knew in 1960 what the future had in store for either man?

On January 17, 1961, President Dwight D. Eisenhower spoke directly to the nation on national television. His "Farewell Address," in which he unexpectedly warned his fellow Americans about the potential dangers posed by our growing "military-industrial complex," ranks in historical importance with another famous farewell—George Washington's farewell warning in 1796 about the dangers of "entangling alliances." Both addresses have had far-reaching impact upon future American public policy. From the White House, President Eisenhower, in his familiar, warm yet serious way, looked directly at the TV camera and said,

*My fellow Americans:*

Three days from now, after half a century in the service of our country, I shall lay down the responsibilities of office as, in traditional and solemn ceremony, the authority of the Presidency is vested in my successor . . .

Throughout America's adventures in free government, our basic purposes have been to keep the peace; to foster progress in human achievement, and to enhance liberty, dignity and integrity among people and among nations. To strive for less would be unworthy of a free and religious people.

\* \* \* \* \* \*

Progress toward these noble goals is persistently threatened by the conflict now engulfing the world. It commands our whole attention, absorbs our very beings. We face a hostile ideology—global in scope, atheistic in character, ruthless in purpose, and insidious in method. Unhappily the danger it poses promises to be of indefinite duration. To meet it successfully, there is called for, not so much the emotional and transitory sacrifices of crisis, but rather those which enable us to carry forward steadily, surely, and without complaint the burdens of a prolonged and complex struggle—with liberty the stake.

\* \* \* \* \* \*

Until the latest of our world conflicts, the United States had no armaments industry. American makers of plowshares could, with time and as required, make swords as well. But now we can no longer risk emergency improvisation of national defense; we have been compelled to create a permanent armaments industry of vast proportions. Added to this, three and a half million men and women are directly engaged in the defense establishment. We annually spend on military security more than the net income of all United States corporations.

This conjunction of an immense military establishment and a large arms industry is new in the American experience. The total influence—economic, political, even spiritual—is felt in every city, every statehouse, every office of the federal government. We recognize the imperative need for this development. Yet we must not fail to comprehend its grave implications. Our toil, resources, and livelihood are all involved; so is the very structure of our society.

In the councils of government, we must guard against the acquisition of unwarranted influence, whether sought or unsought, by the military-industrial complex. The potential for the disastrous rise of misplaced power exists and will persist.

We must never let the weight of this combination endanger our liberties or democratic processes. We should take nothing for granted. Only an alert and knowledgeable citizenry can compel the proper meshing of the huge industrial and military machinery of defense with our peaceful methods and goals, so that security and liberty may prosper together.

\* \* \* \* \* \*

The prospect of domination of the nation's scholars by federal government project allocations, and the power of money is ever present—and is gravely to be regarded.

\* \* \* \* \* \*

. . . . As we peer into society's future, we—you and I, and our government—must avoid the impulse to live only for today, plundering, for our own ease and convenience, the precious resources of tomorrow. We cannot mortgage the material assets of our grandchildren without risking the loss also of their political and spiritual heritage. We want democracy to survive for all generations to come, not to become the insolvent phantom of tomorrow.

\* \* \* \* \* \*

Happily, I can say that war has been avoided. Steady progress toward our ultimate goal has been made. But, so much remains to be done. As a private citizen, I shall never cease to do what little I can to help the world advance along that road . . . .

Dwight D. Eisenhower, mid-Western rough-neck, West Point cadet, General MacArthur's peace-time aide, Commander of all Allied Forces in Europe during World War II, Commander of NATO following the war, President of Columbia University, and ultimately, *President of the United States*, soon retired to his modest farm in Gettysburg, Pennsylvania. Americans still liked Ike. He had led them with dignity and dedication during the Fabulous Fifties. After nearly fifty years of service to his country (1911 to 1961) during good times and bad, Ike deserved some rest.

On Friday, January 20, 1961, following the Inauguration Day ceremony of John F. Kennedy and his "New Frontier," Dwight and Mamie Eisenhower quietly left Washington, D.C., for the only home they had ever owned, their modest farmhouse in Gettysburg, Pennsylvania.[41] Together with their long-time personal servants, Sergeant John Moaney (his wife Delores joined him later in Gettysburg to cook for the Eisenhowers) and Rosie Woods, and their chauffer, Leonard Dry, they unceremoniously piled into one large automobile and headed north on frozen streets. Inside the roomy 1955 Chrysler Imperial that Mamie had purchased for Ike as his sixty-fifth birthday present, everyone was warm and relaxed in spite of the below-freezing weather outside. With no signs of pomp and circumstance besides an

---

[41] Friends later arranged for them to have a second (winter) home in Palm Desert, California.

unmarked Secret Service vehicle to clear their path and lead the way towards Gettysburg, *citizen* Eisenhower was finally free. For some time after World War II ended, Ike had hoped he and Mamie would soon retire to a little town like Gettysburg. A smiling Ike had finally gotten his wish.[42]

---

[42] For a very personal account of Eisenhower's retirement years, see David Eisenhower's *Going Home to Glory* (New York: Simon & Schuster, 2010).

# EPILOGUE

The Eisenhower Years have receded into America's past. Even Ike's famous smile is unfamiliar to many of today's youth. But major reminders of the Eisenhower Years still remain, including the ongoing cease-fire in Korea, our interstate highway system, the St. Lawrence Seaway, integrated schools in all fifty states, Alaska and Hawaii as part of the Union, and NASA's sending of American astronauts safely to the moon and back in 1969. All were the result, at least in part, of Ike's leadership during the Fabulous Fifties.

The Fabulous Fifties was a great decade for the nation's entertainment industry. True, Hollywood studios faced stiff competition from a new and fast-growing rival, *television*. But, with such motion picture super stars as Marlon Brando, Richard Burton, Gary Cooper, Doris Day, James Dean, Kirk Douglas, Cary Grant, Audrey Hepburn, Charlton Heston, William Holden, Rock Hudson, Grace Kelly, Burt Lancaster, Marilyn Monroe, Paul Newman, Gregory Peck, Jimmy Stewart, Elizabeth Taylor, John Wayne, and so many more, Hollywood produced some of its finest films during the Eisenhower Years, including *From Here to Eternity, Stalig 17, Roman Holiday, On the Waterfront, Marty, Giant, The King and I, The Bridge on the River Kwai, Gigi,* and *Ben Hur.*

Television revolutionized America's entertainment industry during the 1950's, and profoundly affected our entire society in the process. At first, motion picture studios and television stations *clashed.* Not so with radio. Television soon became "radio with pictures," and many existing radio networks, including CBS, NBC, and ABC, embraced TV as an expansion of their regular programming. Old radio programs designed for *listening* became "new" TV shows for *watching and listening*. "The Adventures of Ozzie and Harriett" began as a popular radio program in 1944. In 1952, "Ozzie and Harriett" transitioned to television and remained highly popular on TV for the next fourteen years. "The Jack Benny Show," "Our Miss Brooks," "The Lone Ranger," "Gunsmoke," and many others also originated on radio.

"I Love Lucy," starring Lucille Ball and Desi Arnaz, originated on television. It was an instant comedy hit. Other comedians, including Milton Berle, Red Skeleton, and Jackie Gleason became wildly popular as TV personalities. And comedian Bob Hope's "Specials" were a must see. Certainly, no one entertained more of America's children than Walt Disney through his weekly TV shows, or Bill Boyd as TV's most popular cowboy—Hopalong Cassidy. But TV re-runs of the old "Little Rascals" films and "Laurel and Hardy" movies came close.

Television also had its more serious side during the Eisenhower Years, from classical concerts and dramas, to Edward R. Murrow's "See It Now" and "Person to Person" news commentaries and interviews of famous people, to the "CBS Evening News" with Walter Cronkite. And television was an unqualified hit when it came to live broadcasts of major sport events, from professional boxing to World Series baseball games.

No American President since Theodore Roosevelt was a greater advocate of the importance of sports in our daily lives than Dwight Eisenhower. Ike was America's most famous golfer. But he wisely had no plans to turn pro. Ike, although an excellent golfer, left the professional game to the likes of Jimmy Demaret, Ben Hogan, Sam Snead, and Cary Middlecoff. Through the miracle of television, millions of Americans could now watch the nation's best golfers, as well as the finest athletes compete in all the major sports, live or on film from the comfort of their own living rooms. And millions did.

During the Eisenhower Years, one sports fact was clear: New York City dominated major league baseball. From 1947 through 1957, the New York Yankees won a total of *ten* American Leagues pennants, the Brooklyn Dodgers won *six* National League pennants, and the National League's Giants won *two*. One decade. *Eighteen pennants*. No wonder all of America was shocked when the Dodgers and the Giants suddenly moved to California following the end of the 1957 season.

During the Fabulous Fifties, professional boxing was extremely popular with American males. Rocky Marciano was the Heavyweight Champion of the World from September 1952 until he retired *undefeated* in April 1956. To boxing fans, Marciano was *the man*. And welterweight/middleweight Sugar Ray Robinson was, pound-for-pound, one of the greatest practitioners of that "sweet science" who ever lived.

The Indianapolis 500 still dominated auto racing, but NASCAR racing was rapidly gaining in total numbers of fans. In thoroughbred racing, no horse had won the "Triple Crown"—the Kentucky Derby, the Preakness, and the Belmont—since Citation in 1948. And no horse would during Ike's tenure, although four three-year-olds—Native Dancer, Nashua, Neddles, and Tim Tam—each won two of the three races. In women's tennis, "Little Mo" Connelly in 1953 won all four major tournaments—the Australian Open, the French Open, the U.S. Open, and Wimbledon—for a rare "Grand Slam."

Both college football and the NFL grew in popularity during the Eisenhower Years as increasing numbers of games were televised, many coast-to-coast. During Ike's Presidency, college football's national champions included Maryland, UCLA, Oklahoma (twice), Auburn, Ohio State, LSU, and Syracuse. The Heisman Trophy is awarded to college football's "best player" each year by the Downtown Athletic Club of New York City. During the Eisenhower Years, the winners of college football's highest award were: 1953, Johnny Lattner, Notre Dame; 1954, Alan Ameche, Wisconsin; 1955, Howard "Hopalong" Cassidy, Ohio State; 1956, Paul Hornung, Notre Dame; 1957, John David Crow, Texas A & M; 1958, Pete Dawkins, Army; 1959, Billy Cannon, LSU; and 1960, Joe Bellino, Navy. In professional football, NFL championships were won by the Detroit Lions (twice), the Cleveland Browns (twice), the New York Giants, and the Baltimore Colts (twice). All-pros included quarterbacks Otto Graham of the Browns, Y.A. Tittle of the Giants, and Johnny Unitas of the Colts, running back Jim Brown of the Browns, and defensive back Dick "Night Train" Lane of the Lions.

In 1954, a single track event—a mile race held at Oxford, England—made headlines around the world: ROGER BANNISTER BREAKS FOUR MINUTE MILE! And, to prove his time was no fluke, both Dr. Bannister and his rival, Australian John Landy, soon raced each other in Vancouver, Canada. Bannister won, but both men finished the race in under four minutes, putting an end to the age-old myth that it was humanly impossible to run a mile in under four minutes flat.

The rock 'n' roll revolution exploded during the Eisenhower Years. Beginning in the early 1950's as an amalgam of America's popular country-and-Western music, traditional folk music, and "the blues," Elvis Presley took rock 'n' roll to new heights in 1955 as he skyrocketed to stardom. By 1956, Presley was "The King of Rock 'n' Roll" and an international sensation. Privately, President Eisenhower was not pleased when he learned that "O Solo Mio" and "Army Blue," two of his favorite songs, had been "adapted" by Elvis as "It's Now or Never" and "Love Me Tender." And many parents and most clerics saw Elvis' highly suggestive on-stage pelvic gyrations as threats to America's "standards of sexual decency." Nevertheless, Elvis remained "The King."

More traditional pop music, performed by such outstanding vocalist as Frank Sinatra, Nat "King" Cole, Peggy Lee, Rosemary Clooney, Perry Como, Bing Crosby, Doris Day, Frankie Lane, and Julie London, and a host of others, was as good as it gets. And the world still sings songs from the hit Broadway shows of the Fabulous Fifties, including "Damn Yankees" (1955), "My Fair Lady" (1956), "West Side Story" (1957), "Flower Drum Song" (1958), "The Sound of Music" (1959), and "Gypsy" (1959). Sweet.

Dwight Eisenhower was a military man, but he never lost sight of the fact that *private enterprise*—not the national government—was the engine that drives America's economy. Early on, Ike abolished all Federal controls on wages (except for the basic Federal minimum wage), and he returned control of all tidelands oil deposits to the states.

In 1953, the United States contained only six percent of the world's total population, but it had 60% of all the world's automobiles, 58% of all telephones, 45% of all radios, and 34% of all railroads. General Motors was the world's largest manufacturer of automobiles. U.S. Steel was the world's greatest producer of steel. General Electric made the most appliances. DuPont led the world in chemical production. Boeing and Douglas made most of the world's commercial aircraft. AT & T was the world's leader in telecommunications. Exxon Mobil and Texaco were the world's largest oil companies. IBM made most of the world's electric typewriters and calculators. RCA made the most radios, TVs, and phonographs. Armour, Kraft, General Foods, and General Mills led the world in processed food. Procter & Gamble's products kept the world clean. The world drove on Goodyear or Firestone tires. Eastman Kodak Film was the world's finest. Wilson sports products *made in the U.S.A.* reigned supreme. And the entire world drank *Coca-Cola*.

In 1953, the United States faced a growing crisis of transportation gridlock due to its outdated system of highways, bridges, and roads. After consulting the states, Ike presented his National Highway Program to Congress as a solution to the problem. Congress agreed, and the greatest highway construction program in American history began. A similar crisis was looming over many of our nation's public school systems due to the post-war "baby boom." Ike proposed that Congress spend two billion dollars on a national school aid program to help districts in financial trouble due to overcrowded schools. But Federal aid to education was a highly controversial issue during the 1950's in a nation with a long history of *local control* of public schools. Congress put Ike's proposal on hold—until Russia launched its "Sputnik" satellite in October 1957. Meanwhile, the most controversial issue involving public education was not Federal aid; it was the Supreme Court's 1954 decision in *Brown v. Board of Education*. In *Brown v. Board of Education*, the Supreme Court unanimously decided that "separate but equal" schools were unconstitutional. Most of the South had segregated schools. Suddenly, Ike was faced with a new culture war: *Civil Rights vs. Segregation*. One of his most famous responses was sending Federal troops to integrate Central High School in Little Rock, Arkansas, in September 1957.

Throughout his life, Dwight Eisenhower was a voracious reader. During his Presidency, Ike handled stress by playing golf, playing cards with friends, and reading "pulp" Western paperbacks at bedtime. Equally familiar with the writings of such authors as Plato, Shakespeare, Doyle, Kipling, Twain, Nietzsche, and von Clausewitz, Ike enjoyed reading a good Western novel by Zane Grey, Max Brand, Ernest Haycox, Clarence Mulford, Louis L'Amour, and other writers of that all-American genre so dear to his boyhood days in Abilene.

American readers during the Eisenhower Years had a virtual cornucopia of brilliant young authors to choose from: Ray Bradbury, Taylor Caldwell, Thomas B. Costain, James Cozzens, Patrick Dennis, Allen Drury, Edna Feber, Joseph Heller, Ernest Hemingway, John Hersey, James Jones, Mac Kinlay Kantor, Frances Parkinson Keyes,

D.H. Lawrence, Grace Metalious, James A. Mitchener, Edwin O'Connor, John O'Hara, Evan Hunter, Boris Pasternak, Ayn Rand, Harold Robbins, Kenneth Roberts, Bud Schulberg, John Steinbeck, Robert Travier, Leon M. Uris, Sloan Wilson, Herman Wouk, Frank Yerby, and a multitude of others.

The Eisenhower Years witnessed the creation of some of the finest motion pictures, television programs, music, Broadway shows, and literature in American history. The Eisenhower Years—including TV dinners, skating waitresses, hairy wrestlers, and rock 'n' roll—were not the "cultural desert days" some critics may wish us to believe. Quite the contrary, the Fabulous Fifties—warts and all—was an extremely rich and creative decade. America's exuberance in so many areas of the arts and everyday life was omnipresent. As for political and military achievements, President Eisenhower kept us safely out of war, and was wise enough to stay out of the way of America's artists and entrepreneurs. As a result, the Eisenhower Years should forever be remembered as those "Happy Days."

# BIBLIOGRAPHY

Adams, Sherman. *First-Hand Report: The Inside Story of the Eisenhower Administration.* New York: Harper & Brothers, 1961.

Allen, Frederick Lewis. *Only Yesterday: An Informal History of the 1920's.* New York: Harper & Brothers, 1931.

Ambrose, Stephen E. *Eisenhower, the President.* New York: Simon & Schuster, 1984.

_____. *Nixon: The Education of a Politician 1913-1962.* New York: Simon & Schuster, 1987.

*Barron's Profiles of American Colleges.* New York: Barron's Educational Services, Inc., 1985.

Bernstein, Carl, and Bob Woodward. *All the President's Men.* New York: Simon & Schuster, 1974.

_____. *The Final Days.* New York: Simon and Schuster, 1976.

Boller, Paul F., Jr. *Presidential Campaigns: From George Washington to George W. Bush.* New York: Oxford University Press, 2004.

Caroli, Betty Boyd. *The First Ladies*. New York: Madison Park Press, 2009.

Chang, Jung, and John Halliday. *Mao: The Unknown Story*. New York: Alfred A. Knopf, 2005.

Childs, Marquis. *Captive Hero: A Critical Study of the General and the President*. New York: Harcourt Brace, 1958.

Commager, Henry Steele, ed. *Documents of American History*. New York: Appleton-Century-Crofts, 1963.

De'Este, Carlo. *Eisenhower: A Soldier's Life*. New York: Henry Holt and Company, 2002.

Drew, Elizabeth. *Richard M. Nixon*. New York: Times Books, 2007.

Eisenhower, David. *Going Home to Glory: A Memoir of Life With Dwight Eisenhower, 1961-1969*. New York: Simon & Schuster, 2010.

Eisenhower, Dwight D. *At Ease: Stories I Tell to Friends*. Garden City, New York: Doubleday & Company, Inc., 1967.

_____. *Crusade in Europe*. New York: Doubleday, 1948.

_____. "Some Thoughts on the Presidency." *The Reader's Digest* (November 1968).

_____. *The White House Years: Mandate for Change, 1953-56*. Garden City, New York: Doubleday, 1963.

_____. *The White House Years: Waging Peace, 1956-61*. Garden City, New York: Doubleday, 1965.

Farris, Scott. *Almost President: The Men Who Lost the Race But Changed the Nation*. Guilford, Connecticut: Lyons Press, 2012.

Goodrum, Charles and Helen Dalrymple. *Advertising in America: The First 200 Years*. New York: Harry N. Abrams, Inc., Publishers, 1990.

Gould, Lewis L. *The Modern American Presidency*. Lawrence, Kansas: University Press of Kansas, 2003.

Greenstein, Fred J. *The Hidden-Hand Presidency: Eisenhower as Leader*. Baltimore: Johns Hopkins University Press, 1982.

Grun, Bernard. *The Timetables of History*. New York: Simon & Schuster, 1982.

Herring, Hubert. *A History of Latin America*. New York: Alfred A. Knopf, 1960.

Isaacson, Walter. *American Sketches*. New York: Simon & Schuster, 2009.

Katz, Ephraim. *The Film Encyclopedia*, 6th Edition. New York: Harper Collins Publishers, 2008.

Kelley, Kitty. *His Way: The Unauthorized Biography of Frank Sinatra*. New York: Bantam Books, 1986.

Kennedy, John F. *Profiles in Courage*. New York: Harper & Row, Publishers, 1956.

Kennedy, Paul. *The Rise and Fall of the Great Powers: Economic Change and Military Conflict from 1500 to 2000*. New York: Random House, 1986.

Lederer, William J. and Eugene Burdick. *The Ugly American*. New York: W.W. Norton & Company, 1958.

Lewis, Jerry and James Kaplan. *Dean & Me*. New York: Doubleday, 2005.

MacArthur, Douglas. *Reminiscences*. New York: McGraw-Hill, 1964.

McCullough, David. *Truman*. New York: Simon & Schuster, 1992.

Morrison, Samuel Eliott, and Henry Steel Commager. *The Growth of the American Republic*. New York: Oxford University Press, vol. 2, 1960.

Nelson, Kevin. *The Golden Game: The Story of California Baseball*. San Francisco: California Historical Society Press, 2004.

Newton, Jim. *Eisenhower: The White House Years*. New York: Doubleday, 2011.

Nichols, David A. *Eisenhower 1956: Suez and the Brink of War*. New York: Simon & Schuster, 2011.

Packard, Vance. *The Status Seekers*. New York: David McKay Co., 1959.

Smith, Carter. *Presidents: Every Question Answered*. New York: Hylas Publishing Group, 2005.

Smith, Jean Edward. *Eisenhower: In War and Peace*. New York: Random House, 2012.

*Stanford University Bulletin*, Series 9, No. 79, October 1, 1957.

Stanley, Richard T. *A Humorous Account of America's Past: 1945 to 2001*. Bloomington: iUniverse, Inc., 2011.

Stokes, Melvyn. *D.W. Griffith's The Birth of a Nation*. New York: Oxford University Press, 2007.

Summers, Anthony. *Official and Confidential: The Secret Life of J. Edgar Hoover*. New York: G.P. Putnam's Sons, 1993.

_____. *Goddess: The Secret Lives of Marilyn Monroe*. New York: Macmillan, 1985.

_____. *Sinatra: The Life*. New York: Alfred A. Knopf, 2005.

*The Baseball Encyclopedia*, 8th Edition. New York: Macmillan Publishing Company, 1990.

*The Basketball Book*. New York: Sports Illustrated Books, 2007.

*The New Encyclopedia of American Scandal* (ed. George Childs Kohn). New York: Checkmark Books, 1991.

*The New Funk & Wagnalls Encyclopedia Yearbook*. New York: Unicorn Yearbook Services, Annual 1953 through 1960 editions.

*The 1991 Sports Almanac* (ed. Mike Mserole). Boston: Houghton Mifflin Company, 1991.

*The USA Today College Football Encyclopedia*. (ed. Bob Boyles and Paul Guido). New York: Skyhouse Publishing, 2011.

Tocqueville, Alexis de. *Democracy in America*. Chicago: The University of Chicago Press, 2000 edition.

Wallis, Michael. *David Crockett: The Lion of the West*. New York: W.W. Norton & Company, 2011.

Whitney, David C. *The American Presidents*. New York: Doubleday & Company, Inc., 1978.

*Wikipedia.*

Wilson, Vincent Jr. *The Book of the States*. Brookeville, Md.: American History Research Associates, 1986.

Wright, Jordan M. *Campaigning for President*. New York: Harper Collins Publishers, 2008.

Zinn, Howard. *A People's History of the United States: 1492-Present*. New York: Harper Collins Publishers, 1999.

# INDEX

Aaron, Henry  77, 91
Ace, Johnny  104
Adams, Don  57
Adams, Sherman  5-6, 112
Adamson, Joy  150
Adler, Buddy  45
Adler and Ross  105
Adler, Mortimer  133
Adenauer, Konrad  13
Akins, Virgil  82
Aldrin, Edwin, Jr.  141
Alexander, Dale  150
Allen, Fred  53
Allen, Gracie  53, 59
Allen, Phog  75
Allen, Steve  57
Allyson, June  26, 40
Alston, Walter  89
Ameche, Alan  97, 171
Anderson, Eddie "Rochester"  53, 55
Andrews, Julie  106
Anka, Paul  106
Antonelli, Johnny  89
Aparicio, Luis  93
Arbenz, Jacobo  12-13
Arden, Eve  53, 55
Armas, Carlos  13

Armstrong, Louis  100
Armstrong, Neil  141
Arnaz, Desi  54, 58-59, 170
Arness, James  54, 56-57
Astaire, Fred  26
Auerbach, "Red"  86, 88
Autry, Gene  35, 53-54, 56, 60-61
Avila, Bobby  89

Bacall, Lauren  26
Backus, Jim  54
Baker, Art  98
Ball, Lucille  54, 58-59, 170
Banky, Vilma  43
Bannister, Roger  88-89, 171
Bardot, Brigitte  26
Barnard, Henry  129
Baruch, Bernard  150
Basie, "Count"  100
Basilio, Carmen  82
Bassey, Hogen "Kid"  82
Batista, Fulgencio  157-58
Bauer, Hank  78, 92
Baylor, Elgin  86
Bell, Alexander Graham  115
Bellamy, Edward  75
Bellamy, Frances  74

Bellino, Joe  98, 171
Bendix, William  54
Bennett, Constance  48
Bennett, Tony  57
Benny, Jack  54-55, 57, 59
Benson, Ezra Taft  7
Bergen, Edgar  54
Bergman, Ingred  26, 33
"Berkeley Plan"  132
Berle, Milton  54, 58, 170
Berlin, Irving  47, 101
Bernstein, Elmer  47
Bernstein, Leonard  47, 54, 106, 109
Bernstein, Morey  149
Berra, Yogi  78, 92
Berry, Chuck  103, 107
Birch, John  157
Bishop, Jim  150
Bishop, Joey  54
Blaik, Red  78-79
Blake, Amanda  57
Blanc, Mel  54-55
Bobbitt, Franklin  131-32
Bogart, Humphrey  25-26
Bond, Ward  54
Boone, Pat  57, 104
Boone, Richard  54
Borgnine, Ernest  26, 54
Born, B.H.  75
Boyd, William  54, 62, 170
Boyer, Charles  54
Bradbury, Ray  146
Brand, Max  148
Brando, Marlon  26, 28-29, 32, 169
Bratton, Johnny  82
Braun, Wernher von  140
Brennan, Walter  54
Bridges, Lloyd  54

Brinkley, David  54
Brooks, Richard  45
Brown, Jim  95, 171
Brown, Joe  82
Brown, John  98
Brown, Les  37
*Brown v. Board of Education*  134-36, 173
Brownell, Herbert  6, 137
Bruce, Lennie  57
Bryant, Bear  94, 97
Brynner, Yul  26, 33
Burdette, Lew  77, 91
Burdick, Eugene L.  146
Burns, George  53, 59
Burr, Raymond  54, 66
Burton, Richard  26, 169
Buttons, Red  54

Caesar, Sid  54, 59
Cahn, Sammy  47
Caldwell, Taylor  146-47
Campanella, Roy  78
Cannon, Billy  171
Capra, Frank  39
Carey, Andy  92
Carmichael, Hoagy  47
Carnegie, Andrew  115
Carney, Art  54
Caron, Leslie  26
Carrillo, Leo  54, 63-64
Carson, Rachel  149
Carter, James  82
Cash, Johnny  105-06
Cassidy, Howard "Hopalong"  84, 97, 171
Castro, Fidel  60, 157
Central High School  135-36

Chamberlain, Wilt 86
"Champion" 54, 61-62
Chandler, Norman 151, 162
Charisse, Cyd 26
Charles, Ray 104, 107
Churchill, Winston 6, 20-21, 149
Chevalier, Maurice 26
CIA 9-15, 160-61
*Civil Rights vs. Segregation* 135, 173
Clark, Dick 54, 109
Clark, Roy 57
Clausewitz, Karl von 143
Clay, Lucias D. 122
Clift, Montgomery 26
Cline, Patsy 57
Clooney, Rosemary 104, 171
Cobb, Lee J. 26
Coca, Imogene 59
Cochrane, Mickey 76
Cody, Iron Eyes 54
Cohn, Roy 17
Cole, Nat "King" 104, 106, 171
Coleman, Ronald 43
Collins, Joe 78
Como, Perry 104, 171
Conant, James B. 132-33
Connelly, Maureen "Little Mo" 84, 171
Connor, Fox 23, 142-43
Conrad, William 56
Coolidge, Calvin 2, 113, 121
Cooper, Gary 26, 31-32, 43-45, 169
Cooper, James Fenimore 144
Costain, Thomas B. 147
Coubertin, Pierre de 153
Counts, George S. 131-32
Cousy, Bob 86
Cox, Billy 78

Cox, Wally 54
Cozzens, James Gould 147
Crane, Stephen 145
Crawford, Broderick 54
Cronkite, Walter 54, 67, 170
Crosby, Bing 26, 31-32, 35, 101, 104, 171
Crosby, Bob 37
Crow, John David 94, 97, 171
Cummings, Robert 54
Curtis, Tony 26, 31

Daley, Richard 164
Damon, Vic 104
Dana, Richard Henry 144
Danny and The Juniors 106-07
Dark, Alvin 89
Darren, Bobby 107
Darwin, Charles 115
Davenport, Bob 85
Davies, Marion 48
Davis, Elmer 149
Davis, Ernie 98
Davis, Miles 106
Dawkins, Pete 97, 171
Day, Dennis 55
Day, Doris 26, 43, 104, 106, 169, 171
Dean, James 26, 28, 32, 169
DeMarco, Paddy 82
Demarco, Tony 82
Demaret, Jimmy 72, 170
DeMille, Cecil B. 24-25, 45, 47, 62
Dempsey, Jack 81
Denning, Richard 58
Dennis, Patrick 147
Devine, Andy 54
Dewey, John 131-32

Dewey, Thomas E. 101
Dickerson, William J. 117
Diddley, Bo 106
Dietrich, Marlene 36
DiMaggio, Joe 30, 92
Disney, Roy 41
Disney, Walt 40, 69-70, 105, 170
Doby, Larry 77, 89
Dole, Sanford B. 159
Domino, "Fats" 103, 105
Donavan, Robert J. 150
Dorsey, Tommy 100-01
Doud, Elvira 18
Doud, John 18
Douglas, Donald 115
Douglas, Kirk 26, 32-33, 42, 169
Douglas, Lloyd C. 147
Doyle, Sir Arthur Connan 148
Drury, Allen 147
Drysdale, Don 93
Duke, James 115
Duncan, Lee 63
Dulles, Allen 9-15, 157
Dulles, John Foster 6, 9-15, 157
Durkin, Martin 7
Duren, Ryne 92
Durante, Jimmy 54
Durocher, Leo 89

Eastwood, Clint 66
Edison, Thomas 24, 115
Edwards, Douglas 67
Edwards, Tommy 107
Eisenhower, Arthur (Brother) 130
Eisenhower, David (Father) 130
"Eisenhower Doctrine," The 156
Eisenhower, Doud "Icky" (Son) 19

Eisenhower, Dwight D.
    As Columbia University President 102, 133
    As football coach 71-72
    Cabinet, of 5-9
    Childhood and adolescence of 1, 71, 130
    Cooking, hobby of 20, 22
    "Farewell Address" of 164-67
    Favorite authors/books of 142-43, 147-48, 173
    Favorite foods of 20, 22
    Favorite movies of 22
    Favorite music of 103
    Favorite TV programs of 60, 72
    "First Inaugural Address" of 1-5
    Foreign Policy 2, 5, 9-15
    Golf and poker pastime of 15, 20, 71-72
    Health of 20, 94, 155
    Leadership/management style of 8-15, 111-12, 119-20
    Military career of 1, 18, 23, 129, 130-31
    National Education Program of 139-41
    National Highway Program of 121-23, 173
    Painting hobby of 21
    Popularity of 156, 169
    Presidential campaigns of 154
    West Point days of 71
Eisenhower, Earl (Brother) 130
Eisenhower, Edgar (Brother) 1
Eisenhower, Ida (Mother) 130
Eisenhower, John Sheldon (Son) 19, 23

Eisenhower, Mamie (wife)  18, 21-22, 23, 167
Eisenhower, Milton (Brother)  130
Eisenhower, Roy (Brother)  130
Ellena, Jack  85
Ellington, Duke  104
Emerson, Ralph Waldo  144
Erskine, Carl  78
Evans, Dale  54, 61
Everly Brothers, the  107
Explorer 1  140

Fabray, Nanette  54
Farillo, Carl  78
Faubus, Orville  136
FBI  10
Feber, Edna  147
Feller, Bob  89
Ferrer, José  26
Firestone, Harvey  115
Fisher, Eddie  28, 57, 104-05
Fitzgerald, F. Scott  146
Flanders, Ralph  17
Fonda, Henry  26, 39-40
Ford, Glen  26, 39
Ford, John  34, 45, 115-16, 118
Ford, Mary  102
Ford, Tennessee Ernie  105
Ford, Whitey  78, 92
Fox, Nellie  93
Freed, Arthur  45
Funicello, Annette  54
Fullmer, Gene  82
Furillo, Carl  92

Gable, Clark  26, 31-32, 39
Gabor, Eva  54
Gabor, Zsa Zsa  54
Gandhi, Mahatma  145
Gann, Ernest K.  147
Garcia, Mike  89
Gardner, Ava  26
Garfield, James A.  2
Garland, Judy  26
Garner, Jack  74
Garner, James  54
Garrett, Bobby  79
Garson, Greer  26
Gavilan, Kid  82
Gershwin, George and Ira  47
Gilliam, Jim "Junior"  78, 93
Gleason, Jackie  54, 59, 170
Godfrey, Arthur  54, 57
Gola, Tom  86
Golden, Harry  150
Goldfine, Bernard  112-13
Goldwater, Barry  157
Goldwyn, Samuel  24
Gomez, Ruben  89
Goodman, Benny  100
Goodyear, Charles  115
Gorbachev, Mikhail  124
Grable, Betty  26
Graham, Billy  68
Graham, Otto  80-81, 95, 171
Grant, Cary  26, 32, 35-37, 169
Grant, Ulysses, S.  2, 113, 143
Graves, Peter  56
Graziano, Rocky  38
Green, Johnny  47
Greene, Lorne  54, 66
Grey, Zane  148
Griffith, Andy  54
Griffith, D.W.  24
Griffith, Hugh  33
Grimm, Charlie  76, 89

Grissom, Marv 89
Guinness, Sir Alec 26
Gunther, John 150

Hagen, Cliff 74, 85-86
Haggerty, James 8, 112
Hale, Barbara 54
Haley, Bill 103, 107
Hall, G. Stanley 131
Hammerstein, Oscar II 47, 101
Harding, Warren G. 2, 16
Hardy, Oliver 54, 65
Harlan, John Marshall 135
Harriman, Averell 155
Harriman, E.H. 115
Harris, Oren 112-13
Harris, Phil 55
Harrison, Benjamin 2, 163
Hart, Moss 150
Hawks, Howard 45
Hawthorne, Nathaniel 145
Hayes, Gabby 61
Hayes, Woody 85, 96
Hayward, Rita 26
Hayward, Susan 26
Head, Edith 46
Hearst, William Randolph 48, 115
Hefner, Hugh 30
Heifetz, Jasha 109
Heinson, Tommy 86
Heller, Joseph 147
Hemingway, Ernest 145, 147, 149
Henry, O. 148
Hepburn, Audrey 26-27, 39, 169
Hepburn, Katherine 26
Hersey, John 147
Herter, Christian A. 160
Heston, Charlton 26, 32, 46, 169

Heyerdahl, Thor 150
Hill, James 115
Hilton, Nicky 28
Hiss, Alger 16
Hitchcock, Alfred 32, 45
Hitler, Adolf 143
Hobby, Oveta Culp 8, 133-34
Hodges, Gil 78
Hogan, Ben 72, 170
Holden, William 25-27, 32, 169
Holiday, Billie 106
Holliday, Judie 26
Holly, Buddy 103, 107
Hooper, Hedda 48
Hoover, Herbert 2, 102
Hoover, J. Edgar 10, 150
Hope, Bob 26, 35, 54, 58-60, 170
Hornung, Paul 97
Houston, John 39
Houtteman, Art 89
Howard, Elston 92
Howe, James Wong 47
Hudson, Rock 26, 32, 37, 42-43, 169
Hughes, Howard 35, 115
Hulme, Kathryn 150
Humphrey, George M. 6
Humphrey, Hubert 161-62
Hunter, Evan 147
Hunter, Tab 26
Huntley, Chet 54, 67
Hutchins, Robert M. 133

Imhoff, Darrall 87-88
Irving, Washington 144

Jackson, "Shoeless" Joe 73
James, Harry 100-01

Janssen, David 54
Jefferson, Thomas 127-28
Johnson, Don 82
Johnson, Lyndon 162
Johnson, Van 26
Jones, James 147
Jones, Jennifer 26
Jones, K.C. 86
Jones, Shirley 26

Kantor, MacKinlay 147
Kaye, Danny 26
Kazan, Elia 29, 45
Keel, Howard 26
Kefauver, Estes 155
Khrushchev, Nikita 160-61
Kelly, Gene 26
Kelly, Grace 26, 31, 36, 44, 169
Kennedy, Bobby 9
Kennedy, John F. 9, 16, 155, 161-64
Kennedy, Joseph P. 162
Kern, Jerome 47
Kerr, Deborah 26
Kerr, Jean 150
Keyes, Frances Parkinson 147
King, Alexander 150
King, Dr. Martin Luther, Jr. 136, 145
Kipling, Rudyard 148
Kluszewski, Ted 93
Knight, Eric 63
Koufax, Sandy 93
Kramer, Stanley 29, 45, 49
Kaupa, Gene 100
Kubek, Tony 92

Labine, Clem 78, 91
Ladd, Alan 26

"Lakewood Plan," the 123
Lamas, Fernando 26
LaMotta, Jake 81
Lamour, Dorothy 26
L'Amour, Louis 149
Lancaster, Burt 26, 169
Landis, Jim 93
Landy, John 89, 171
Landon, Michael 54
Lane, Dick "Night Train" 96, 171
Lane, Frankie 105, 171
Lang, Walter 45
Lange, Hope 26
Larker, Norm 93
LaRosa, Julius 57
Larson, Don 90-92
Lasky, Jessie L. 24
"Lassie" 54, 62-63
LaStarza, Roland 81
Lattner, Johnny 97, 171
Laurel, Stan 54, 65
Laurie, Piper 26
Lawford, Peter 26
Lawrence, D.H. 147
Lee, Peggy 42, 104, 171
Lee, Robert E. 142
Leigh, Vivien 26
Lemon, Bob 89, 92
Lemon, Jack 26, 31
Leonard, Bob 75
Lerner, Jay 101, 106
Levine, Joseph E. 48
Lewis, Jerry 26, 49
Lewis, Jerry Lee 103, 107
Lewis, Robert Q. 54
Lewis, Sinclair 145
Liberace 54
Lindbergh, Charles A. 40

Lindbergh, Anne Morrow 149
Linkletter, Art 54
Livingston, Mary 55
Lockhart, June 54
Lodge, Henry Cabot 163
Loes, Billy 78
Loewe, Frederick 47, 101, 106
Logan, Joshua 39
Lollobrigida, Gina 26
London, Julie 105, 171
Longfellow, Henry Wadsworth 144
Lopat, Eddie 78
Lord, Walter 150
Loren, Sophia 26, 36
Louise, Tina 54
Lucas, Jerry 87-88
Lynch, Dick 96

MacArthur, Douglas 5, 73, 112
MacLaine, Shirley 26
MacRae, Gordon 26
Madison, Guy 54
Magile, Sal "The Barber" 89-90
Mancini, Henry 47
Mankiewiez, Joseph L. 45
Mann, Horace 128-29
Mann, Woodrow Wilson 137
Mantle, Mickey 77-78, 90, 92
Marciano, Rocky 81, 171
Marshall, George C. 13, 16
Marshall, Catherine 149
Martin, Billy 78
Martin, Dean 26, 49
Martin, Tony 105
Massey, Raymond 31
Marx, Groucho 54, 57
Marx, Karl 124
Mastroianni, Marcello 26

Mature, Victor 26
Mayo, Elton 117
Mayo, Virginia 26
Mays, Willie 77, 89, 92
McCarthy, Joe 76
McCarthy, Sen. Joseph R. 16-18
McClintock, Bill 87
McCraken, Branch 75
McDonald, Jim 78
McDougald, Gil 78, 92
McFarland, Spanky 64-65
McGavin, Darren 54
McGuffey, William Homes 129
McGuire, Frank 86
McKay, Douglas 7
McKinley, William 2
McQueen, Steve 54
Melville, Herman 145
Mercer, Johnny 47
Merman, Ethel 108
Metalious, Grace 147, 149
Michener, James A. 147
Middlecoff, Cary 72, 170
Mikan, George 76, 88
Milland, Ray 54
Miller, Arthur 30
Miller, Glenn 40, 100
Miller, Mitch 105
Mise, Johnny 78
Mitchell, James P. 7
Mitchum, Robert 26
Moaney, John 167
Monroe, Marilyn 26, 29-31, 169
Montalban, Ricardo 26
Montand, Yves 26
Montgomery, Robert 51, 54, 120
Moon, Wally 93-94
Moore, Archie 81

Moore, Clayton  54-55
Moore, Davy  82
Morgan, J.P.  115
Mossadegh, Muhammed  11
Mueller, Don  89
Mulford, Clarence E.  148
Murphy, Auddie  26
Murrow, Edward R.  16-17, 54, 66-67, 170

Nabokov, Vladimir  149
Nasser, Gamal Abdel  14, 155
National Aeronautics and Space Act  141
National Defense Education Act  141
NATO  13, 73
Neal, Charlie  93
Nelson, David  54-55
Nelson, Harriett  54-55
Nelson, Ozzie  54-55
Nelson, Ricky  54-55
Newell, Pete  87
Newman, Alfred  47
Newman, Paul  26, 38, 169
Nietzsche, Friedrich William  143
Nillson, Brigit  109
Niven, David  26, 39, 54
Nixon, Richard  21, 94-95, 124-25, 151-52, 161-64
Nolan, Lloyd  54
Norris, Frank  145
Novak, Kim  26

O'Brian, Hugh  54
O'Connor, Donald  54
O'Connor, Edwin  147
O'Hara, John  147
O'Hara, Maureen  26
Olivier, Sir Lawrence  31
Olson, Carl "Bobo"  82
O'Malley, Walter  91
Owens, Jim  99

Packard, Vance  123, 150
Padres, Johnny  78, 90, 93
Pagent, Debra  26
Pahlavi, Shaw Muhammed  11
Palance, Jack  26
Pardee, Jack  94
Parker, Fess  42, 54, 105
Parks, Rosa  136
Parr, Jack  54
Parsons, Louella  48
Paul, Les  102
Peale, Norman Vincent  149
Peck, Gregory  26-27, 32, 38-39, 169
Pemberton, John  115
Pep, Willie  82
Perkins, Anthony  26
Perkins, Carl  107
Persons, Wilton B.  6, 120
Pettit, Bob  86
Petty, Lee  83
Plato  142-43
*Plessy v. Ferguson*  134-35
Poe, Edgar Allan  145
Poitier, Sidney  26
Porter, Cole  47
Porter, Edwin S.  24
Power, Tyrone  26
Powers, Francis Gary  160-61
Preminger, Otto  45, 49
Presley, Elvis  26, 36-37, 102-05, 107, 171

Previn, André 47
Price, Lloyd 103
Price, Vincent 26

Quinn, Anthony 26

Rainier III, Prince 32
Ramsey, Frank 85
Rand, Ayn 147
Randall, Tony 54
Rawls, Betsy 72
Ray, Aldo 26
Ray, Johnny 105
Reagan, Ronald 43, 54, 66, 126
Reed, Donna 26, 54
Reese, "Pee Wee" 78
Reiner, Carl 54
Remick, Lee 26
Renaldo, Duncan 54, 63-64
Reynolds, Allie 78
Reynolds, Debbie 26
Rhodes, Dusty 89
Richard, Little 103, 107
Rickey, Branch 76
Rickover, Hyman G. 12
"Rin Tin Tin" 62-63
Rizzuto, Phil 78
Roach, Hal 64-65
Robbins, Harold 147, 149
Roberts, Fireball 83
Roberts, Kenneth 147
Robertson, Oscar 86-87
Robinson, Henry Morton 147
Robinson, Jackie 76, 78, 91-92
Robinson, Sugar Ray 81-82, 171
Rockefeller, John D. 115
Rockwell, Norman 44
Rodgers, Richard 47

Roe, Preacher 78
Roethlisberger, Fritz J. 117
Rogers and Hammerstein 101, 107-08
Rogers, Roy 54, 56, 60-61
Romero, Cesar 26
Rooney, Mickey 54
Roosevelt, Eleanor 19
Roosevelt, Franklin D. 2, 9, 12, 14, 114, 118, 132
Roosevelt, Theodore 2, 71, 156, 170
Rosen, Al 89
Rosenberg, Julius and Ethel 16
Rosenbluth, Lennie 86
Rosewall, Ken 84
Ruark, Robert 147
Rupp, Adolph 74-75, 85, 87
Rush, Barbara 26
Russell, Bill 86, 88
Russell, Jane 26
Ryan, Robert 26

Saddler, Sandy 82
Sain, Johnny 78
Saint, Eva Marie 26, 29
Salas, Lauro 82
Salinger, J.D. 147
Salk, Dr. Jonas 140
Salisbury, Jim 85
Sanders, Henry "Red" 80, 94
Saxton, Johnny 82
Schloredt, Bob 98
Schlundt, Don 75
Schulberg, Budd 147
Scott, Randolph 26, 32, 34-35
Sears, Jessie B. 131-32
Seaton, Frederick A. 7

Seixas, Vic 84
Selinko, Annemarie 147
Selig, William N. 24
Selvy, Frank 86
Serling, Rod 54, 66
Sevaried, Eric 66
Seward, William H. 158-59
Shakespeare, William 142
Shaw, Artie 100
Sheen, Bishop Fulton J. 67
Sheridan, Phil 143
Sherry, Larry 93
Shirer, William 150
Shute, Nevil 147
Sinclaire, Upton 145
Silvers, Phil 54, 63
Silverheels, Jay 54-55
Sinatra, Frank 26, 36-37, 101-02, 104-07, 171
Skeleton, Red 26, 54, 58-59, 170
Skowron, Bill 92
Slaughter, Enos 91
Smith, Bedell 5, 11
Smith, Huey 107
Smith, Wallace "Bud" 82
Snead, Sam 72, 170
Snyder, Duke 77-78, 90, 92-94
Southern, Ann 54
Spahn, Warren 77, 91
Spencer, Herbert 116
Spivey, Bill 74
Sputnik 1 140
Stallings, Gene 94
Stanwyck, Barbara 54
Stephens, Thomas E. 21
Steinbeck, John 146-47
Stengel, Casey 76, 93
Stern, Bill 69

Stevens, George 33
Stevenson, Adlai 2, 52, 155
Stewart, Jimmy 26, 32, 39-40, 44-45, 169
Stoneham, Horace 91
Strasberg, Lee 30
Strasberg, Paula 30
Strategic Air Command 12
Stroheim, Erich von 25
Sturgess, John 45
Styne, Julie 108
Sullivan, Ed 54, 60, 157
Summerfield, Arthur Ellsworth 7
Swanson, Gloria 25
Swayze, John Cameron 67
Swift, Gustavus 115

Tacitus, Cornelius 142-43
Taft, William Howard 2, 158
Taylor, Elizabeth 26-28, 38, 169
Taylor, Frederick Winslow 116-17, 142
Taylor, Maxwell 137
Taylor, Robert 26, 39
Teagarden, Jack 100
Terman, Lewis M. 129
The Comets 103, 107
The Cords 104
The Crickets 107
The Moonglows 104
The Orioles 104
The Penquins 104
The Platters 105
The Teenagers 105
The Three Stooges (Curly, Moe & Larry) 54
Thomas, Danny 54, 64
Thomas, Herb 82

Thomas, Lowell  54, 67
Thompson, Hank  89
Thompson, Kay  147
Thompson, Morton  147
Thompson, Speedy  83
Thoreau, Henry David  144-45
Tierney, Gene  26
Tiomkin, Dimitri  47
Tittle, Y.A.  96, 171
Tocqueville, Alexis de  8, 151-52
Todd, Mike  28
"Topper"  62
Trabert, Tony  84
Tracy, Spencer  26, 32
Traver, Robert  147
Trevor, Claire  26
"Trigger"  54, 61-62
Trout, Robert  66
Truman, Bess  19
Truman, Harry S.  2, 73, 101, 164
Tse-tung, Mao  11
Tsioropoulos, Lou  85
Turley, Bob  91-92
Turner, Lana  26
Turpin, Randy  82
Twain, Mark  145

Unitas, Johnny  95, 171
United Nations  5, 14-15
Uris, Leon M.  147
"U-2 Affair", the  160-61

Van Buren, Martin  16
Van Doren, Charles  65-66, 108
Veeck, Bill  76
Villanueva, Primo  85
Vincent, Gene  106
Vukovich, Bill  83

Wagner, Robert  26
Walcott, Jersey Joe  81
Wallis, Hal B.  45, 49
Walsh, Raul  45
Warren, Earl  135, 157
Washington, George  2, 148
Waterfield, Bob  95
Wayne, John  26, 32-34, 44-45, 56-57, 169
Webb, Jack  54, 57
Webster, Beveridge  109, 115
Weeks, Sinclair  7
Welch, Robert  157
Wellman, William  45
West, Jerry  86-87
West, Mae  36
Westinghouse, George  115
Weyerhauser, Frederick  115
Whitehead, Donald  150
Widmark, Richard  26, 32
Wilcox, Deida  24
Wilde, Cornel  26
Wilder, Billy  27, 46
Wilding, Michael  26
Wilhelm, Hoyt  89
Wilkenson, Bud  96
Williams, Hank  104
Williams, Ike  82
Williams, Ted  92
Williams, Tennessee  29
Wilson, Charles E.  6
Wilson, Don  55
Wilson, Meredith  106
Wilson, Sloan  147
Wilson, Woodrow  2, 129
Winchell, Walter  60
Winsor, Kathleen  147
Winters, Shelly  26

Wise, Robert 46
Wood, Natalie 26
Wooden, John 86
Woodling, Gene 78
Woods, Rosie 167
Woodward, Bob 152
Woodward, Joanne 26, 38
Woolpert, Phil 86
Wouk, Herman 147
Wyatt, Jane 54
Wyler, William 33, 46
Wyman, Jane 43
Wynn, Early 89

Yerby, Frank 147
Young, Loretta 36, 54, 66
Young, Robert 54, 64

Zaharias, Babe 72
Zanuck, Daryl F. 39, 63
Zimbalist, Jr., Efrem 66
Zimmer, Don 92
Zinnemann, Fred 46

CPSIA information can be obtained
at www.ICGtesting.com
Printed in the USA
LVHW090853170421
684782LV00007B/199